GUN FAG MANIFESTO
Edited by Hollister Kopp.
Foreword by Jim Goad.
Nine-Banded Books & Underworld Amusements

Gun Fag Manifesto
©2013 by David E. Scott

Copyright to all contributed content retained by original authors and artists.

ISBN: 978-0-9896972-0-0

Special thanks to Cletus J. Mauser, Ann Sterzinger and Jim Goad.

Production managed by Chip Smith.

All new material designed by Kevin I. Slaughter

Co-published by
Nine-Banded Books
ninebandedbooks.com
and
Underworld Amusements
underworldamusements.com

"Today we live so cowed under the bombardment of this intellectual artillery (the media) that hardly anyone can attain to the inward detachment that is required for a clear view of the monstrous drama. The will-to-power operating under a pure democratic disguise has finished off its masterpiece so well that the object's sense of freedom is actually flattered by the most thoroughgoing enslavement that has ever existed."

—Oswald Spengler,
The Decline of the West

SUCCESSFUL SHOTGUN SHOOTING

By Andrew Montague with S.V. Beckwith
Easy-to-understand, easy-to-follow shotgun shooting and hunting know-how. All about your gun and how it shoots. How to hit moving targets. Hints on hunting. How to select and care for shotguns and accessories.

Item No.	No.	List
27830192	92	$5.95

THE COMPLETE BOOK OF TRICK AND FANCY SHOOTING

By Ernie Lind
Here are step-by-step instructions to help you acquire the whole range of skills for trick and fancy shooting with rifle, pistol and shotgun. Illustrated.

The Complete Book of Trick and Fancy Shooting

Item No.	No.	List
27830190	90	$5.95

THE GOLDEN AGE OF SHOTGUNNING

By Bob Hinman
A goldmine of information about guns, shells, hunting and target equipment of the last 30 years of the 19th century. Includes the most complete listing anywhere of shotgun makers' names, dates, histories.

The Golden Age of Shotgunning

Item No.	No.	List
27830169	169	$8.95

GOUGH THOMAS'S GUN BOOK

By G.T. Garwood
Wide-ranging coverage of every aspect of shotgun use, performance, care and lore in this practical and entertaining book. Illustrated.

Gough Thomas's Gun Book

Item No.	No.	List
27830163	163	$8.95

THE HISTORY OF WINCHESTER FIREARMS

1866-1966, Third Edition by George M. Watrous
A complete authorative, meticulously accurate reference to the entire Winchester production. Essential for all serious collectors.

The History of Winchester Firearms

Item No.	No.	List
27830115	115	$10.00

SCORE BETTER AT TRAP

By Fred Missildine With Nick Karas
The history of the sport and complete, fully illustrated step-by-step instructions on mastering the finer points of trap shooting.

Score Better At Trap

Item No.	No.	List
27830121	121	$5.95

SCORE BETTER AT SKEET

By Fred Missildine With Nick Karas
Detailed, fully illustrated station-by-station recommendations on how to stand and where to point out. How to pick up and break the bird for every shot in the game. Plus a station-by-station analysis of how and why skeet shooters miss.

Score Better At Skeet

Item No.	No.	List
27830118	118	$5.95

GUN FAG MANIFESTO: RELOADED AND VINDICATED

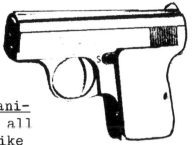

Seeing <u>Gun Fag Manifesto</u> again after all these years was like being pistol-whipped with the realization that our culture has gotten much worse since it was first published.

I never met Gun Fag Dave, AKA Hollister Kopp, although we both lived in Southern California in the early 1990s right before the Internet rendered the "zine revolution" a technologically impotent dodo bird. We swapped our publications via what used to be known as "mail," and though I liked very few zines, <u>Gun Fag Manifesto</u> made the idea of spraying street scum with megatons of

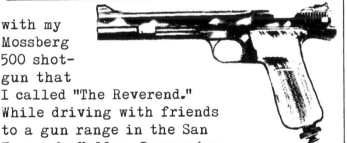

hot lead seem funny, charming, and downright delightful.

This was back when I'd become quite the Gun Fag myself. If it were medically possible, I would have had babies

with my Mossberg 500 shotgun that I called "The Reverend." While driving with friends to a gun range in the San Fernando Valley, I remember whipping out my Ruger pistol and pointing it at a carful of Mexicans who'd cut us off in traffic and asking them if they really had any sincere interest in fucking with us. (As luck would have it, they didn't. When the light turned green, they pulled away respectfully and, I might add, very quickly.)

What fun, freewheeling times those were. Reading Gun Fag Manifesto again bathed me in an exhilarating rush of wistful nostalgia.

This was all right before lesbians, cell phones, antidepressants, and the Internet came along to ruin this once-great Republic. In the interim, most Americans have become neutered into silence, straitjacketed by totalitarian PC psychosis. What's worse, they haven't even put up a fight.

Since all governments seek to monopolize violence, today's compliant, pro-statist mainstream media selectively filter reality and sculpt the narrative to create an impression that "gun control" is one of the nation's top priorities.

I agree. I would like to personally control all of the government's guns.

Despite the media-created racial hysteria around the Trayvon Martin case, the deeper subtext was whether ordinary citizens should be able to use guns to defend themselves when someone's smashing their head into the concrete...or whether they should wait 20 minutes till police to arrive and they're already dead.

Gun-grabbing, chopped-liver-gobbling US Senators such as Dianne Feinstein and Charles Schumer—who faced scorn in these pages—are still steaming merrily along, still in power, still surrounded by gun-toting bodyguards, and still agitating to disarm the public. And now we have the black president who talks dismissively of people who cling bitterly to guns. We also have ever-expanding official definitions of "hate speech" and "terrorism" that could possibly even cover reprints of self-published magazines from a mere two decades ago.

Yet since Gun Fag Manifesto was first published, gun ownership in America has ballooned. Violent crime has plummeted. You were right all along, Hol-

lister Kopp. And when the shit hits the fan as most of us seem certain it will, you will rise from the status of zine publisher to that of prophet.

Jim Goad
October, 2013

Lawman MK III

Heavy "bull" barrel. Used widely by State Police, highway patrol and sheriffs.

.357 Magnum Caliber; Blue Finish

Item No.	B.L.	No.	List
03292700	2"	J1247	$149.50

Item No.	B.L.	No.	List
03292705	4"	J1245	$149.50

Detective Special

Tough all-steel short barreled handgun, delivering more stability for repeat shot accuracy.

28

Detective Special
.38 Special Caliber; Blue Finish

Item No.	B.L.	No.	List
03294775	2"	D1425	$140.00

.38 Special Caliber; Nickel Finish

Item No.	B.L.	No.	List
03294800	2"	D1426	$149.50

Trooper MK III

Tremendous penetration power in the magnum caliber makes this hard-hitting handgun ideal for big game hunters and for police officers. Target stocks, target hammer, wide smooth trigger.

Trooper MK III
.357 Magnum Caliber; Blue Finish

Item No.	B.L.	No.	List
03293075	4"	J4241	$188.00
03293600	6"	J4261	$188.00

SINGLE ACTION REVOLVERS

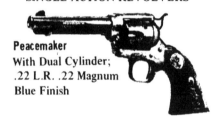

Peacemaker
With Dual Cylinder;
.22 L.R. .22 Magnum
Blue Finish

A steel frame true .22 caliber version of the famous Colt's .45 caliber "Peacemaker." Color case hardened frame and smooth action set it apart from all copies.
Fixed sights.

Item No.	B.L.	No.	List
03290875	4¾"	G1441	$ 96.50
03291975	6"	G1461	$ 96.50
03291650	7½"	G1471	$102.50
	Buntline		

New Frontier
With Dual Cylinder;
.22 L.R./.22 Magnum
Blue Finish

A .22 caliber version of the famous Colt's New Frontier Model, boasting ramped front side and adjustable rear sight. as well as a color case hardened frame in the classic Colt tradition.

Item No.	B.L.	No.	List
03291900	4¾"	G2441	$108.00
03292000	6"	G2461	$108.00
03292075	7½"	G2471	$113.50

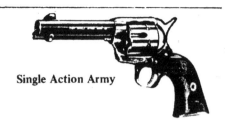

Single Action Army

The classic American handgun, the original, fixed sight. "Peacemaker," with superb balance, reassuring feel and complete failproof action.

.45 Colt Caliber; Rubber Stocks; Blue Finish

03296900	5½"	P1850	$246.50
03297050	7½"	P1870	$253.00

Interarms

MODEL HSc MAUSER

Positive thumb safety, magazine safety, exposed hammer for added safety. matted non-glare sight channel, checkered genuine Walnut grips, Inertiatype firing pin, Bright Blue finish.
CALIBER: .380 ACP
BARREL LENGTH: 3.375"
WEIGHT: 23.3 oz.
MAG. CAPACITY: 7 rounds

Item No.	No.		List
03358625	3580		$199.00

MODEL VIRGINIAN
Single Action Revolver

Hammerli triple action Swissafe Safety System, "Olympic Match" barrel finish in mirror blue, chromed trigger guard and back strap, select walnut one piece.
CALIBER: .357 Mag. & .45 Long Colt.
BBL. LENGTH: 4-5/8", 5½", 7½".
NO. ROUNDS: 6
NOTE: .357 Magnum chamber also accommodates .38 Special

.357 Magnum

Item No.	No.	B.L.	List
03359000	3634	4-5/8"	$220.00
03359010	3635	5 1/2"	$220.00
03359020	3637	7 1/2"	$220.00

.45 Long Colt

Item No.	No.	B.L.	List
03359030	3640	4-5/8"	$220.00
03359040	3645	5 1/2"	$220.00
03359050	3647	7 1/2"	$220.00

Prices
Subject to Change
Without Notice

INTRODUCTION

1994 doesn't seem so long
ago. I just read about
100 pages of Gun Fag Man-
ifesto for the first time
in 17 years, and I laughed
good and hard for a bit
and then had to stop. Wow.
That time is gone.

I've always been a fan
of guns. The craftsmanship, the
heritage, the traditions, the Ameri-
cana. I loved Gunsmoke and all those
cowboy movies on TV when I was a
kid. I just about wore out the Mar-
ty Robbins album Gunfighter Ballads
and Trail Songs. I'd listen to those
great songs and be transported to a
different time, imagining myself in
those scenarios. El Paso. Big Iron.
Running Gun. They're Hanging Me
Tonight. The Strawberry Roan. I'll
bet I could still recite the lyrics

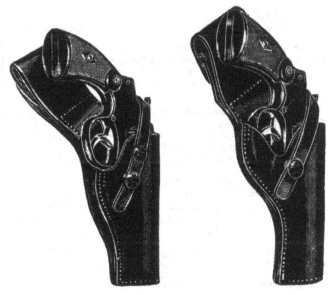

to all those songs. My dad was a cop,
and he showed me how to clean the
Smith & Wesson Model 15 .357 Magnum
he carried at work (I now have that
gun, and I cherish it). He taught me
how to shoot when I was seven years
old, with a Smith & Wesson .32-20 he
inherited from his father. I still
have that gun as well.

Even so, I wouldn't have considered

myself a gun fag at that time. Even
while serving as one of our nation's ri-
fle-packin' bullet-stoppers I considered
the M-16 nothing more than a cheap, gim-
micky .22 caliber toy. This all changed
in the spring of 1992.

The race riots in Los Angeles after
the Rodney King verdicts — when the
cops were exonerated for taking down a
drug-fueled maniac after a high-speed
chase — changed the perspective of a lot
of people. People who hadn't given any
thought to being armed were suddenly
all for the second amendment. I remember sitting around with my buddies in my
backyard watching all the black smoke
from the city (we lived in Burbank, and
a riot wouldn't last five seconds there)
and we all agreed that we needed more
guns. There were five of us, and between
us we had a grand total of two shotguns
and two handguns. Pathetic. We all be-

came gun fags that day.

I'll skip back to 1994 here, and offer
some perspective: Cell phones were about
as common as Bentleys. I didn't know
what an "internet" looked like, although
I had heard of them. Jeeps had square
headlights. Burbank, California was
blue-collar and middle-class, and I could
afford to live there. William Jefferson Clinton was president of the United States, and we thought we had it bad.
The New York Times, Los Angeles Times and
Chicago Tribune had a lock on the information you were allowed to read. NBC,
CBS and ABC ruled the air for information you were allowed to see. Yeah, CNN
was there, but inconsequential, as they
still are. The economy was terrible if
you didn't feel like looking for a job.

If you were to communicate with someone it was face-to-face, by phone (your

home phone, with a cord attached to it), or the U.S. Mail. That was it. It seemed a healthier time, but it's hard to be nostalgic in light of instant communications and the huge amount of information available to us today. The old networks and papers are hemorrhaging customers and going bankrupt, and they won't be missed much.

* * *

There was a bookstore called Amok, on Vermont Avenue in the now-trendy and upscale Los Feliz district. I don't

know if it's still there, and don't really care - I lived in California for ten years and that's enough for me. I

frequented this bookstore mostly for its impressive collection of unpopular and difficult-to-find "fringe" publications.

By the counter was a curious display of little self-published pamphlets and

rants that looked like they were put together by a third grade class with a punk rock teacher. Ugly Xerox graphics and poor grammar seemed to be intentional, and they were "irreverent" and "edgy," so one day I bought a copy of each and took them home. These publications, I was soon to learn, were known as "zines." In reading through them, a

couple of aspects of this odd trend struck me. Firts, it was apparent that the only people who read zines were

the people who wrote them. Next was the strident uniformity of cultural and political opinion. How can you be irreverent and edgy and "brave" (that word was tossed around an awful lot) when you're raging against suburbia,

homophobia, sexism, racism, hillbillies, Nazis, American cars, Republicans, cops, chain restaurants, etc.?

You get what I mean. They were in lockstep with the prevailing culture and stroking themselves and each other as some kind of underground revolutionaries. I doubted they even had jobs, or needed them. I despised these people. They were small. I hated their tattoos and pierced faces and fake poverty. I had a good mind to poison that bookstore display with a zine of my own.

Everything they hated and feared was quickly and quite easily packaged into a digest-size zine that was just

as ugly as the rest of them, although probably better written. A cartoon redneck by the name of Hollister Kopp would confirm their most cherished prejudices. It was so much fun writing it that I figured I was on to something even before I dropped the first copies off at Amok. I also sent a copy to Factsheet 5, a sort of clear-

ing house for the zine scene, who would give you a short review and list your address and price. A local bookstore was one thing, but Factsheet 5 had countrywide distribution, and my P.O. box soon filled up with some interesting correspondence.

Gun Fag Manifesto was hated and loved, but man, there was nothing in

between. I fully expected the hate - after all, that's what I was going for - but the love rattled me some. I actually like fringe kooks (of course)

and some of the publications I received in the mail were the fringiest, kookiest things I had ever seen. There was a world out there I never knew existed. My reaction was keep 'em coming! I looked forward to stopping by the post office every day after work and col-

lecting the letters, many containing the niggardly two dollars and a return address, quite a few puking sanctimonious venom toward the evils of redneckery, still more sporting pamphlets

for militias, fliers for Klan rallies, and my favorite, a gun totin' cross-dresser who was naturally attracted to the title and bought a copy at Amok. A real gun fag! I think I still have the photos he sent me.

I also discovered a few zines that didn't fit the mold, and I was grateful

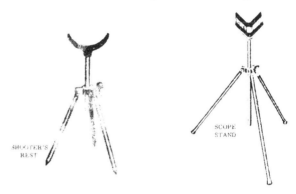

SHOOTER'S REST

SCOPE STAND

for that. The clear standout was ANSWER Me! - considered a zine only because it was self-published. It was a professional magazine done by a real journalist doing real research, with a depth of quality the zines couldn't touch. So of course the zinesters yammered on about it in their gossipy way. Many of them were clearly inspired by it, which is fine. But I remember trying hard not to sound imitative, a difficult task that I'm not sure I accomplished. The editor of ANSWER Me! is to this day a prolific and influential writer and philosopher. I think Jim Goad has got a bright future.

I made some good friends through correspondence — a few actually face-to-face — who seemed to get what I was doing. We were in the minority and happy to be there. They are some of the most interesting people I've had the pleasure of meeting. I've lost touch with most of them, what with everyone moving around to different states and countries (heck, I even lived in Spain for a year, and that's a whole 'nother story), but their contri-

butions live on, and you can read them here. One of those old pen pals is Chip Smith of The Hoover Hog and Nine Banded Books, who somehow tracked me down after all these years and suggested publishing all three issues in one book. So this whole thing is his fault.

* * *

1994. Those were some good times. I and my circle of friends drank too much beer for sure, and we all should have been married off by then, or jailed. The crazy stuff we used to pull off could have been the subject of a zine all its own, with dozens of issues. Spinning donuts in Bob Hope's front lawn in a dually pickup truck. Ripping around town in a real police car (one of my friends worked

for a prop house), scaring the bejeezus out of gangbangers and dopeheads. Shooting my truck because I thought it needed some bullet holes, then hiding from the cops when they drove around looking into reports of gunfire. I've got a million of those stories, and they're all true.

Some of our nuttiness made its way into the pages of Gun Fag, where I mostly stretched the truth. Maybe I shouldn't have, because the straight truth would have been just as entertaining if written properly. An example would be the boar hunt in Issue #3: We didn't see any bow hunters. I felt that the story needed some sort of crescendo, and it fit the theme of irresponsible gun ownership. In fact I have never discharged a firearm in an unsafe direction, although it can be argued that drinking and shooting is not a recommended practice for most people.

Now, 2013. I'm a construction guy with a mortgage and a family. Not a bad life, really. Money has been scarce the last few years, but I'm not alone there. We all bitch and complain about the times. When have we not? Although it could be argued that we have very good reason to bitch now more than ever, with government at all levels overstepping its authority with an audacity never before seen in this country. Good God, the EPA has its own SWAT team, for cryin' out loud! Aw, don't get me started...

I remember years ago sitting in a barber shop, and there was a young guy getting a haircut by a barber who was probably 80 years old. They were making conversation as is the norm, and the kid asked the barber in which era he thought the country was at its best. The old man walked around to face the kid and said, "For you, young man, it's right now. Just get off your ass." By God, he was right.

When it was my turn for a haircut I

felt honored to be in the presence of such a man.

* * *

Enjoy the book. It may be banned in the near future.

Hollister Kopp
September 2013

HIGH STANDARD REVOLVERS

Sentinel Mark I & Mark IV

A completely redesigned and improved version of the .22 Cal. Sentinel revolver which, for years, filled the need of shooters and sportsmen throughout the country.

At home, in the field, or in camp, it's now a steel framed revolver with classic styling, chambered for 22 long rifle or magnum. Available in 2, 3, or 4" barrel lengths, with fixed or adjustable rear sights, this gun is unequal in its versatility.

Impressive ballistics of the 22 magnum, coupled with the mild recoil, makes it an excellant off duty gun for policemen or policewomen. Available in Trophy Blue or Nickel finish, with wrap around American Walnut stocks. White outline rear sights with red ramp front sight, standard with Nickel finish adjustable sight models.

Item No.	Model	Features	Finish	Cal.	Bbl.	List
MARK I						
03338250	9350	Fixed Sights	Trophy Blue	.22LR	2"	$109.00
03338251	9351	Fixed Sights	Nickel	.22LR	2"	$119.00
03338256	9356	Fixed Sights	Trophy Blue	.22LR	4"	$109.00
03338257	9357	Adj. Sights	Trophy Blue	.22LR	4"	$119.00
03338259	9359	Adj. Sights	Nickel	.22LR	4"	$129.00
MARK IV						
03338260	9360	Fixed Sights	Trophy Blue	Mag.	2"	$109.00
03338261	9361	Fixed Sights	Nickel	Mag.	2"	$119.00
03338262	9362	Fixed Sights	Trophy Blue	Mag.	3"	$109.00
03338264	9364	Adj. Sights	Trophy Blue	Mag.	3"	$119.00
03338268	9368	Adj. Sights	Trophy Blue	Mag.	4"	$119.00
03338269	9369	Adj. Sights	Nickel	Mag.	4"	$129.00

REMINGTON HANDGUNS

Long Range Single Shot Model XP-100 Pistol — Bolt Action, Center Fire, For Varmints, Hunting and Target Shooting

The XP-100 long range pistol is a super-accurate handgun chambered for the extremly fast-shooting 221 Remington "Fire Ball" cartridge that has a muzzle velocity of 2650 feet per second (50 grain soft point bullet). Bolt action is the strongest — same as featured on Remington center fire rifles.

Over all length 16¾ in., barrel length 10½ in., drilled and tapped for telescope mount; weight each 3¾ lbs. Complete with zippered carrying case.

Model XP-100

Caliber: .221 Rem "Fire Ball"

Item No.	No.	List
03029700	5470	$144.95

CHARTER ARMS HANDGUNS

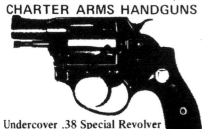

Undercover .38 Special Revolver

The smallest, lightest .38 special steel frame revolver made in the United States weighs only 16 ounces. The new handgun incorporates a five-shot swing out cylinder which may be unlatched by pushing either the cylinder latch or ejector rod forward.

Item No.	No.	List
Regular Grips		
03233950	1382	$104.00
Bulldog Grips		
03233975	13821	$111.00
Regular Grips, Nickel Finish		
03233900	138201	$115.00

Pathfinder .22 Long Rifle Revolver

A new .22 long rifle incorporating many design features of the famed UNDERCOVER .38 special. The PATHFINDER is perfect for the hunter. Great for fun. Six shot, single and double action. Swing-out cylinder latch. Hammer is completely blocked. The three-inch barrel is button rifled with six grooves to insure the highest possible degree of accuracy.

Item No.	No.	List
03230200	2223	$114.00

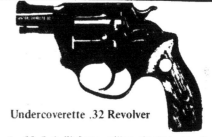

Undercoverette .32 Revolver

A .32 S & W Long caliber six-shot repeater adapted from the famed UNDERCOVER .38 special incorporating all the superb design and performance features of the UNDERCOVER. A natural for anyone favoring a .32 caliber revolver. Offers a 2 in. barrel, button rifled with 8 grooves instead of the conventional 6. Sights are a 9/64 in. serrated ramp front and square notch rear for fast alignment.

.32 S & W Long Caliber

Item No.	No.	List
03232200	1322	$105.00

Bull Dog Grips — For any Charter Arms Revolver —

Item No.	No.	List
09682700	100	$10.00

Bulldog .44 Special

Continued on next page.

GUN FAG

#1

$2

MANIFESTO

THIS IS ISSUE #1. BUY AT LEAST 20 COPIES AND HANG ONTO THEM.

GUN FAG MANIFESTO

is published whenever the Publisher feels that there is enough material to
assemble an issue. This could be weeks, months, years or never.

THE STRATEGIC GUN FAG COMMAND:

HOLLISTER KOPP
Publisher, Editor and Supreme Commandant

JAKE JOSEPH L.Z. KILROY KOWALSKI IV (aka RED)
Special Guest Columnist and Border Area Correspondent

and a few others who, for the sake of national security, must remain anonymous

---

Send $2.00 per copy, plus $1.00 to cover the postage & handling
(We'll ship First Class, of course)

Free postage & handling for orders of 20 or more copies.

Understand that to order *Gun Fag Manifesto* you must send **CASH**, as
Commander Kopp does not believe in bank accounts, and *GFM* is not (yet)
looked upon by the slimy liberal authorities as being a legitimate business. If you
really need to write a check, make it payable to CASH.

Anyone caught reprinting, publicly exhibiting or badmouthing any of the contents
of *Gun Fag Manifesto* without express permission of the Publisher will be shot.

COPYRIGHT © MARCH, 1994

The cover art features a detail from *The Orator* by Ferdinand Hodler

URBAN RENEWAL

There is a dangerously popular misconception being rammed down our throats these days by newspaper columnists, multiculturalist faggots and Red scum that there are "too many guns on our streets." Balderdash. There are too many *people* on our streets, and not *nearly* enough guns! In what's left of this rotten, bloated corpse of a society, guns are all we have left to keep us alive! Think about it! No cranked-up street scum is immune to bullets, and none but the craziest of shit-stained winos or self

righteous "it's-your-fault-I'm-homeless" vermin will talk tough to the gaping barrel of a .45 Colt. Everyone should carry a handgun! Preferably two or three! Hell, carry a riot shotgun if you can keep it concealed!

It's appalling that we aren't *encouraged* to carry firearms. They should be issued by the authorities like driver's licenses. They should be *mandatory* in most L.A. neighborhoods. There wouldn't be half the crime or joblessness in this city if jobless criminals were routinely shot. And it doesn't stop there! Think of the revenue generated by selling urban hunting licenses! There could be thrilling inner-city safaris guided by friendly natives! And imagine the positive crime deterrent when potential young punks see men in pickups on their way to the taxidermist with freshly-bagged gangbangers strapped to the hood! Call me Bwana!

The term *gun fag* is commonly used in law-enforcement circles and refers to men like Randy Weaver and David Koresh. Men with more guns in their houses than windows. I'm a gun fag. I represent what has become a last-ditch line of defense against the other kind of fag (those liberal goons and intrusive, sick busybodies in our government who theoretically represent We the People). I live for guns. I eat, drink, sleep, shit shower and shave for guns. I'm fat and white. I have a subscription to every gun, hunter, military and police-oriented magazine available, and I'm on the mailing list of every extremist right-wing cause in the U.S. and Europe. I'm a life member of the NRA, NGFP, NSDAP, CCFG, NHRA and Club Coors. I've studied and pondered so many neat ways to kill you that the subject doesn't even give me a hard-on any more. I *love* goddamn guns, and I'm never without at *least* one. I'm the expert here, so what I say goes. Get it? Good.

There wouldn't be half the crime or joblessness in this city if jobless criminals were routinely shot

GUN FAG MANIFESTO is a guide not only to urban survival, but *urban renewal*. Every miserable apartment-dweller in this fetid rat hole of a city should pay close attention to the messages contained herein. THIS IS IMPORTANT. We cannot survive the scourge of human filth that is now sodomizing our very heritage, UNLESS WE KEEP AND BEAR ARMS! We must stem this hideous tide and beat it back with whatever means necessary. This will probably include killing on a massive scale, so as a public service, I will share with you my knowledge, experience and expertise in the field of firearms.

The emphasis will remain mostly on reviewing effective, cheap firepower and tactical home defense (and *offense*), but I will stray now and then to present an article on something luxurious and expensive for your voyeuristic titillation, such as the sensuous Smith & Wesson model 586, reviewed in this issue. The editorial content will be bigoted, remorseless and ugly, just like me. If you have a problem with that, YOU CAN CALL THE GODDAMNED COMMUNIST ACLU AND SNIVEL ALL YOU WANT. This is my magazine, and this is my gun. That makes me the boss!

This and future issues of this important work may someday be regarded as the testimony of a great statesman and champion of the people. Few others have the *cojones* to speak pure truth. Very little printed media escapes the watchful, beady eyes of the Thought Police, who have a cold and clammy grip on the throttle of our runaway culture. WE NEED THE TRUTH, AND WE NEED ACTION! ARE WE MEN, OR ARE WE COWARDLY SISSIES? *WHEN THE BASTARDS COME FOR OUR GUNS, WE HAD BETTER BE PREPARED TO SHOOT BACK!*

CASH-N-CARRY FIREPOWER?
NOT FOR LONG! BUY NOW!

Pure and simple, folks. Gun laws are unconstitutional. They're also *unconscionable* and *un-American*. Gun laws smack of repression, totalitarianism, communism and faggotism. They do absolutely *no good*. Craven politicians tell us that gun laws are "for our protection." Which would you rather use for protection - a *gun,* or a gun *law?* Which is the more effective deterrent to an attack by dope-addled "at-risk youth" in an unlighted parking lot? Right!

A couple of years ago, the maggots in the California Legislature decided, in their imminent wisdom, to expand the mandatory 15-day waiting period for the purchase of handguns to include rifles and shotguns. A lot of people didn't know this, and were unpleasantly surprised when they went to their local gun dealers during the riots of April '92, looking to buy some protection. SOME OF THOSE POOR SAPS ARE DEAD NOW! Granted, they should have been better prepared in the first place, but let this be on the conscience of the criminal bastards who take it upon themselves to "Protect" us with restrictive, unconstitutional gun laws! THIS IS OUTRAGEOUS!

> **Which would you rather use for protection - a GUN, or a gun LAW?**

In this segment I will reveal to you a couple of ways to get around some of this insanity. This article will be especially informative if you're a convicted felon or have ever been committed in a mental health facility (both of these categories disqualify you from owning firearms under the present discriminatory law). Now remember, I'M NOT ENCOURAGING YOU TO DO ANYTHING ILLEGAL (clever, trendy disclaimer). I'm not your mommy, so if you decide to take some decisive action for your community and assassinate several hundred people, don't come bitching to *me* when the cops nail you and the politicians turn you into a poster boy for gun control.

The first thing that comes to mind when one brings up the subject of circumventing unconstitutional gun laws is the *black market.* We've all heard lurid stories (and seen episodes of Starsky & Hutch) which involve a beat-up van full of machine guns and rocket launchers in some trash-strewn vacant lot. A couple of slimeballs (always white, in need of a shave and wearing stocking caps) are selling the stuff cheap to 12-year old gangbangers. If this actually happens I wouldn't know about it; I don't associate with criminals, I shoot them. I do know a little about current gun laws, however, and this is how they work:

What the law considers "curios" and "antiques" are allowed to be sold over the counter on a cash-and-carry basis; no waiting period, no registration or background check. As all guns should be!

Percussion-fired blackpowder replica guns are considered "curios" under the law, and although they take too damned long to load, making them inefficient for mowing down criminals, they are a lot of fun to shoot, and surprisingly powerful. In this issue I review an Italian-made replica of the Colt 1860 Army revolver, which was carried by the

Union Army during their dastardly invasion of the Confederate States of America. Also worth note here are muzzle-loading rifles in huge calibers, and sawed-off "stagecoach style" double barreled 10 gauge shotguns. I recommend the latter for home defense, loaded with piano wire and roofing nails.

The "antiques" are the ones that lovingly tug at my heart strings. This category includes guns manufactured during and prior to WWII: The feared M1 Garand, the roaring little M1 Carbine (which I review in this issue), the popular British Enfields, smooth and rugged Russian Nagants and the legendary German Mauser. And they're cheap! The Enfields and Nagants almost always sell for less than a hundred bucks. You can pick up Garands and Mausers for around $300. I bought my M1 Carbine for $195, and I've seen them even cheaper.

Yes, they're inexpensive and plentiful, and that's not even the good news. My friends, these are *assault weapons!* Fire-belching, flesh-ripping, screaming meat grinders! They were designed 50 years ago to efficiently kill large numbers of men, and believe me, they are just as effective today.

You might ask, "How could these guns be legal in today's political climate?" Beats the crap outta me. The rabid fiends in our government who salivate and jump at every chance to take away any and all of our God-given rights would *undoubtedly* jizz with joy in outlawing more guns, particularly the bargains described above. I frankly don't have a clue as to why they haven't yanked these guns off the market, but I can tell you with absolute certainty that *these few freedoms won't last.*

Remember what that geek Patrick

Purdy did for the AK-47's image? Shot it all to hell, so to speak. It's only a matter of time before some spoil-sport sets up his "antique" .303 British Enfield in another schoolyard and starts dropping the little whippersnappers in their tracks. This will cause another law-making feeding frenzy in Sacramento, probably even in Washington. The fact that more laws mean nothing to the lawless never seems to enter their feeble little minds.

Gun control is *the* hot topic these days among the egalitarian cretins who invent our laws for us, and it seems to be accumulating momentum with each passing day. Everyone is trying to outdo each other: Senator Wankelweiner and his staff of bumper-sticker authors theorize that if hollowpoint bullets were illegal, then punks would stop robbing and killing each other over dope. This elicits a somewhat favorable response from a mysterious newspaper poll (have they ever asked *your* opinion? I didn't think so) which in turn inspires Congressman Weaselfelch to propose a 10,000% tax on all handgun ammo, and it soon snowballs into a competition among the snickering rats in the vomit-spattered halls of our government and the drooling, leering media fucks who blindly regurgitate the Doctrine of the Day to see who is "tougher on guns." Meanwhile, as they run roughshod over the Constitution and smear their ego-smegma over the very soul of America, you and I - the people who pay for their society dinners, their sleazy affairs and their crack habits - suffer greatly.

These are the vilest subspecies to ever walk the face of the planet. Most of them are lawyers, and all of them are criminal opportunists. They are the same smarmy punks who kissed the principal's ass in high-school, volunteered to become hall monitors and snitched on you for every minor infraction of the rules. *Now they make the rules.* There has been a movement during the last couple of years to impose term limits to "throw the bums out" (it has actually become law here in California), but this indirect, half-baked measure misses the point. The answer is not to "throw the bums out" or to vote them out or even to prosecute them. The answer is to simply **KILL THEM.** They all should be staked to ant hills until death, but logistics and time constraints make this unrealistic. An all-out attack with crossbows would be fun, and would have the added advantage of making their gun control measures look ironic and silly for the benefit of posterity. However, it may take a far more profound statement from the gun fags of America - nuclear, chemical and/or biological warfare - before the creeps even begin to get the message.

My advice is to stock up on ammo *in a big way* and buy as many guns as possible, before they "protect" us with more of their insanity! Criminals will always have guns! And when hoards of screaming, cranked-up, *armed* crazies descend upon you and your family, our chancrous government sodomites expect you to keep them at bay with a rolling pin and an empty Evian bottle!

Godspeed!

Top to bottom: M1 Garand, M1903 Springfield, M1 Carbine

ARMY SURPLUS M1 CARBINE
SERIOUS CHOPPER FOR CHEAP

Ever since my grubby-faced boyhood, I've been enamored with the M1 Carbine. My GI Joe doll had one, some of the guys in the TV series *Combat* carried them and it showed up in countless war photographs; in the grip of grimacing, determined GIs spewing lead and scattering spent casings like confetti or lying mournfully silent next to dead guys in the mud. The thing just looked cool, and I wanted one.

I'm not one to shun an important part of my childhood, so naturally I now own an M1 Carbine. I am not disappointed. The first time I fired the thing was a joyous experience, the memory of which stirs my heart to this day. It was about ten miles east of Mojave: just my truck, my Carbine, myself and a warm desert breeze. I loaded up two 30-round magazines and gently slid one into the magazine well, the Carbine responding with a loving CLICK as the deadly little package found home. Trembling with sweet anticipation, I released the bolt catch, took aim at nothing in particular and emptied the magazine in about four seconds. The vicious burst of fire could only be equalled by my bounding joy. My cackling and shrieks could probably be heard all the way to Edwards Air Force Base.

OK, I'm queer for Carbines. But not without justification: this is probably the most efficient and practical all around self-defense weapon you can buy. Its .30 caliber round packs plenty of punch (it was designed to kill *men*), it's small and light enough for fast action in close quarters (hallways, stairwells etc.) and its capacity is only limited to how many magazines you can carry.

NOTE: *If you're trapped in your apartment and a crazed meth-head has just beat down your door, use your shotgun on him, loaded with #4 buck shot (this will waste the creep without inflicting too much collateral damage to neighboring apartments). But if for any reason the son of a bitch gets away and you have to go after him, your M1 Carbine, with its quick handling and substantial firepower will be the proper tool for the task.*

Expect to spend as little as $175, and not more than $250 on a perfectly functional weapon. Check the bolt for sloppiness or worn areas and work the charging handle back and forth, feeling the action for smoothness and hearty spring tension. Check the sights for signs of abuse, and see that the rear sight adjusts to the left and right without binding up. Lock the bolt in the open position by pulling the charging handle to the rear and depressing the little spring-loaded button which holds it in place. Hold the weapon up to the light and peer down the bore, making sure there is no damage to the rifling or pitting in the steel. Now *gently* let the bolt forward, or you could damage the breech and/or the bolt face (and the gun store owner might in turn damage *your* face). Only let the bolt slam forward when there is a full magazine in place (this ensures that the bolt locks into full battery and that the round makes it all the way into the chamber). The condition of the stock should be secondary in your purchase decision, as it doesn't interfere with the operation of the firearm, and refinishing is easy. If the Carbine meets the above criteria - and they usually do - give your money to the nice man behind the counter and take your beautiful new baby home while she's still legal (remember - *no waiting period*).

A number of companies were contracted during WWII to make the Carbine, including Winchester, Inland, IBM and Rock Ola (yep, the juke box company), and these companies operated under strict quality control, not only to ensure reliability under rigorous combat conditions, but all the parts had to be interchangeable. My Carbine is an Inland with some Rock Ola parts. I really doubt if one manufacturer is superior over the others, but I recommend making sure that the weapon you consider for purchase is genuine surplus: there are Carbines on the market of recent manufacture which have proven to be of inferior quality. They may be pretty, but looks - especially when it comes to combat arms - aren't everything.

Speaking of looks, keep in mind the fact that a stock, run-of-the-mill M1 Carbine is pretty innocent looking, as far as assault weapons go. This will be in your favor should your Carbine become People's Exhibit #1 when the geek you shoot lives, and decides to sue you or press criminal charges against you. Contrary to the blather that the controlled media would like us to believe, juries *are* biased. And when it comes to gun fags, juries are downright prejudiced. Think of what it must look like to an average jury (mostly inner-city black women who hate you) when the prosecution displays the weapon with which you've defended yourself. If the thing is equipped with a bipod, folding stock with a pistol grip, flash suppressor, machine-gun style heat shield and "God Bless America" engraved in gold leaf on the side of the receiver, you are not going to get a fair trial. Hollywood doo-dads such as these are available for the

Carbine, but in my opinion, it's better to leave them in the movies.

In light of the above, it's always best to make sure that the douche bag whom you've shot is dead. In this insane, litigation-happy era we live in, you can be vigorously prosecuted for violating the "civil rights" of burglars, muggers and rapists! I personally would like to violate the civil rights of a few lawyers!

Ammo for the M1 Carbine is fairly cheap; usually seven or eight bucks a box, and frequently on sale for considerably less. Also, gun shows are a good place to find real bargains. Regular military ball ammo should work just fine (it has for 50 years), but softpoints are readily available and offer a little more stopping power, as they expand upon entering the target. I haven't seen any hollowpoints in .30 Carbine, and I wouldn't recommend them anyway: they're bound to cause feeding problems, and the last thing you need in an emergency is a jammed weapon.

If you don't buy an M1 Carbine soon, you're either crazy, stupid or you believe everything you read in the treasonous commie newspapers who claim that a gun in the house is more likely to be used against you or your family than against an intruder. That's a vicious lie! Don't be duped by degenerate propaganda! Empower yourself with the American Way!

Nothing else will do.

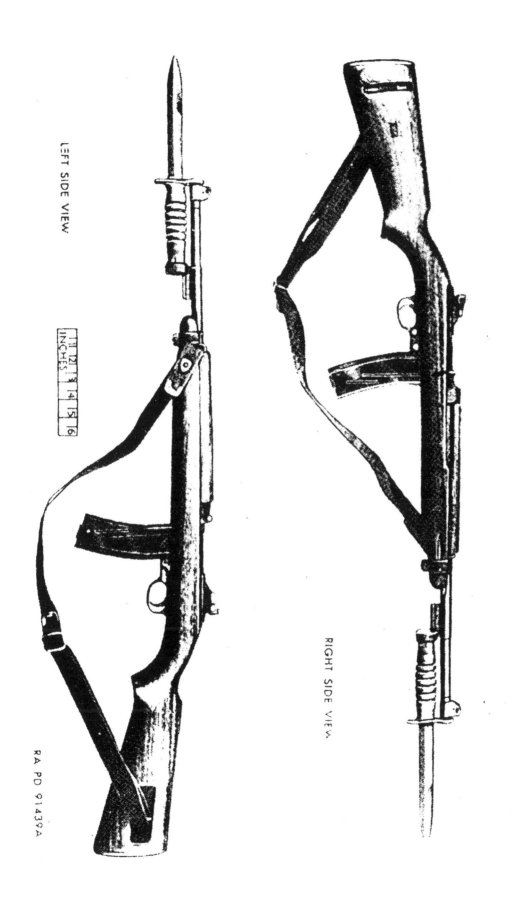

LEFT SIDE VIEW

INCHES 11 12 13 14 15 16

M1 CARBINE

RIGHT SIDE VIEW

RA PD 91439A

21

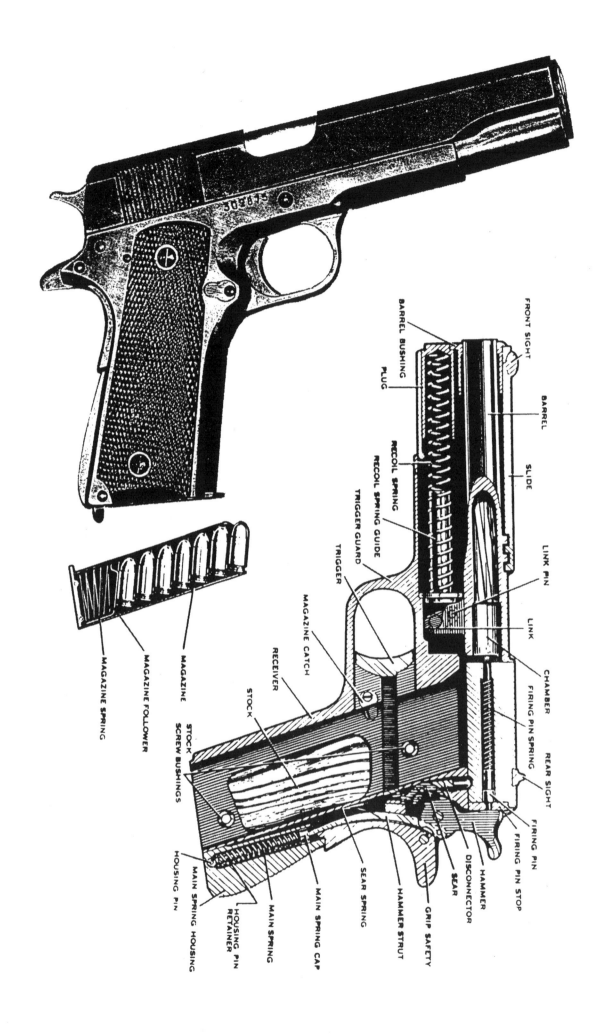

FRONT SIGHT

BARREL BUSHING

PLUG

RECOIL SPRING

RECOIL SPRING GUIDE

TRIGGER GUARD

TRIGGER

MAGAZINE CATCH

RECEIVER

STOCK

STOCK SCREW BUSHINGS

HOUSING PIN

MAIN SPRING HOUSING

HOUSING PIN RETAINER

MAIN SPRING

MAIN SPRING CAP

SEAR SPRING

HAMMER STRUT

GRIP SAFETY

SEAR

DISCONNECTOR

HAMMER

FIRING PIN

FIRING PIN STOP

REAR SIGHT

FIRING PIN SPRING

CHAMBER

LINK

LINK PIN

SLIDE

BARREL

MAGAZINE

MAGAZINE FOLLOWER

MAGAZINE SPRING

NORINCO M1911A1 .45 AUTO

In the early part of this century, the U.S. Marine Corps didn't just sit around letting its talent go to waste. They were called upon to put down scores of uprisings and uppity third-world regimes with the utmost valor. They encountered some fearsome opponents; among these were coca-crazed Nicaraguans and Colombians who would fight viciously in close-quarters with several .38 slugs lodged in their amped-up bodies. The military needed a sidearm that would incapacitate these punks. Hence, the birth of the Colt 1911 Government Model .45.

The Government .45 is probably the most popular semi-automatic pistol in America. It has been copied by countless arms manufacturers over the years, and there is a plethora of companies specializing in aftermarket parts, "race" kits and sporty gizmos for the hardcore fans of the .45. Gunsmiths all over the country are kept in business by modifying and customizing the heck out of .45s for competition matches or for combat. They're used for everything. Even the water pistols I had when I was a kid were replicas of .45s. And what *good* movie would be complete without a .45 or two? Can you imagine Humphrey Bogart or James Cagney packing a 9mm? Perish the thought! Speaking of movies, there's a graphic scene in a film called "Fingered" starring Lydia Lunch where a guy uses a .45 on Lydia the way a normal guy would use his wedding tackle! She seems to like this, and later, while she has the gun and he's doing it to her the regular way on the hood of a car, she fires off a few rounds in ecstasy. Yahoo!

Of the copies, the Norinco .45 is probably the best bargain going right now. It's an exact replica of the famed G.I. "A1" model (the later version of the 1911, incorporating a shorter trigger pull and an arched, *rather* than flat mainspring housing) issued from WWII up until very recently, when the Pentageeks decided that all military sidearms will be chambered for the vastly inferior 9mm Parabellum.

Norinco firearms are made in China. Now before you go into your hysterical "Buy American" tirade, hear me out: They're made in prison camps using slave labor! America could learn a lesson or two from China, even if they *are* commies. But politics aside, here's the scoop on the gun itself:

This is a semi-automatic .45 caliber handgun with a capacity of eight rounds (seven in the magazine and one in the chamber). They come either parkerized (matte-black "G.I." style) or with the more civilized blued finish. Mine is of the latter variety. Coming soon are a couple of pimpish-looking hard-chrome and nickel plated models, as well as a "Combat Commander" version (shorter barrel) in all finishes. The gun comes with an owner's manual, a bore brush and two magazines.

Upon taking it out of the box for the first time, I jacked a few rounds through it by yanking the slide back and forth with a full magazine, just to check smoothness of functioning. The bullets (plain lead round-nose) chambered and ejected with no problem, but the slide action was pretty rough. Examination of the slide and lower receiver after field-stripping revealed tooling marks on the bearing surfaces which, while admittedly shoddy, poses no risk and doesn't interfere with functioning at all. And what do you expect for $275.00, a Colt Gold Cup? Nevertheless, the roughness all but disappeared after firing a couple hundred rounds. The grip panels, true to the G.I. model, are cheap-looking ugly brown plastic, which I discarded immediately in favor of a beautiful pair made of endangered hardwood. If you don't like wood, Pachmayr makes an excellent set of wrap-around rubber combat grips for about $25.

Firing the Norinco is a pleasant enough experience. Like the Colt, the gun fits comfortably in the hand and points naturally, making for fast target acquisition. Recoil is quite tame for a large-caliber handgun; it's nothing compared to a .357 or .44 magnum. You can fire this gun all day long without enduring any of the punishment associated with the above-mentioned magnums.

Accuracy with this gun is not all that great. But so what? 99.99 per cent of the situations encountered in the city requiring the use of deadly force happen at point-blank range. The idea is to stop the creep with one shot if possible (fire three or four times anyway), and for this you need a bullet big and heavy enough to remove meat. Pinpoint accuracy doesn't even come into the picture here.

The only problem encountered so far: This gun does not like Black Talon ammo (it's hard to find anyway, since Winchester, in a disgusting act of spinelessness, recently agreed under Clintonian pressure to limit all sales of Black Talon ammo to the law-enforcement community). After loading up with Black Talons, I tried to empty the gun, only to find that I couldn't remove the chambered round, no matter how hard I jerked the slide. The only way to unload the thing was to pull the trigger! I removed the magazine,

pointed the gun out my apartment window and let 'er rip, being sure to aim toward Hollywood Boulevard (that way no one *innocent* would get hurt). The Black Talon bullet appears to be a little fatter at the tip than most others, and thus achieves an interference-fit in the chamber, which in the case of this particular gun was probably made just a little bit too small. I've never heard of this happening before, so I don't think it's a common problem. Everything else I've fired with this gun works without a hitch, including man-stoppers like Federal Hydra Shok and CCI Lawman jacketed hollowpoints.

But don't worry about problems with the gun. Buy one, load it and fire it. Fire it all day. Take it with you to work, school and play. Shoot drug dealers and car thieves with it. Impress girls with it. Pistol-whip the squeegee guy in the grocery store parking lot with it. Walk with the confidence you deserve as an American. No longer must you tolerate the panhandler with the vomit on his pants who claims to be hungry. No longer must you avert your eyes in submission upon crossing the path of an *untermensch*. No longer are you a prisoner in your own home, confined by lawless vultures who look upon you as carrion. You are *armed*. You are *dangerous*. You are king.

If what you're looking for is more bang for the buck, I recommend this gun.

PLACES TO SHOOT, THINGS TO SHOOT

There was time not so long ago, a healthier time, when man and gun went and did as they damned well pleased. A fella could step out onto his back porch and dispatch a pesky varmint with his trusty old "side b' side" or venture into the woods for weeks at a time, returning home with a harvest of deer, elk and bear. We no longer live in a healthy time, and that varmint out by the back porch is not likely to be of the four-legged variety. But we still need to keep our shooting skills finely honed, and unfortunately we can't shoot like free men anymore. Here are a few guidelines to keep in mind:

Supervised ranges are for those who feel the need to be supervised. True gun fags, being men of *freedom,* do not fit into this category. We need to be where the deer and the antelope play (or at least to where *something* plays - scoring a hit on a moving target is much more challenging and satisfying than poking holes in paper). And add to this the sad fact that established ranges never allow us to exercise our constitutional right to DRINK BEER.

OUTDOOR RANGES: Just a mile or so up the road from the hallowed spot where that well-known punk got his ass whipped by the L.A.P.D.'s Foothill Division (they should have just shot the son of a bitch), is the Angeles Crest Shooting Range. They charge ten bucks to get in, with a $1 discount for NRA members. The place is alright if standing shoulder to shoulder with a bunch of armpit-smelling ragheads firing cheesy little .25 autos is something you consider fun. I personally am not allowed back into that range, since they kicked me out for drinking beer. Can you believe that shit? They probably even supported the Brady Bill! Fuckin' pansies!

INDOOR RANGES: They're stuffy, they smell bad and they're always full of non-english speaking immigrants who have no business handling guns in the first place. Avoid them.

Save your money. There are plenty of places - even outside the city - where you can fire at will all day long without suffering through annoying "safety" rules. FUCK RULES! Of course, it's a sad fact that experienced shooters generally don't drink and shoot, so for safety's sake, I recommend shooting with experienced drinkers.

Just start driving north or east out of L.A., and after about an hour and a half look for a place to pull off the road. You should set up in a place out of earshot, and not visible from the road; a lot of family types get nervous at the sight of gun fags with beer, and they're liable to call the cops or, worse, the fuckin' Sierra Club. Not that any *smart* cop or bunny-hugging Bolshevik is likely to approach a dozen or so drunks under a hail of roaring gunfire, but they like to report our activities, which eventually leads to legislation, and we certainly do not need any more of *that!*

TARGETS: These can range anywhere from the previous night's beer cans to your ex-girlfriend's car. One of my favorite targets makes some people nervous, but you can't beat it for ballistics observation: a human corpse. If you know anyone who works for the city or county in any law-enforcement capacity, it's pretty easy to claim a John Doe from the morgue; the coroners are more than happy to get rid of them. Be sure to bring a shovel, because

A smug Lee Harvey Oswald about a minute before he ate lead

when you're finished with the target you'll have to bury it deep enough to where the coyotes can't get at it. When some do-good hiker spots a coyote gnawing on an arm, he's bound to report it, and again, this is something we do not need.

AMMO: Bring plenty, and don't waste your money on the expensive stuff. It's surprising how fast you can burn up a thousand rounds, even if you're only firing revolvers.

FIRST AID KIT: Will do you no good. In case of an accident, the above-referenced shovel will be all you'll need. Hospitals are required by law to report gunshot wounds to the police, so it's best to not deal with them at all. It should be understood by all parties involved that if a guy acquires lead, he ain't coming back.

Happy shooting!

SMITH & WESSON
MODEL 586 DISTINGUISHED COMBAT MAGNUM

There is almost nothing as simply elegant as a Smith & Wesson revolver. The only thing I can think of that comes close is Colt's spendy Python, which is a little too high falutin' for this blue collar man. On the other end of the spectrum are Ruger's double-action revolvers, which, while tough enough to be used as framing hammers (this has been proven by guest-columnist Red) just don't have that Smith & Wesson grace.

The Model 586 .357 magnum was a worthy addition to the proud Smith & Wesson line, and while there are still plenty of them on dealers' shelves, this model has unfortunately been discontinued. *What the hell are they thinking? This is quite possibly the ultimate revolver!* Well, it turns out that it's not the fault of Smith & Wesson; the American public just wasn't buying the 586 in quantities sufficient to justify its continued production. The popularity of traditional blued steel revolvers is evidently on the wane. The relatively few people who buy wheel-guns anymore lean toward stainless steel in their preference (the model 686, still in production and selling well, is a stainless version of the 586). This trend of abandoning traditional handguns in favor of flashy stainless steel revolvers, ridiculous-capacity 9mm autos, polymer stocks and plastic composite frames gets this gun fag a little misty-eyed for the good old days when guns were black and men were white. This decline of firearms tradition parallels society's abandonment of traditional values, which is creating a reprehensible moral vacuum in this country. Our one-peaceful world is being torn apart by liberal hyenas and leftist jackals at the same time our once-proud gun marketplace is being flooded with newfangled toys. I'm no conspiracy theorist, but this glaring "coincidence" is disturbing.

There aren't enough adjectives in the English language to describe the stunning beauty of this gun. It is almost perfect. Maybe it *is* perfect. Its heavy, fully-lugged 6" barrel projects an air of indisputable masculinity (while helping to keep the big guy's stout recoil down to a manageable level). To gaze at this masterpiece is to feed the very soul. The elegant curve of the trigger housing gently draws the viewer's eye up over the immaculately machined thumbpiece, pausing for a moment to absorb the artfully swept-back hammer spur before continuing on to reflect nostalgically on Smith & Wesson's trademark adjustable rear sight, which has been unsuccessfully mimicked by lesser companies for years. The lovingly crafted checkered hardwood grip fills the heart as well as the hand. The finish is flawless in its application as well as its mystique. It is a monument to all things good and right. This is one beautiful gat.

And accurate as all get-out! Before I was 86'ed from the Angeles Crest Shooting Range for drinking beer I was able to fire several hundred rounds through the 586 in their ridiculously - *anally* - controlled environment at silhouette targets placed at 25 and 50 yards. After a couple clicks of windage adjustment to the rear sight, I was able to hit consistently dead on.

I did have one problem with this piece, which has been cleared up by the factory, under warranty. I suspect that the problem was an aberration, and should in no way influence your decision should you decide to plunk down the dough for one of these beauties: while fresh out of the box, the thing shaved lead like crazy.

I'll explain: if the cylinder does not line up perfectly with the barrel, if the gap between the barrel and cylinder is too large or if the forcing cone is slightly misshapen, a piece of the bullet will be shaved off on its way through the cylinder gap and launch out the side of the gun at enormous velocity. If you happen to be standing off to the side of the shooter when this happens, you'll definitely notice. *It fuckin' hurts!*

Federal Express is too politically correct to ship firearms - which is a good reason to boycott their sniveling liberal asses - so I shipped the gun via U.P.S. to the factory in Springfield, Mass. with a brief explanation of the problem. I got it back two weeks later. There was no charge, and the problem has been completely eliminated.

Go buy a 586 now, before they become pricey collectibles. You will treasure it 'till the day you die, and then your grandchildren can fight over it.

S&W Model 586 – One Beautiful Gat

REQUIEM FOR A GUN FAG

He was a fearless visionary, a man with purpose and the will to do the right thing. He was a quiet man; his actions having spoke louder than his words. His courage and his unflinching fortitude proved to be bigger than his enormous girth. He engaged the enemy with a style and grace rarely seen among modern men. Sadly, this great revolutionary is no longer with us, for his pride and dignity would not allow him to be taken prisoner. In the face of overwhelming odds, he took his own life on July 7, 1993. He bid a final farewell to his trusty sidearm, the Norinco 1911A1 .45 auto, and turned it upon himself.

Gian-Luigi Ferri, we hardly knew ye, but your legend will live on in our hearts, and your spirit will not falter in the face of our foes. You big fat Gun Fag, rest in peace.

BLACKPOWDER SIX-SHOOTERS
SMOKE, HONOR & MANHOOD

There is a small subculture of cowboy buffs and Civil War fetishists who swear that blackpowder cap-and-ball guns are every bit as useful and effective as modern firearms. This is obvious horseshit, but the irresistible charm of these smoke-belching dinosaurs is understandable. Hold a Colt Walker or Dragoon six-shooter in your hand and you automatically imagine yourself scowling around a soggy old cigar as you draw a bead on the dirty four-flusher across the card table whom you've just caught cheating. With a resounding *DOOM!* smoke billows forth from four pounds of gun at the end of your arm as you send that low-down galoot to meet the big trail boss in the sky.

I've had a hankerin' to own one of these coal-burners for quite some time, but never thought of them as being practical enough to justify spending the money (about $200). As it turns out, I won an Italian-made Colt 1860 Army .44 caliber sixgun in a poker game (a much different game, unfortunately, than the one described above). This gun has put me in touch with my manhood like no other.

Step aside, boys. There's a new sheriff in town, and he ain't likely to take any guff. He's fixin' to set things right around these parts, and y'all best behave yourselves whilst he's a-workin.' Sheriff Hollister Kopp: one-man posse. Judge, jury and executioner. Old gravel-guts. Step aside, boys.

The cap and ball sixgun is reduced to a handsome paperweight without the accessories that go with it: you'll need 3F black powder (a can with enough powder for hundreds of shots goes for $8.00) and a powder flask ($18.00 for a deluxe model which precisely measures the powder for each cylinder). You'll also need .44 caliber felt wads ($3.50 for a bag of 100) to place in the chambers on top of the powder before cramming the bullet in (this prevents powder from coming loose and igniting the neighboring chambers, an unsettling situation known as a *chain fire*), #11 percussion caps ($3.50 for a can of 100) and .44 caliber lead balls (about $4.50 per bag of 100). Since a blackpowder hogleg gets badly gummed up and is only good for about 18 shots before cleaning, you should always keep some kind of cleaning agent handy while shooting. The best - though not in keeping with the old west flavor - is a can of carburetor cleaner: after about the third reload, just spray around the cylinder and barrel. The black goop runs right off and the cleaner evaporates instantly. Don't buy expensive gun cleaning spray; it's only carburetor cleaner (trichloroethane solvent) with a different label.

Loading one of these relics is a ritual unto itself. Pull the hammer back to half-cock so the cylinder spins freely. With your left hand holding the gun barrel skyward and butt resting on the shooting bench or pickup hood or whatever, grab the powder flask with your right hand. Turn the flask upside down and work the lever back and forth with your thumb, while your index finger covers the nozzle. You now have a measured charge. Dump it into a chamber and repeat this process for the other five chambers. Next, stick a felt wad into each chamber. To load the balls, place one on the chamber just to the right of the barrel and rotate the cylinder so that the ball rests beneath the loading lever. Ram it in tight. A ball of the correct size will leave a small ring which has been shaved off, as the ball fits tightly into the chamber. Keeping the gun at half-cock, stick the caps onto the nipples on the back side of the cylinder. They should stay just fine, but sometimes you have to squeeze them a little before you put them on, giving them a tighter fit. As you practice this procedure a few times, it becomes fairly easy; a seasoned gun fag such as myself can accomplish the task in well under a minute.

The gun is now ready to go!

Aside from the above-mentioned chain fire, safety concerns are about the same as any other single-action revolver (i.e., if you're going to carry it around, leave the hammer resting on an empty chamber). And this note of caution: if you're going to fire a blackpowder gun in any public situation (ranges, etc.) be sure to at *least* wear boots and a hat. If you disgrace one of these celebrated shootin' irons by wearing some pansy-assed jogging suit, you're going to raise the ire of surly blackpowder enthusiasts who'll have you drawn & quartered. Show some respect!

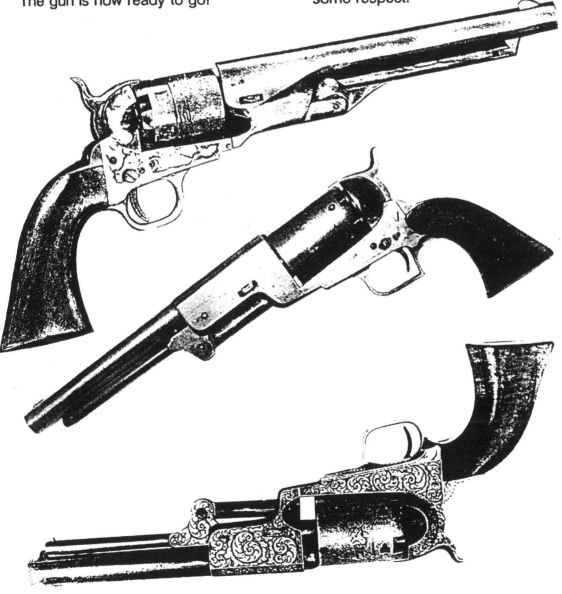

Top to bottom: Colt 1860 Army, Walker and Dragoon

CRIME COULD BE BROUGHT UNDER CONTROL
BUT AS LONG AS THE GEEKS ARE IN POWER, IT WON'T BE

So the heathen liberal filth in Sacramento have finally - after kicking and screaming for years against it - passed an enormously popular (that is, popular with *citizens*) bill through the Assembly known as Three Strikes You're Out, which allegedly means that a person convicted of a violent or serious felony for the third time would spend the rest of his life in the joint. This bill is a namby-pamby approach to an out-of-control problem, but it is a step in the right direction. The arguments against the bill range from the ridiculous (the prisons are already overcrowded) to the naive (convicted felons need a chance to be rehabilitated - give them jobs!).

Boo fuckin' hoo. Look, you grovelling political perverts, nobody cares if prisons are overcrowded, and rehabilitation is nothing more than a vote-grabbing hollow promise that you fuckers callously hand down to your stinking, illiterate ghetto constituencies. That they are allowed to vote at all flies in the face of reason. And if I'm wrong about you cynical bastards, then what the hell are you afraid of? Are you afraid that you might hurt the feelings of a three-time convicted felon? And why do you insist on calling the guerilla war in our cities a crime wave? Democrats! Republicans! For all practical purposes you're one and the same! That leaves us, the bewildered, frustrated and bitter taxpayers with no voice in government. There needs to be an officially recognized Nationalist Gun Fag Party, whose candidates would *literally* stomp the teeth out of pansy-ass Republicans and faggot Democrats. Sadly, this will never happen as long as THEY control the television networks and print media, thereby controlling and shaping public opinion to satisfy their own craven agendas. Bastards!

If we are to get any handle on crime at all, most major Supreme Court decisions from the last hundred years will have to be immediately overturned. The Bill of Rights needs to be suspended; only the second amendment should remain intact. American jurisprudence needs to be rolled back by at least two centuries. And the idea of imprisonment - sending a criminal to a huge human warehouse to spend a couple of years watching TV with his buddies - is relatively new to Western Culture. In healthier times, common forms of punishment included branding, mutilation (this is still practiced to good effect in the Middle East), indentured servitude or death. And with a television in nearly every household these days, getting the message to a wide audience would not be a problem, should the need arise to make an example of someone. Short of this, logic dictates that criminals should at the *very least* be sterilized; allowing them to reproduce is a crime in itself.

The above methods are unrealistic only because they make sense. Our only recourse is to work with what we've got, which means the cops have a big job ahead of them. Their hands are tied, however - a la Vietnam - in a war which they are not allowed to win. The politicians' claim that cops are outgunned by the criminal element is a stupidly transparent lie: when was the last time you heard of a dope dealer or gangbanger use an attack helicopter or a fighter jet? How about an M1 Abrams Main Battle Tank? The cops are not outgunned, they are just forced to take orders from snivelling desk-jockeys who have never been to the Front and are themselves under orders from Western Civilization's sworn enemies at the L.A. Times and CBS/NBC/ABC. The police can't even use a nightstick anymore, for crying out loud, let alone a real weapon!

If the scum politicians really wanted to reduce crime, they wouldn't be actively involved in disarming law-abiding taxpayers and sending cops to jail for doing their jobs. They wouldn't insult us by deifying the likes of Rodney King. They wouldn't subsidize worthless simpletons who refuse to contribute to society, yet bear litters of moronic children who will in turn depend upon the Welfare State - and crime - for their survival. They wouldn't look the other way as swarms of brazen, uneducated peasants invade our country *every day,* bringing with them disease, crime and more children! They wouldn't coddle looters, arsonists and killers by referring to a fucking riot as "civil unrest!"

And they wouldn't assume that a placebo like the Three Strikes You're Out bill is going to pacify an angry citizenry who one day soon could become *genuinely* fed up. Fed up enough to support for President someone like Hollister Kopp. Then we'll see the sonsabitches squirm.

Salus populi suprema est lex.

The Reverend Jesse Jackson on a good day.

RED'S LAST WORD

Jake Joseph L.Z. Kilroy Kowalski IV aka Red

MY AGENT CALLED ME THE OTHER DAY ABOUT A WRITING ASSIGNMENT FOR A NEW GUN MAGAZINE COMING OUT THIS SPRING CALLED GUN FAGS ARE US OR SOMETHING LIKE THAT FUCKING SHIT...WELL I AM NOT REALLY TOO SURE THAT GUNS AND FAGS GO TOGETHER OR THAT FAGS SHOULD HAVE GUNS...THE ONLY TIME THAT THEY DO GO TOGETHER IS WHEN YOU'RE AIMING A BIG OLD THREE FIVE SEVEN AT ONE OF THEM LIMP WRISTED LIBERALS LIKE THOSE IN WASHINGTON...WELL FUCK I WILL GET TO THAT ANOTHER TIME...SINCE I HAVE NOT BEEN MAKING MUCH MONEY RUNNING MY METH AND RELOADING LAB GODDAMN EXPENSES AND GOOD HELP IS HARD TO COME BY THESE DAYS WHAT'S WRONG WITH THIS FUCKING COUNTRY...EVERYONE WANTS FUCKING HANDOUTS WELL HOW BOUT KICKING SOME MY WAY...SINATRA...I DON'T GIVE A FUCK ABOUT MY FUCKING PRIDE OR I WOULD NOT BE WRITING THIS FUCKING PIECE OF SHIT COLUMN TO PAY MY FUCKING RENT...MY AGENT TOLD ME THAT I WOULD BE PAID ONE THOUSAND AMERICAN DOLLARS UP FRONT PLUS MILAGE AND ALL THE BEER I COULD STOMACH FROM SOME TITTY BAR CALLED CECIL'S...I GUESS CECIL'S IS THE FAGS' HEADQUARTERS WHICH SOUNDS WEIRDER THAN FUCKING SHIT TO ME BUT MONEY IS MONEY WHAT THE FUCK...AND MY AGENT GOT THEM TO THROW IN A STOLEN OR CONFISCATED GUN OF MY CHOICE...WELL FUCK SINCE THE LAST GREAT PIECE OF SHIT THAT I WROTE BESIDES THE RENT CHECK WAS TWENTY YEARS AGO NO MORE LIKE TEN WAS ENTITLED THE GUNS OF BURBANK...THAT GOT ME IN SOME TROUBLE WITH THE

LOCAL LAW ENFORCEMENT CUNTS...NOW I LIVE BY THE SALTON SEA...I DECIDED TO GO MEET THESE FUCKING FAGS...AS LONG AS THERE'S NO POLE IN MOTION I THOUGHT I'D BE ALRIGHT...SO I LOCKED UP MY AIRSTREAM...A TWENTY FOOTER...TOLD FOUR BALLS TOMMY TO KEEP AN EYE ON THINGS AND HEADED FOR MY SCARY FUCKING DESTINATION...UNCERTAIN FATE...WHAT A WAY TO FUCKING GO...I HOPPED INTO MY '62 CHEVY TRUCK WITH A CASE OF P.B.R. TALLBOYS AND A COLT .45 LOADED WITH MY OWN FUCKING VERSION OF BLACK TALONS...FUCKING PANTYWAISTS AT WINCHESTER...WELL WHAT THE FUCK MINE ARE BETTER AND FUCKING CHEAPER...I HAVE NOT BEEN TO BURBANK SINCE THE GUNS OF BURBANK CAME OUT IN THE SPRING OF EIGHTY-FOUR...PLACES LIKE BURBANK DON'T CHANGE MUCH THANK GOD...EXCEPT FOR THIS TITTY BAR CALLED CECIL'S...FUCK WHAT KIND OF TITTY BAR COULD THIS BE IF FAGS WERE HANGING OUT THERE...WERE THE WOMEN CRANK-SPENT GRANDMAS TRYING TO RELIVE THEIR NOT-SO-GLORIOUS YOUTH OR DID THESE FAGS SEE PARTS OF HILLARY FUCKING RODHAM IN THEM THAT NO NORMAL MALE COULD EVER SEE EVEN WITH EIGHTEEN FUCKING P.B.R. TALLBOYS IN THEIR GUTS...WELL IT WAS SOMEWHERE AROUND MY NINTH TALLBOY THAT I GOT A CRACKLE ON MY OLD TUBE CITIZENS BAND RADIO...THE THING CAN FUCKING SCRAMBLE TV SATELLITE DISHES AND BLOW CELLULAR PHONES FOR A FUCKING GODDAMN THREE MILE RADIUS DAMN I LOVE THIS FUCKING THING SOMETIMES MORE THAN MY FUCKING GUNS AND MY FUCKING P.B.R. BECAUSE OF ALL THE HAVOC I CAN INFLICT ON A LOT OF SUPPOSEDLY INNOCENT FUCKING PEOPLE FOR FREE AND IT IS LEGAL...WELL ALMOST...

*THIS IS THREE NINER NINER FIVE CALLING TWO ALPHA BRAVO CHARLEY SIX FIVE HOTEL TANGO OR SOMETHING MOTHER DO YOU COPY...*I TOSSED MY BEER CAN OUT THE WINDOW ALMOST CAUSING AN ACCIDENT...MAYBE NEXT TIME...WHAT IN GOD'S ASS CREATION DO YOU FUCKING WANT FOUR BALLS TOMMY...*THIS IS THREE NINER NINER...*CUT THE FUCKING MILITARY LINGO THE FUCKING WAR IS OVER...*RED THEY'RE COMING TO GET ME RED THE MEN IN BLACK...*HOW MUCH FUCKING CRANK HAVE YOU DONE IN THE LAST THREE FUCKING HOURS YOU FUCKING IDIOT...*A FUCKING LOT AND DON'T CALL ME AN IDIOT YOU FUCKING BASTARD OR I WILL KILL YOU AND YOUR FUCKING FAMILY SOME FUCKING DAY...*FUCK YOUR FUCKING ASS FOUR BALLS AND TELL ME WHAT THE FUCK IS GOING ON...

ABOUT THIS TIME SOME RICH FUCK WAS TAPPING HIS CELLULAR PHONE ON THE DASH OF HIS BMW WHICH MADE ME HAPPY...I WAS GETTING A WOODY AND COULDN'T WAIT TO GET TO CECIL'S NO MATTER HOW BUTT ASS UGLY THE TITTY SHAKERS WERE GOING TO BE...

FUCK YOU ALL I WILL NOT BE TAKEN ALIVE YOU FUCKING SHIT EATING FUCKERS IN BLACK...

FOUR BALLS TOMMY WAS TOTALLY PINNED AND I KNEW THAT THERE WAS NOTHING I COULD DO NOR DID I REALLY CARE ABOUT THAT PIECE OF SHIT SKELETAL METH-SPENT HUMAN...FOUR BALLS TOMMY WAS TWO SANDWICHES SHORT OF A PICNIC...EVER SINCE THE FALL OF '87 WHEN HIS MOTHER AND SISTER DIED IN BANGKOK DOING GOD KNOWS WHAT...THERE WAS JUST LONELY STATIC ON THE CB FOR ABOUT TEN SECONDS...THEN A HAIL OF GUNFIRE...CALIBERS OF MANY DENOMINATIONS WERE GOING OFF AND IT MADE ME HAPPY WITH MEAN-ASS AMERICAN ANGER...THEN

37

SILENCE AND I KNEW THAT FOUR BALLS TOMMY WAS NO LONGER WITH US...HE WOULD NOT BE MISSED BUT WHO THE FUCK WAS GOING TO FEED MY DOG...I TURNED OFF THE CB PLUGGED IN A CD AND ZEPPELIN FOUR BOUNCED AROUND THE CAB OF MY TRUCK AND I WAS ON MY TENTH OR MAYBE ELEVENTH P.B.R. AND TEN MINUTES SOUTH OF BURBANK...MY FUCKING TRIUMPHANT RETURN AND I GOTTA SEE A BUNCH OF QUEERS·WITH GUNS...SHIT...I PARKED MY TRUCK RIGHT IN FRONT OF CECIL'S WHICH IS AN OLD CINDER BLOCK BUILDING ON VICTORY IN THE DIRTY INDUSTRIAL PART OF BURBANK...CRACK WHORES AND MEXICAN AUTOBODY SHOPS LITTERED THIS PART OF BURBANK NOW WHICH YEARS EARLIER WAS THE GLORIOUS HOME OF LOCKHEED AIRCRAFT...HOME OF THE SR-71 AND THE P3 ORION AND HONEST HARD WORKING TAX PAYING WHITE MEN BUT LONG GONE NOW...NO FORWARDING ADDRESS...THE STRONG STENCH OF URINE AND FUCKING MOLDY YELLOW VOMIT STAINS UP AND DOWN THE BLOCK...I THINK I MIGHT FEEL AT HOME HERE...LIKE DEER IN THE HEADLIGHTS LIKE SOME DUMB DELIRIOUS FUCK IN MY GUNSIGHTS...I WAS SINGING...I WALKED INTO THE PLACE EXPECTING THE FUCKING WORST BUT FOUND IT RATHER NICE WITH ITS DISCO BALL SPINNING BETWEEN TWO FUCKING GIANT STAGES WITH SIX FUCKING BEAUTIFUL GIRLS STRAIGHT OUT OF SWANK WEARING NOTHING BUT ENGINEER BOOTS...THEIR HAIR ALL UP IN BUNS WITH FUCKING PENCILS STUCK THROUGH THEM AND ALL SIX WEARING BUDDY HOLLY GLASSES...WEIRD...THE PLACE WAS PACKED UP FRONT BUT NOT TOO BAD AT THE BAR...THE GIRLS WERE GYRATING THEIR SWEET PELVISES AND SHAKING THEIR AMAZING HOOTERS TO THE SOUNDS OF THE FUCKING BOILERMAKERS...WHICH I FOUND OUT LATER WAS BURBANK'S BEST KEPT SECRET SINCE RIBS U.S.A...THERE WAS NO POLE-SMOKING OR FUCKING HAND HOLDING GOING ON...WHEN BULLETS RAIN AND STRAINS DUMBFUCK BRAINS I FEEL NO PAIN...I WAS FORTY FIVE MINUTES AND THREE FIFTY SEVEN FUCKING EARLY...SO I TOOK A STOLEN BAR STOOL FROM THE BLUE SALOON AND DRANK THIRTY-OUGHT-SIX OUNCE PITCHERS OF WIDMER HEFEWEIZEN FOR A DOLLAR SIXTY EIGHT...I GUESS THE EARTHQUAKE TAX FOR THE DUMBFUCKS WHO LIVE ON FAULTS...NOT MY FUCKING FAULT...WITH A COUPLE OF WWII AND KOREAN WAR VETS...NAM VETS AND GULF WAR VETS WERE NOT ALLOWED AS BOTH WERE FUCKING FAG WARS...THE PHONE RANG AND I HAD A GUT-ACHE FEELING IT WAS FOR MY SORRY ASS...WERE THE FAGS GOING TO BE LATE BECAUSE OF SOME AIDS TEST OR GIVING KNOBBERS IN GRIFFITH PARK TO PAY THEIR FUCKING FAGGOTY LACE PINK-ASS SILVERLAKE FUCKING RENT OR SOME FUCKING SHIT...THE BARTENDER COULD BARELY TALK BETWEEN HIS PALL MALLS AND GASPING BONG-LIKE ON HIS FUCKING RESPIRATOR...GIVE ME THE FUCKING PHONE I SAID AS HE INCOHERENTLY BABBLED AND BOTCHED MY BEAUTIFUL SWEETASS ALL FUCKING AMERICAN NAME...IT WAS MY AGENT AND PART TIME LAWYER SAMUEL SIMON SIMONSAMUELSTEINBERGSTEIN AND HE SAID IT WAS ABOUT FOUR BALLS TOMMY...I SAID SPARE ME THE FUCKING POLITICALLY CORRECT EULOGY WITH ALL THE FUCKING PRETTY ADJECTIVES WE USE ON DEAD DUMBFUCKS...THE CHINESE INVENTED GUNPOWDER THE FRENCH MADE WINE AND THE FUCKING GLORIOUS U.S. OF A. INVENTED THE NRA AND WHY OH FUCKING WHY ALSO THE ACLU...SIX DEAD FROM THE IMPERIAL COUNTY SHERIFF'S DEPARTMENT AND A HOLE IN THE GROUND THE SIZE OF A FOOTBALL FIELD AND THE SALTON SEA HAS BEEN REVERSED AND IS FLOWING INTO MEXICO...FUCKING HOLY FUCKING FUCK...IT WAS CALEB

AND JARED JUST STOPPED BY TO PICK UP THEIR AMMO FOR THE ANNUAL TURKEY SHOOT WITH THE BORDER PATROL NEXT MONTH...FUCK...YEAH FUCK...FOUR BALLS TOMMY DUMBFUCK WENT FUCKING APE SHIT...ALRIGHT SAMUEL SIMON SIMONSAMUELSTEINBERGSTEIN I WILL TAKE CARE OF IT FROM HERE...I HUNG UP THE PHONE...MY DOG...FUCK...

ARE YOU JAKE JOSEPH L.Z. KILROY KOWALSKI THE FOURTH AKA RED...FUCK YES I AM...GLAD TO MEET YOU I'M DAVE I'LL BE YOUR CONTACT MAN FOR COMMANDER KOPP WHO'S PUTTING TOGETHER GUN FAG MANIFESTO...NICE TO MEET YOUR FUCKING SORRY ASS FUCKING SWEATY ASS FUCKING FACE...HE DIDN'T LOOK LIKE A FAG SO I SHOOK HIS HAND WITH THE KILLER KILROY DEATH GRIP...HE TOOK IT LIKE A MAN...HE SAYS TELL ME ABOUT THE GUNS OF BURBANK AND I SAY SOME OTHER TIME...HE SAYS IT MUST HAVE BEEN ROUGH AND I TELL HIM FUCK YOU FUCK YEAH IT WAS ROUGH AND I STILL WANNA CRY EVERY TIME I SEE A COPY OF IT IN THE USED BIN AT

BIFF BIZ FUCKING BOOK EMPORIUM...DAVE SAYS HOLLISTER KOPP WANTS TO WRITE ABOUT IT AND I SAY FUCK YOU...NO FUCKING WAY...HE SAYS WHAT THE FUCK DO THEY GET FOR THEIR MONEY AND I SAY WHATEVER I FUCKING FEEL LIKE WRITING AND I DON'T WRITE ABOUT THE FUCKING GUNS OF BURBANK OR THE FUCKING NRA...AND GUNS KILL PEOPLE FUCK YEAH GUNS KILL PEOPLE THAT IS WHAT I LOVE ABOUT THEM...EVER TRY TO KILL SOME DUMBASS WITH A COLD FUCKING BUTTER KNIFE...I DIDN'T FUCKING THINK SO...FUCK...

NEXT ISSUE: FOUR BALL TOMMY'S FUNERAL AND COVERAGE OF THE 33RD ANNUAL BORDER TURKEY SHOOT FEATURING WHATS LEFT OF THE IMPERIAL COUNTY SHERIFF'S DEPARTMENT VS THE BORDER PATROL. THAT IS UNLESS THE IMPERIAL COUNTY GRAND JURY HANDS DOWN AN INDICTMENT...

EDITOR'S NOTE
Red's views and behavior are not necessarily compatible with the ethos of *GUN FAG MANIFESTO*. However, his participation in the events of 1984 in Burbank, and his subsequent testimony regarding those events (The Guns of Burbank - now out of print) qualify him as a gun fag of the highest caliber. We are proud to have him aboard.

GUN FAG
~~MANIFESTO~~

Hollister Kopp
EDITOR-IN-CHIEF

March 1, 1994

My Fellow Gun Fags:

THE NEXT ISSUE of *GFM* will feature the excellent
Mossberg Model 500 12-gauge shotgun, which is a proven
killer (ask the Menendez brothers) and a favorite riot-
stopper with police departments all over the country.
Also on next issue's agenda is the Ruger Security Six
.357 magnum revolver, the single-action Ruger New Model
Blackhawk and a couple of other guns not yet decided
upon as of this writing.
　　　You can also depend on *GFM* to deliver more of my
fair and objective political commentary, as well as
reasonable solutions to some of the problems that we
gun fags in particular, and American citizens in
general, face daily. I will keep you posted on any
recent developments regarding the government gun-
grabbers as well.
　　　Letters to the Editor are welcome, and I plan to
run some of them in the next issue. They should be
addressed to Hollister Kopp, ███████████████████████
███████████████.
　　　Until then, my friends, peel an eye and keep your
powder dry; it's going to get worse before it gets
better.

Peace

HK

Hollister Kopp

GUN FAG

MANIFESTO

2

$4

ENTERTAINMENT FOR THE ARMED SOCIOPATH

GUN FAG MANIFESTO

is published whenever the Publisher feels that there is enough material to assemble an issue. This could be weeks, months, years or never.

STAFF:

HOLLISTER KOPP
Publisher, Editor

JAKE JOSEPH L.Z. KILROY KOWALSKI IV (aka RED)
Society Columnist

CONTRIBUTING GUN FAGS:

CHET ANTONINI
POLLYANNE HORNBECK
JAMES STEINBACH

All articles by Hollister Kopp unless otherwise noted

**For additional copies of GFM
SEND $4.00 CASH TO**

Anyone caught reprinting, publicly exhibiting or badmouthing any of the contents of *Gun Fag Manifesto* without express permission of the Publisher will be shot.

Copyright © September, 1994

**Elvis on the cover drawn by the amazing STEVE KIDWILER
who carries a Glock .40 S&W
and scanned into the Mac by the esteemed MALKA YOUNGSTEIN
who packs a Colt Police Positive .38 Special**

THIS IS THE CITY. LOS ANGELES, CALIFORNIA.

HOME TO A ONCE-BOOMING FALSE ECONOMY WHICH ATE ITSELF ALIVE LIKE A SELF-LOATHING AND GLUTTONOUS MONSTER.
HOME TO MOVIE STARS AND MAYHEM, RACE RIOTS AND TERROR. EVERY MINUTE OF EVERY DAY A CAR IS STOLEN, A WOMAN IS RAPED AND A CHILD IS BEATEN. POLICE MORALE IS AT ITS LOWEST POINT IN L.A.'S HISTORY. NEWBORN BABIES ARE FOUND DEAD IN DUMPSTERS. THE ENTIRE CITY IS COATED WITH A GRIMY, LEAD AND BENZINE-LADEN DUST, AND ITS INHABITANTS ARE CHOKED WITH AN OPRESSIVE AND PERVASIVE SMELL OF AUTOMOBILE EXHAUST, ROTTING GARBAGE AND URINE. SIRENS SCREAM BY, HOVERING HELICOPTERS RATTLE WINDOWS AND KICK UP MORE DUST, TIRES SCREECH AND HORNS BLARE. GUNFIGHTS ERUPT OVER IMPROPER LANE CHANGES. ROBBERY IS AS COMMON AND CASUAL AS LITTERING. INSANE TRANSIENTS BABBLE AND SHOUT AT HALLUCINATIONS, FOREVER TRAPPED IN THEIR OWN PRIVATE HELL, AND NO ONE CARES ENOUGH TO SHOOT THEM.

WELFARE CHECKS ARE ROUTINELY GIVEN TO FERTILE MORONS, ENSURING A NEVER-ENDING CYCLE OF MISERY AND HOPELESSNESS.

LOOK AROUND, AND IN EVERY DIRECTION THERE ARE PRIMITIVE HUMAN BEINGS FROM UNGODLY THIRD-WORLD COUNTRIES WITH CULTURES REPUGNANT AND OFFENSIVE TO WESTERN CIVILIZATION. THERE ARE MILLIONS OF THEM, ALL CLOISTERED TOGETHER IN THE CITY LIKE CATTLE.
ONLY THEY'RE FAR WORSE THAN CATTLE:
- THEIR BREEDING IS COMPLETELY UNREGULATED -
- THEY'RE ALLOWED TO MAKE DECISIONS -
- THEY HAVEN'T BEEN FENCED IN -

FITFUL SLEEP IS CONSTANTLY INTERRUPTED BY SOME SELF-IMPORTANT YUPPIE'S SCREAMING CAR ALARM. MAYBE THE CAR IS BEING BROKEN INTO. GOOD! THE FUCKING ALARM IS INFURIATING. I GET UP AND SIT IN THE OPEN WINDOW OF MY CHEAP, DILAPIDATED LITTLE APARTMENT WEARING BOXER SHORTS AND A SHOTGUN. IT'S FUCKING HOT.
THE CITY IS HISSING AND BELCHING LIKE A HUGE, UGLY DEMON.

I PRAY FOR ANOTHER EARTHQUAKE.

GUN FAG ~~MANIFESTO~~

It's my LIFE...

Hollister Kopp
EDITOR & PUBLISHER

September 1, 1994

Fellow Gun Fags:

Welcome to issue #2 of *GUN FAG MANIFESTO*: bigger, better and more expensive than issue #1. A lot has happened since issue #1. Mrs. Kopp and I spent a fun-filled month up in Oregon - hiking, fishing, camping, drinking beer, recklessly discharging firearms, basically living it up - and during this time I had my mail temporarily forwarded, which turned out to be a bad idea: our wonderful postal service screwed up my mail in a big way. So if you've sent me an order or a letter and haven't heard back, try again and I'll set you straight.

How 'bout that crime bill, eh? It seems our country is on the fast track to all-out communism (communism, according to my pals over at the John Birch Society, is just socialism in a hurry). We've got a pair of socialists in the White House who are in a hurry and doing their best to destroy the very fabric of civilization. They're going to outlaw all guns which have revolutionary potential (assault weapons), which is exactly why you should own several of them, along with a few thousand rounds of ammo. Do you think the feds (the enemy) are going to give up *their* assault weapons? Not bloody likely. A few years ago I never would have thought that there would come a time when I would be genuinely afraid of my government. Among other villainous schemes, Clinton is stacking the U.S. Supreme Court in favor of totalitarian political correctness. In the next few years the court will make it illegal to question the Official Version of recent world history. You probably think I'm kidding.

Soon the federal government will dictate all aspects of our lives. Total control of the populace is their goal, and the momentum they've gained is appalling. Haven't they had enough? Do they know who they're fooling with? Good God, we're Americans! We hit back! We *shoot* back! We don't need any more goddamn laws! We'll see to it that every greasy politician, bureaucrat and newsroom collaborator is TIED TO A POST WITH THEIR OWN RED TAPE AND SHOT! We cannot live with the United States federal government. It is a cancer that is very close to saturating and killing its victim (western civilization). The time has come to eradicate the disease. I believe it was Thomas Jefferson who said that "the tree of liberty must from time to time be watered with the blood of tyrants, and the blood of patriots."

We don't need the federal government, and we don't need any more laws. The only law worth living by is the law of property rights. Do not take anything from anybody. Period. This includes a person's time, their material possessions, and certainly their life. Anyone who cannot or will not abide by this one simple law should be deported or put to sleep. Now, do we need a big fat slobbering government with its clammy hands forever groping in our pockets to enforce one law? I don't think so.

OK, I had to get that off my chest. You'll notice in this issue a couple of articles submitted by some armed and talented characters. Feel free to send me an essay on your favorite gun (or even a gun you hate) for issue #3. If I decide to run it, I'll send you a confirmation letter. You might also notice an inaccuracy or two in my assessment of gun laws. This is because our oppressors in Washington are attacking our rights at such a brutal pace that I have to edit and re-edit articles to try and keep up with the bastards. I've given up editing for this issue. For example, in *"The President and his Cronies..."* I left in the MAK-90 and SKS rifles (and their average prices as of June '94), even though the world's most powerful draft-dodger has banned the import of Chinese-made firearms in a compromise to Feinstein/Schumer and the Congressional Black Caucus, in order to retain China's most-favored trade status. Pretty sneaky, eh? Next time he tries something like that, I hope he at least uses a condom and a lubricant. You might still find a couple of these rifles around, but Lord only knows what kind of money you'll have to shell out to actually purchase one.

While the Second and Fourth Amendments are being systematically destroyed, we can at least (for now) enjoy the benefits of the *First* Amendment. Recommended reading in this category are some publications that take free speech to the extreme. *Loompanics Unlimited* (████████████████████████) is a book catalog that you cannot live without. Some real treasures are to be found in here; how-to books on homemade explosives and booby traps, electronic surveillance, CIA methods of killing people with your bare hands, you name it. *ANSWER Me!* (████████████████████████) is a beautifully-done hate-fest, #3 having probably the best gun article ever written. It might be sold out by the time you read this, but it's worth looking for. And an upstanding fella by the name of Sick-O puts together a righteously angry mag from the deep, dark jungles of Las Vegas called *Nice Guys Finish Last*✶ (████████████████████████). Send him four bucks for a copy of issue #2 and tell him I sent ya. He tells me that #3 should be out soon.

I'm dedicating this issue to Dianne Feinstein and Charles Schumer. I hope you enjoy it; I know they will.

Peace, love & ammo   *HK*

✶ Don't order NGFL -
Your money will disappear.
- Ed.

INCOMING

SOME RANDOM SHOTS AND UNEXPLODED DUDS FROM THE GFM MAILBOX

Dear Hollister,

Just the other day, I was bitching to a friend of mine that somebody ought to put out a zine that speaks to real gun lovers, without all the candy-ass warnings to be safe and responsible that have crept into the NRA's propaganda lately. Fuckin A, guns kill people, that's why I own them! When my friend handed me a copy of Gun Fag Manifesto, I fell in love. Hollister, darlin', you are the voice of reason.

Your piece on the Smith & Wesson Model 586 in Gun Fag #1 was particularly good. I understand the strong emotion evoked by the S&W sidearm. I possess but a modest arsenal myself. A Norinco SKS (the only true offensive weapon I own), a Glock 17 (my warm-up, "fun" gun) and a stainless-steel Smith & Wesson .38 Special, Model 640, a 5-shot with an internal hammer and a 2-inch barrel. Naturally, it's the gun I carry concealed, and I love it. I *adore* this fucking gun. The only thing I've done to it is exchange the rubber grips for some a little longer, to keep the little beast from kicking so hard into the web of my right hand. You can bemoan the demise of black guns if you like, Hollister, but I think even you would appreciate the sight of this lovely silver revolver strapped to my soft, flat belly. When I take it off in the evening, the sweet 640 is as hot to the touch as my skin and smells of Liz Claiborne's Vivid and KleenBore gun oil. If I waved it under your nose, you'd get a hard-on.

The beauty of the 640 isn't just skin deep. In my opinion, this gun's elegant menace is unmatched. Draw it, and anyone within range can see immediately that this is a man-killer, not some plastic gizmo or a small-caliber beesting. Fill the cylinder with Federal HydraShocks and the business end looks positively demonic. You name it, the 640's got it: Reliable simplicity, an easy-to-conceal profile, no hammer to snag on clothing and pure double-action shooting all the way. This tough little wheel-gun will deliver five guaranteed shots into the center mass of any street punk who strays within 21 feet of my tender body and so much as looks at me the wrong way! Honestly, any woman who *doesn't* carry a 640 is either packing something bigger or living in a state of complete denial about the nature of our mean streets. I take this gun everywhere I go and sleep with it at night. I've even thought about using it to beat off, but I don't like to get it wet.

Sincerely,

Peach

Hollister— Would you like to trade gun fag for porno. Here's a sample.

HAIL, GUN WACKOS !!

I am a gun freak and proud of it. Fuck the Liberal humanist pussies, the stinking filthy, hollow mouthed sons of bitches!!
I would like to bomb that bitch brady in the mouth, watch her teeth fly with blood gushing out.....HA HA!
DO YOU FEEL SAFE BITCH,HUh?....WHERE THE FUCK ARE YOU GONN RUN! Man, I would like to rape that stupid bitch, forget her old dry, fucked up pussy,......I WOULD GO FOR THAT BIG WRINKL-ed ASS! I wanna bruise her fuckin back pound her and then knock her a couple of shots in her airhead with my .22 and can.

That stupid bitch has to die!!!!
who the fuck do they think they are?........to put it short they whant all our guns so they can have us like little conte nt rats on the basis of some"safety" or "crime" bullshit.
THEY DONT WHANT US TO HAVE OUR FUCKING "ASSUAULT"GUNS,, CAUSE THEY WHANT TO ENSLAVE US AND SINCE THIS IS AMERICA, IT WOULD BE INEVITABLE THAT DUDES LIKE ME AND H.K WILL FORM GUERRILLA/PARTISAN/"terrorist"/etc,etc. AND THEY KNOW,HEART IS HARDER TO KILL THAN POWER...........
I AM ONLY 16 AND I GOT ME AN AKM FOR THOSE DAYS+ I CAN SEE IT NOW........riddled bodies of stupid u.n troops, from every nation who tried and failed to estimate the stren-gth of a kid with heart,140 i.q. and an AK LOADED WITH 7.62x19 FULL METAL JACKET!!!!!!!!
I AM GOING TO GET ME A GLOCK .45 LOADED WITH GLASERS,AND HPs......ior those stupid'jtf.and 'incen' when they try to sneek up on me when im taking a shit in the woods.
I am so pissed i cant even type right!
we better organize now.......goto the surplus get some clo thing,boots,some crates of cup o' noodles and lots of mags and ammo for your M1 carbines, ARs,AKs,MAKs,SKS`.and whatever else you got......IF YOUR TO LATE, TO STUPID,OR TO "AFRAID" YOU DESERVE WHAT YOU GET......SLAVERY OR DEATH!!!!!
I AM SATANIST,GUN FREAK,ARTIST AND ALOT OF OTHER SHIT IF YOUR YOUNG AND THE SAME WRITE ME, IF YOUR A SATANIC GIRL WHO LOVES GUNS,MUSIC,FUCKING AND STAYING UP TOO LATE...I WHANT TO TALK TO YOU.......
Load your magazines all the way up,take a sip of coke,put your sights on the real EVIL politicians and let your suppress-ors thump!

HAIL, VICTORY!!!!

demon
P.O.box 421184
L.a.., CA 90042

Kids these days! sheesh!

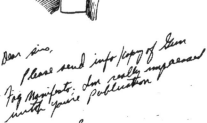

Dear sirs,
Please send info/copy of Gun Fag Manifesto. I'm really impressed with your'e publication.

Sincerely
Geoff Milner
1204 Q Elm St.
Austin TX
78703

Red: 5/26/94 — This guy owes me three bucks. Take care of him, will ya? —HK

small changes

316 Terry Avenue North
P.O. Box 19048
Seattle, WA 98109
PHONE 206-382-1980
FAX 206-382-1814

Dear Publisher:

After careful consideration, we have decided not to carry your work.
Thank you for the opportunity to see your work.

Sincerely,
Small Changes

May 5, 1994

-Dear Gun Fag Magazine-

Where have you been all my life? I fired my first shot out my Grandfather's Jeep. Was in the passenger's side window, doing about 60 across the Arizona desert. I fricken nailed a Gila Monster right between the eyes. The fricken reptile made eye contact with me when I shot it. In fact we had a telepathic conversation for a split second about head and sex and food. Gramps said "Fricken good shot Ernie." Ernie was my name before I changed it to Kutz. Kutz is taunting Ernie is a fricken sock puppet. ~~Put me~~ ... Jump ahead to high school. Jesuit College Preparatory school in the middle of the desert. Initiated into a secret club by Christian Morck, instructor. Attend meeting mostly attended for the free beer and pastries. Invited on a "hunting" trip which turned into a bizarr Jesuit Initiation ceremony which included peyot and mezcal concoctions brewed in a large sea turtle shell

brightly adorned with Rubies and Blue Topaz. Went through 2 months of Jesuit poot camp which I will not describe for there is no explanation. There are no words. Coincidentally a Jesuit missionary was killed execution style in a nameless Central American ville. For my Sins I was given a Mission Search and Destroy. Search and Destroy I did? Can't explain. Mission accomplished. 24 hours I was the only passenger on a C5-A Galaxy on my way to Las Vegas of all places. Lived in Vegas for two years working the Craps tables at the Mint. Met a dancer who calmed my nerves and my angst. Angst Smoged — by fricken beck. I'm back!!! I'm fickin pissed off becauz some fuckin 15 year old cholito carved his fuckin gang sign into the table next to me. I said "Hey pepe! Que til pinche Cayron? He said what you want you white mother fucker?" I said "okay, lookey here Pepe Say hello to Señor Treint. Treinte and pulled my nickel plated 1894 and shot his white dome cap right off his shaved head. Got attention. Problem solved. Like one... Too pissed to write more.

Kutz Kila

A BEAUTIFUL DAY
MR. & MRS. KOPP GO TO THE GUN SHOW

A couple of Sundays ago Mrs. Kopp and I went to the firearms manufacturer's exhibition at the Angeles Shooting Range. If you've read the first issue of *GFM*, you know how I feel about that place. So I was hesitant at first, but my distaste for the range was ultimately overpowered by my lust for guns. On this day there were thousands of them, all ready to fire. Hand the guy a buck and point out the weapon of your choice. He'll even load it for you. We must have fired a hundred different rifles, pistols and shotguns; all brand new, some not even on the market yet (because of this, cameras and recording devices were not allowed on the range).

It was a beautiful day. We showed up at 9:00 sharp, riding the motorcycle to avoid traffic and parking hassles (which turned out to be a mistake, as we had to limit the amount of free brochures, catalogs, stickers, patches, etc. to how much we could carry on the bike), and parked right next to the booth for the California Department of Fish & Game. They had an interesting display of confiscated weapons, some clever and some just plain retarded (like a stick with a fork tied to it) as well as maps to shooting areas and the usual boring booklets on safe hunting.

There were a couple of other booths sponsored by gun shops, but we spent very little time there. Our trigger fingers were getting itchy, and there were a thousand guns waiting for us. It was time to go up to the firing line and do some shootin.'

Up on the line, the manufacturers each had their own areas separate from each other, with banners bearing their company logos and guns guns guns everywhere you looked. The thought crossed my mind that maybe we had crashed the bike and now were in heaven. But alas, they called a cease-fire to replace the targets. They would never call a cease-fire in heaven.

After gazing wide-eyed and child-like at the wonderful spectacle before us, we picked Smith & Wesson for our first stop. I fired the new .40 S&W Sigma Series pistol, which looks like and is designed much like a Glock. Smith & Wesson is apparently going after the police market with this one. It was too light for my taste, but I suppose I could get used to it. Its light weight made for a pretty sharp recoil, but the trigger action was buttery-smooth and the sights were perfect. Mrs. Kopp went straight for the Model 29 .44 magnum, and men all up and down the range gaped in awe as she deftly destroyed her targets, the big magnum roaring its undisputed authority and rattling the awning from one end of the range to the other. There is no more awe-inspiring sight in the world than this woman firing a handgun. She assumes the Weaver stance as naturally and easily as a gold-medal gymnast on a balance beam. She handles violent recoil without batting an eyelash, as if it were nothing more than flipping a pancake on a lazy Saturday morning.

And she drives the men crazy. They stumble over each other like slobbering fools trying to win a mere flicker of acknowledgement from what they know to be a superior being, a goddess. They *pray* to her, even as she flicks them away like ants. I've seen them as she walks by; mopping their brows, loosening collars, fidgeting, adjusting jeans to make room for the only natural response. But watch it, Bub. She may be a radiant vision of supreme godhood, but keep in mind the fact that she's *armed and extremely dangerous.*

Next stop, Ruger. Again, Mrs. Kopp went for a .44 magnum, this one a Super Redhawk with an 9½" barrel. I was so horny I couldn't swallow. I picked up a Vaquero .45 caliber single-action sixgun and blasted away. Very, very cool gun. I then tried out the Ruger Mini-14 Ranch Rifle.

"That's Mrs. Kopp. If you try anything she'll kick the shit outta ya!"

YES! Definitely my next firearm purchase. What a great company! I'm turning into a hard-core Ruger fan. About this time Mrs. Kopp was firing a SIG Sauer P229 pistol, and I had to turn away; the sight was just too much for me. I sauntered over to a big display of Remington shotguns, thinking of what we would be doing after the gun show. Some couples go for the missionary position, others like doing it doggy-style. Mr. & Mrs. Kopp - gun fag & gun fag-ette - are into the Weaver stance. Try it sometime.

As I approached the Remington display I witnessed a true NRA moment. A beaming, tow-headed little kid of about nine years old was getting a hug from his loving mom as the proud father tousled the kid's hair, congratulating him on some mighty fine shooting. He had just downed three out of four sporting clays with a Remington 870 Magnum Express. I saluted the kid, and he saluted back. I had a warm feeling that there may be hope for this country after all.

All up and down the range were red-blooded men, women and children who have not given up hope for the fading American way of life. This was a robust crowd, everyone friendly and talkative. I couldn't believe I was in Los Angeles county. The fact that these poor souls are represented in government by the likes of Dianne Feinstein and Henry Waxman - who would like to see these people in jail or dead - is chilling indeed.

I had to brush aside such thoughts. I spend every day of my life in a boiling, poisonous rage and I need a break now and then. I struck up a conversation with the man at the Browning table, who was showing me some gorgeous shotguns. I chose a fine-looking over/under job and popped in a shell. **"PULL!"** The yellow target zinged up and away, seeming to pause for a moment as it reached the apex of its trajectory. I smoked it with a round from a three thousand dollar shotgun. It was a beautiful day.

THE PRESIDENT AND HIS CRONIES ARE ON A ROLL!
FIRST YOUR MONEY...THEN YOUR FREEDOM...THEN YOUR GUNS...
LIBERTY? THEY'D RATHER KILL YOU

The scum in Washington have big plans for us, my friends. The impending ban on so-called "assault weapons" (which sooner or later will include anything that will deliver a projectile) is only a small cog in a monstrous machine being developed by Big Brother for the New World Order. "Legitimate sportsmen don't need weapons like these for hunting and target practice," is a common argument used by the government vermin, which is true, if left at face value. But taken in the context of the Second Amendment, the argument falls flatter than the trajectory of a .460 Weatherby. They would like us to believe that the Second Amendment was designed to protect the rights of Americans to shoot beer cans and paper targets, which is a bit like saying the *First* Amendment was written to guarantee the rights of school children to write *See Spot Run.*

"We need to get these devastating weapons out of the hands of criminals!" is another headline-grabbing diatribe puking forth from their fetid mouths. This argument is as laughable as it is downright stupid. The use of "assault weapons" in crime is so negligible as to be virtually nonexistent. They are too big for concealed carry, and most of them are prohibitively expensive for the common street thug. Armed robberies and muggings are nearly always carried out using cheap handguns. So why all the fuss? Listen up:

The Second Amendment was written at a time when American citizens were in very real danger of government tyranny, much like our present situation. The "well regulated militia" consisted of every free (white) man between the ages of 16 and 45, and the

arms they had the right - *the duty* - to keep and bear were *exactly the same arms as those which were carried by the standing army.* If the government decided to use its armed forces and/or police for despotic purposes, well, they were going to have a fight on their hands. A fight that they could very well lose.

The New World Order which is being designed and constructed right under our noses is going to be so repugnant, so un-American, so *anti*-American that when finally unveiled (and a thin veil it is) the average citizen - who for the last twenty years has been keeping up on football statistics and sitcoms on television while ignoring the real world - is going to be in for an ugly shock. He'll be angry enough to realize that America needs another Revolution, and by this time it'll be too late. He'll be unarmed. Emasculated. Hoodwinked by carpetbagging gangsters who take from him a bigger and bigger chunk of his paycheck at the same time they strip him of his most basic freedoms. It may take a couple of years before the firm of Clinton, Reno, Feinstein & Schumer tie up the loose ends (like the Second Amendment), But don't think for a moment that they aren't working night and day to achieve their despicable goal.

Gun fags know the truth behind the campaign to disarm Americans, and we refuse to descend meekly and quietly into the hell which they are preparing for us. The crafty government punks know as well as we do that the only effective defense against a heavily-armed and hostile state is a heavily-armed populace. Handguns are fine for fending off muggers, rapists and the homeless, but when you're next

on Janet Reno's hit list, you, your family and your entire neighborhood had better be prepared for war.

For the individual citizen concerned with the preservation of his or her freedom, the ideal rifle will be an M16 or an AK-47. These are, of course, hard to come by. However, they have close relatives which are on the list of weapons to be banned, but are still available (not for long! Get your ass to the gun store *now!*).

In the M16/AR-15 category there are several manufacturers, most notably Colt. The **Colt Sporter** comes in a few variations, all of which are excellent. Expect to spend $1,000 to $2,500 on one (ouch!). You can choose a Colt Sporter chambered either in .223 Remington or 7.62 x 39mm. I recommend the former, as it is used by American armed forces, and in the event of a total breakdown of society, we may have to acquire ammo from captured enemy trucks, armories and the lifeless bodies of yellow traitors who would fight on the side of the government.

In the family of the AK-47 is the relatively new **MAK-90**, which for all practical purposes is an AK with a different stock. They cost around $500 and, like the AK, are pretty cheaply built. They're imported from China, and China doesn't give two shits about the safety of Americans, so if you buy one, have it looked over by a gunsmith before you fire it. The MAK-90 is chambered for the 7.62 x 39mm round which does a decent job of killing people (it's the most popular military round in the world), but as stated above, it's not an *American* military cartridge, so when all hell breaks loose you'll have to establish your own supply line. You can bet that

Mizz Reno will make damn sure the gun and sporting-goods stores are closed when she declares war on the United States of America.

Also made in China and very attractive for the patriot on a budget is the **SKS** rifle (reviewed in this issue), which, like the AK-47 and MAK-90, uses the 7.62 x 39mm cartridge. They sell for about $150, and you get what you pay for. Definitely get it checked by a gunsmith, and definitely *keep it clean! Dirty guns - especially cheap ones - are prone to malfunction.* The SKS has been known to take shooters by surprise with some horrid little quirks. One poor dumb bastard had one get away from him at a shooting range. The thing suddenly went full-auto and wouldn't stop. The guy freaked and dropped the gun like a little girl, getting his shit blow away in the process. People scrambled for cover as the insane rifle danced around the range, destroying everything in its path until finally lodging under the tire of a pick-up and running out of ammo. It was undoubtedly an exiting few seconds.

> **Once upon a time the American government enjoyed the fierce support of men like us**

Favored by farmers and ranchers across the country for dispatching varmints and I.R.S. agents is the Ruger **Mini-14**, chambered for the .223 Remington. Rugged and reliable, it's been a staple of defense-minded individuals, "paranoid" survivalists and God-fearin' white supremacist groups for years. It comes standard with a five-round magazine, which needs to be discarded immediately. 30-round mags are available at gun shows and your better gun shops, and highly recommended. Ruger also makes the **Mini-30**, basically a Mini-14 chambered in 7.62 x 39mm. Both models are available in either stainless steel or a blued finish. Just the other day I went to pick up my new Mini-14 after the 15 day wait, only to find out that the Dept. of "Justice" turned me down. *Oh yeah, you slimy bastards?* That same day, I got my money back and bought an M1 Garand and a thousand rounds of ammo. *And took it home on the bus.* Fuck 'em.

M1 Carbine and **M1 Garand**: I reviewed the Carbine in the last issue of *GFM*, so you know by now how I feel about the lovely little killer. I've heard people bitch about the .30 Carbine round not being punchy enough, and I say bull-hockey. Try firing that round from a handgun (ruger makes one) and then tell me it ain't punchy. It may not be a cannon, but the idea is to kill *men*, not water buffalo. The M1 Garand, on the other hand, can rip your goddanged head off; the .30-06 round is devastating (see the M1 article in this issue). This rifle only holds eight rounds (no detachable mag), and because of this shortcoming, the rifle demands that you make every shot count (the "spray & pray" technique is inadvisable with any firearm, let alone one holding only eight rounds). Most other WWII-era rifles are of the bolt-action variety and thus not very competitive with modern assault weapons, unless you're Sgt. York. Don't forget that the most attractive feature of WWII-era rifles is the absence of a background check and waiting period. Prost!

A very high quality (and very expensive at around 3,500 plunks) combat rifle is the U.S. **M14**. It fires a .308 round (7.62 NATO) which is the same cartridge used in the murderous M60 machine gun. Since you're reading *Gun Fag Manifesto*, it's a safe bet that you've seen *Full Metal Jacket*. In the movie, the M14 is the weapon the jar-heads were issued during boot camp (they switched to M16s upon arriving in Vietnam). It is also the rifle with which Private Pyle, in a Zen-like trance, smoked his Drill Instructor before fouling the latrine wall with his own tormented brain.

Other "assault weapons" slated for the banned wagon include variations of the **MAC-10** and the **Uzi** submachine gun, which are chambered for the limp-wristed 9mm Parabellum cartridge. These (in their semi-auto, politically correct state) are nothing more than clumsy handguns, and won't be of much use to you during the Great Fall of America. They are designed for very specialized purposes (anti-terrorist operations, hostage situations, drug raids, etc.), and need to be fully automatic to be truly effective.

Any of the above weapons will be reduced to an expensive club if you run out of ammo. Stock up. THAT IS AN ORDER. Set aside a percentage of each paycheck for more ammo. Even just one box per week will add up after a couple of years. Some people worry about ammo getting old and "stale," which is pure horse pucky. Hell, I'm still firing ammo from the Spanish Civil War. Stock up and don't worry about the ammo getting old.

We are all familiar with the Second Amendment, but there is another - the Fourth - which will be the next target of the Clinton Regime once the Second Amendment sustains sufficient damage. The Fourth Amendment guarantees Americans protection from unreasonable search and seizure. The bilge-lapping wharf rats are already molesting search and seizure laws, and it won't be long before a couple of brainwashed Bolsheviks with cheap suits and badges knock on your door and "ask" to see your gun cabinet. This scenario is not far-fetched, and not far off. Use your own judgement on timing, but pretty soon we'll have to start

THIS IS HOW THEY TAKE YOUR TAXES

HOW DO YOU THINK THEY'RE GOING TO TAKE YOUR GUNS?

burying stuff.

Most surplus stores carry containers of all shapes and sizes, some hermetically sealable, and some not. Military ammo boxes are ideal for burying handguns, knives, blackjacks, and of course, ammo. They're made of heavy-gauge steel with tight-fitting, sealed lids. It's also wise to bury a couple hundred bucks, fake ID, passport, etc., and an ammo box is perfect for this. Larger containers are needed for burying rifles and shotguns. TOW missile containers are available, and are well-suited for this purpose. At about 3 ½ feet long, they are made of heavy plastic and seal up nicely. Newly available from *The Sportsman's Guide* (you're not a true gun fag unless you're on their mailing list. Write to them at 411 Farwell Avenue, So. St. Paul, MN 55075-0239 for a free catalog) is a handy device called the Patriot Safe. It's made of heavy-gauge PVC and is airtight, watertight, and comes in three different sizes. Burial vaults designed specifically for firearms are also available from Vanguard Security Systems (they hold two assault rifles and 500 rounds of ammo with room to spare). Write to them at P.O. Box 330, Hillsboro, WV 24946, and don't forget to ask for the National Vanguard Book Catalog. It contains *essential* gun fag reading material! Break the weapon down, oil it well, seal the container and bury it at least four feet deep. Use a post-hole digger, and bury rifles vertically (that way they're harder to find with a metal detector). If the containers you use don't have rubber gaskets on the lids, a careful application of bee's wax will do the trick. Now for God's sake, remember where you buried the stuff! And don't draw some cutesy little map. The authorities are bound to find it, dig up your contraband and send your sorry ass up the well-known creek.

A few years ago, red-blooded gun fags would have considered this article nothing less than subversive. These days, however, an article like this is merely practical. The reason for this is the fact that the United States of America is in a moral tailspin. The government has crossed the line between existing for the *people* and existing for *itself.* This government, feeding hideously on rotten avarice, has turned into something big, ugly and dangerous.

Once upon a time the American government enjoyed the fierce support of men like us. An off-color remark about our government would likely get you a mouth full of knuckles, followed by an impromptu haircut, a bucket of tar and a bag of feathers. We stood by America and the way of life it afforded us through good times and very, very bad times. We did what we were told to do, even if it meant fighting, killing and dying *on the wrong side* of two world wars. We pledged our allegiance to the Flag and we meant it. Now the beneficiaries of over 200 years of protection and loyalty by patriotic gun fags are in position to assume total power. Our job is finished; we're no longer needed or wanted. So they're coming for our guns. They sold us out.

Does all this sound paranoid? Lemme tell ya a little story. In August of 1991, in Idaho, Federal agents staked out a man's house who was accused of selling two shotguns that were a quarter of an inch shorter than the legal length. When the man's 12 year-old son, Sammy, and his dog stumbled upon the camouflaged and heavily armed men hiding outside their house, the dog barked and was shot dead with a burst of automatic gunfire. The boy hollered and received the same treatment. Later, an FBI sniper tried to take the accused out of the picture with a round fired from some 200 yards away. The bullet entered the back of his arm, exiting through his armpit. *Damn! Bad shot!* The next target to present itself was the man's wife, Vicki, as she stood just inside the front door, holding her baby girl. This time, all that expensive government training paid off; a good clean head shot. The baby girl survived the sudden drop from her dead mother's arms, but Kevin Harris (a young friend of the family), who was standing nearby, was seriously injured by flying skull fragments. A siege commenced, and lasted six days before they had to medevac Harris to a hospital in Spokane, Washington (he survived). The next day Randy Weaver (the accused), with his baby girl Elisheba and his teen-aged daughter Sara, surrendered to the authorities as Vicki Weaver lay dead inside the house, most of her head missing.

It turns out that the feds were not all that concerned with the shotgun sale after all, but were zeroing in on this man because of his unpopular political beliefs (he believed in having the government *leave him alone*). He had no illegal firearms, no criminal record, and was a decorated Green Beret combat veteran. The charges against him were eventually dropped (some comfort, eh?). This happened in the United States, friends. Land of the free, home of the brave.

The Orwellian scenario described above happened on George "Kinder Gentler" Bush's watch. And if you think that's scary, wait until Clinton and his band of jackbooted hippies and dope-crazed perverts get their sinister agenda into high gear (Waco, Texas was - pardon the pun - just a warm-up).

Are you willing to die for freedom? You might have to. See you at the gun store.

KNOW YOUR ENEMY

BY RAY LUSTIG—THE WASHINGTON POST

Members of the winning side in the House on the issue of an assault weapons ban in the pending anti-crime bill exult with Sen. Dianne Feinstein (D-Calif.), center, at a Capitol news conference yesterday after the close vote. From left, they are Democratic Reps. Charles E. Schumer (N.Y.) and Mel Reynolds (Ill.).

55

SPECIFICALLY BANNED:

AK, All models
Uzi
Galil
Beretta AR-70
Colt AR-15
FN/FAL, FN/LAR and FNC
Cobray/SWD M-10, M-11 and M-12
Steyr AUG
Intratec TEC-9, TEC-DC9 and TEC-22

AND THIS IS WHERE IT GETS REALLY UGLY:

Any semi-automatic weapon with more than one *assault style feature*.
What the fuck is that!?! Goddamn bastards. This is what they mean by *assault style features*:

- Detachable magazine with a capacity of more than ten rounds
- Pistol grip "which protrudes conspicuously beneath the action of the weapon" (cute fuckin' language, eh?)
- Bayonet mount
- Folding or telescoping stock
- Flash suppressor or threaded barrel
- Grenade launcher (no shit!)

Any semi-automatic pistol which accepts a detachable magazine and has at least two of the following features:

- Magazine which attaches to the pistol outside of the grip
- Threaded barrel
- A shroud which is attached to the barrel and permits the shooter to hold the pistol with the non-trigger hand without being burned (a definite menace to society)
- Manufactured weight of 50 ounces or more unloaded
- Semi-automatic version of an automatic firearm

Any semi-automatic shotgun which has at least two of the following features:

- Folding or telescoping stock
- Pistol grip "which protrudes conspicuously beneath..." blah blah fuckin' blah
- Fixed magazine capacity greater than five rounds
- Ability to accept a detachable magazine

And any shotgun which contains its ammo in a rotating cylinder, such as (but not limited to) the Street Sweeper and Striker 12

Thursday, May 5, 1994. A day which will be remembered and reviled for all time. A day of terrible infamy, of deceit and treachery. The maggots in the House got away with it. They passed the now-famous bill sponsored by that greasy little semite known as Rep. Charles E. Schumer (D-NY). This horrid thing happened, we must keep in mind, soon after the bitchy mall-fly Dianne Feinstein gave birth to a similarly revolting bill in the Senate. Now the House and the Senate are going to compare bills and pass into law something truly terrifying, maybe even before this issue goes to print.

THE DIRTY TRAITORS
MUST DIE!

You treacherous commies will someday soon become worm food. You and your disgusting, soiled collaborators will meet violent death. You have pissed off a lot of taxpayers who until now were law-abiding folks. Taxpayers who until now were not considered dangerous. You rotten scum! You vile human tapeworms! You stinking, lousy, chancrous philistines! Just who the FUCK do you think you are? You punks! You rats! You slithering bastard spawn of lowly slugs! By the way, SHITBIRDS, gun sales are booming. What does that tell you?

SURE A THOMPSON
SUBMACHINE GUN IS COOL
BUT I CAN'T HIDE ONE IN MY PANTIES

By Pollyanne Hornbeck

If I turn a lever on my 1936 Thompson submachine gun I can instantly pop it from semi to full automatic. I can blast off bursts of .45 caliber hot lead to the tune of five rounds per second. My Tommy has little recoil and virtually no muzzle jump for an old carbine, thanks to the addition of the handy Cutts Compensator. Pretty aims as Pretty kills! Neat, huh? And this is a fuckin' relic! But when do I need that kind of firepower, and where am I going to find me a sugar daddy to pick up the tab for 18,000 rounds an hour? I told you it was cool, but just think of what it would do to my panty line.

It's hard. It's black. It fits nicely in my hand. It's even gone inside my undies before. OK, so it isn't black, it's blued. But if it was good enough for 007 (only Sean Connery counts) then goddammit it's good enough for me. My Walther PPK .380 is my precious little pal with a punch.

An unloaded gun is as good as a hammer, so I keep my little one packed, chambered and real friendly like with two other magazines. If I gotta kill somebody who has "mistakenly" wandered into my house I want to do the job right. And I don't want to worry about my bullets gliding through a chunk of crack-infested viscera and ending up in my neighbor's TV set, so I use Winchester Silvertip Hollowpoints at home. You should too.

During "The Riots" I drove around in confidence with my .380 inches away on the console of my Cougar. Around town I look like just another jerk with a butt bag. But what people don't know is that this is a Bianchi Ranger Series Fanny Pack, size small. With a tug on the corner of the zippered coinpurse (either side just in case you're a southpaw plinker) the Velcro separates to reveal a secret padded slot just big enough to hold my heater. If it's a little chilly out, I just slip my comfy Shooting Systems shoulder holster under my leather jacket. With a muzzle velocity of 955 fps and the stopping power of 9mm Kurz ammo (that translates into a short 9mm bullet going almost a thousand feet per second for those of you out there who shot a Daisy BB gun once) this 21-oz. palmer of a gun smacks a whallop. I've always had consistent direction of discards from the ejection port. The slide has a great ride to it. The firearm is beautifully designed and easy to take apart. I can dismantle and reassemble my pistol in the dark, can you?

Besides the usual manual safety found on most semi-automatic pistols, my Walther has a signal pin protruding from the rear of the slide. This pin can be seen or felt to indicate if a cartridge is chambered in the weapon. This saves time figuring out how hot your gat is, so you can kill faster.

1. Barrel (muzzle end)
2. Front sight
3. Recoil spring
4. Bore
5. Slide
6. Cartridge in chamber
7. Barrel (chamber end)
8. Firing pin
9. Rear sight
10. Safety
11. Loaded chamber signal pin
12. Hammer
13. Frame
14. Sear
15. Magazine
16. Magazine extension
17. Cartridges in magazine
18. Trigger
19. Trigger guard

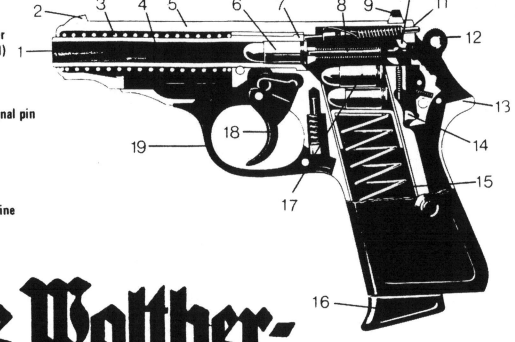

Die Walther-Polizeipiſtolen
PP u. PPK
Kal. 7,65 %m

Beſchreibung, Hand-
habung und Pflege

Mit Abbildungen

Power versus size keeps this gun perfect for self defense. Most incidents of urban violence occur within a fifteen foot space. The accuracy of the PPK is designed for short distances. If concealable close-range self defense is your goal then this is the right tool for the right job. But the diminutive size of the PPK in relation to its caliber makes for a harsh, snappy recoil. So if shooting pleasure is your goal you'd be better off with a full size 9mm.

I once forgot I had it with me when I was going to a nightclub. I wasn't about to leave it in the car, but I certainly didn't want to chance getting searched by some commie longhair bouncer/doorman ape. I unloaded my weapon. I put the magazine in my boot and stuck James Bond's best friend down the front of my panties. I wasn't wearing a G-string. It stayed in place. I was wearing a dress, and the gun was undetectable. The guy at the door patted down my jacket and let me in. Once inside, I visited the little girl's room. There was a single blond pubic hair caught in the ejection port. I reloaded my rod and zipped in my jacket pocket. No muss no fuss. No cumbersome belts. No sticky adhesive. Now no one ever asks me if I'm on the rag.

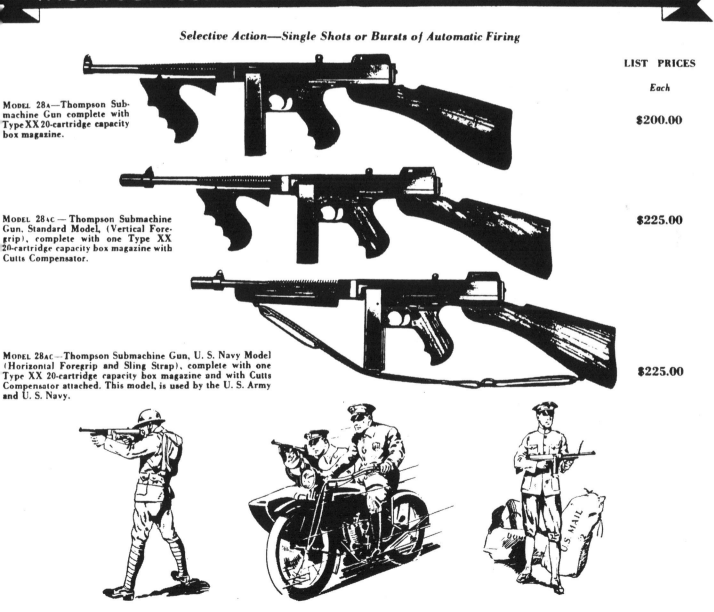

THOMPSON SUBMACHINE GUN MODEL Nos. 28A and 28AC

Selective Action—Single Shots or Bursts of Automatic Firing

LIST PRICES

Each

MODEL 28A—Thompson Sub-machine Gun complete with Type XX 20-cartridge capacity box magazine.

$200.00

MODEL 28AC — Thompson Submachine Gun, Standard Model, (Vertical Fore-grip), complete with one Type XX 20-cartridge capacity box magazine with Cutts Compensator.

$225.00

MODEL 28AC—Thompson Submachine Gun, U. S. Navy Model (Horizontal Foregrip and Sling Strap), complete with one Type XX 20-cartridge capacity box magazine and with Cutts Compensator attached. This model, is used by the U. S. Army and U. S. Navy.

$225.00

Pollyanne Hornbeck writes for the Angry Thoreauan and is currently involved in weapons research for the Turkish Border Patrol.

M1 GARAND

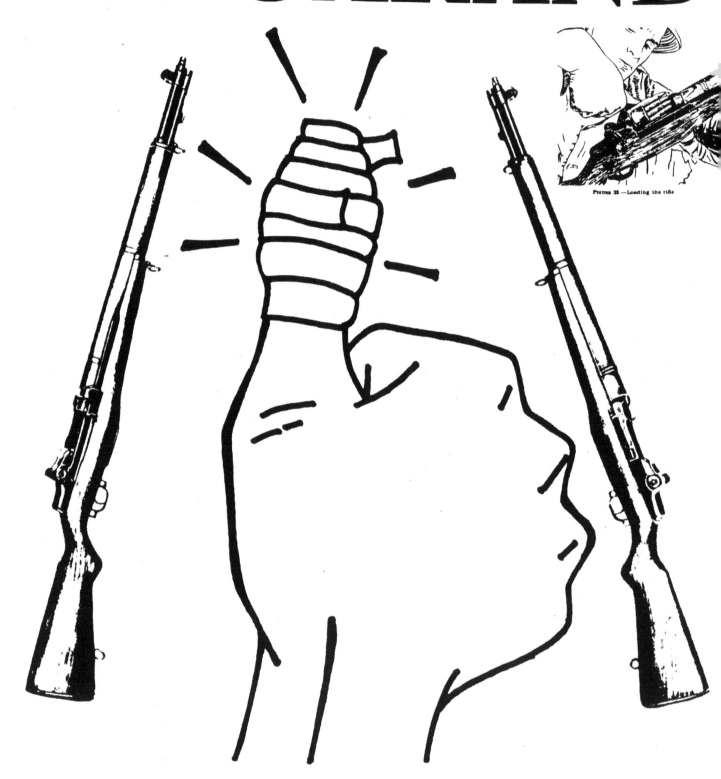

Figure 23.—Loading the rifle.

THUMBS UP!

THE MIGHTY M1 GARAND
IT'S KILLED BEFORE AND IT'LL KILL AGAIN!

General Patton called the M1 rifle "the greatest battle implement ever devised." If allowed to live after the U.S.-Soviet invasion and subsequent takeover of Western Europe, he would probably reiterate that statement on a regular basis. There has never in military history been a more successful rifle than the legendary M1 Garand. Millions have fallen before its mighty roar. Empires were built and maintained under the threat of the M1's deadly authority. Grizzled infantrymen with smoking M1s have slaughtered countless thousands of japs, wops, gooks, krauts, kikes, chinks, polacks, limeys, wogs, frogs, micks, spics, spades, zipperheads, ragheads, dune-coons and geeks of all persuasions from the M1's introduction to the U.S. Army in 1936 until the late 1950s when it was phased out in favor of the M14.

The M1 Garand was the first semi-automatic rifle in the world to become a standard-issue military arm. This proved to be a tremendous advantage to the U.S. armed forces during WWII. Its accuracy and high rate of fire tipped the scales in the allies' favor in innumerable battles. All the other armies of the time were still issuing to their hapless foot soldiers bolt-action rifles of turn-of-the-century design.

> **I often wonder how many men have been brutally annihilated by this very rifle.**

Weirdly enough, the army originally wanted the M1 to be chambered for a wispy little .276 caliber round, until Gen. Douglas MacArthur vetoed the idea in favor of the proven .30-06. His argument was that everything else the army was using (M1903 Springfield, 1917 Enfield and the soon-to-be-unveiled Browning Automatic Rifle) was chambered for the robust and respected old "thirty-ought-six," and in the event of mobilization, a diversity in rifle cartridges was bound to induce a major clusterfuck. Thank you, General!

During and after WWII millions of M1s were exported to countries all over the world to assist them in killing each other on a scale unprecedented in history. Of course, these armies have been modernizing their arsenals over the years (most of them are mowing down humans with AK-47s and M16s nowadays) and when this happens, the old M1s go on sale at bargain-basement prices and find their way back to the States for people like us to purchase and savor.

One of my most prized possessions is my M1 Garand. Even though it's a little beat up, it remains a thing of beauty. I coddle my M1 as if it were a newborn baby. I fashioned a candle-lit shrine for it in my otherwise unsightly, run-down little apartment. The rifle is prominently displayed amidst a wreath made of spent brass and dummy grenades all glued to surplus bandoliers which encircle the holy death-dealer like a golden glow around the Virgin Guadalupe. Serving as a backdrop are old Time & Life photos of WWII beach landings, exploding tanks, screaming Stukas, guys on fire, etc. Topping the whole spectacle off is an orange-and-gold painted tanker's helmet, which was Patton's design (never officially approved by the army, unfortunately) with a bayonet jammed through it. I think the shrine really spruces up the old place.

I often wonder how many men have been brutally annihilated by this very rifle. And therein lies the mystique of owning surplus military weapons. Between my M1 Garand, my M1 Carbine and Mrs. Kopp's Smith & Wesson Model 15 (previously owned by the L.A. County Sheriff's Dept.) there would undoubtedly be some great stories if these weapons could only talk.

As an urban assault rifle, the M1 leaves a little to be desired, until you get used to it.

Its most glaring shortcoming would be magazine capacity: the rifle has no detachable magazine, and is loaded via an 8-round clip. That's right; a CLIP:

This is where the goatfuck antigunners really piss me off: you've all heard their shrieking and sniveling about "these horrible clips that hold 30 or 40 bullets." Well next time you hear that crap, tell them to go fuck themselves, and since they don't know what the hell they're talking about, how can they possibly join a debate? First of all, until the round is fired, it's a goddamn CARTRIDGE, not a bullet, and a CLIP, you ignorant geeks, is something to hold the cartridges together as a unit (in the Garand's case, it's eight), making them more convenient to shove into the MAGAZINE, from which the firearm is fed its ammunition. What you alfalfa-munching crybabies are really blubbering about are high-capacity detachable magazines, and we know this. But your choice of words reveals your ignorance on the subject, and should automatically disqualify you from any say in the matter. Now since you unshaven, sandal-wearing perverts don't know anything about guns and obviously don't care to learn, then just stay the fuck away from guns, and stay WAY the fuck away from gun owners.

Another drawback is the fact that it weighs ten pounds, which doesn't sound like much until you try lugging the thing around all day.

Ah, but there are endearing characteristics aplenty with this rifle. Foremost among these is the fact that a shot placed anywhere on the target *will put the target down* (and probably the guy behind him as well). This thing is a cannon. A clip of .30-06 cartridges resembles something that would be loaded into an anti-aircraft gun. There is a *lot* of powder being burned with each round. After firing just three or four clips in rapid succession, the barrel gets so hot that it will sizzle if you spit on it.

Even with the hot barrel, I can consistently accomplish 3" shot groups at 150 yards. That's certainly no record, but keep in mind that in addition to the crude combat-style sights and stiff trigger, the rifle has been through 50 years of abuse from God-knows-what kind of sad-sack, third-world army in God-knows-what kind of

climate. Also keep in mind that the M1 kicks like a stud quarter horse in a patch of loco weed. All told, we conclude that this is an inherently accurate rifle.

I learned while in the military that there are three ways of doing things; the right way, the wrong way and the army way. Of course, I'm not old enough to have had the honor of packing an M1, but according to an old manual I found, the army way to load the M1 is also the way to lose a substantial portion of your thumb. Old-timers will affectionately recall a common ailment known as "M1 Thumb."

The right way to load an M1 Garand takes a little practice, but you'll get the hang of it. Hold the rifle by its handguard with your left hand, with the butt resting against your thigh. With the bolt locked in its rearmost position and a full clip in your right hand, lay the clip atop the follower in the magazine well. Now place your right hand along side the rifle in front of the bolt handle, so that the heel of your hand will prevent the bolt from slamming forward, which is what will happen when the follower gets pushed down. Now with your right hand in position, ram the clip down into the magazine all the way, until it clicks into place. Timing is crucial here: you need to GET YOUR FUCKING THUMB OUT OF THE WAY OF THE BOLT. In a single *quick* motion, whip your hand up and to the right while the bolt goes forward and everything snaps into place. The rifle is now ready to kill something.

If you decide to get an M1 Garand, you will not be sorry. You will have in your possession a piece of our heritage. It will be as at home on display in a museum as it will be out in the freezing rain on your next poaching expedition. Its versatility and reliability are legend. And the next time L.A. has to endure an "uprising," I plan to take my M1 up to the roof of my apartment building and dispatch a few uppity looters.

I can't wait!

MOSSBERG MODEL 500 12 GAUGE SHOTGUN
A SWEET DEAL ON A SWEET GUN!

chk-chk...**BLAM!** Ah, there's nothing like a shotgun. *What're you lookin' at, punk?* chk-chk **BLAM!** *Huh?* chk-chk **BLAM** chk-chk **BLAM** chk-chk **BLAM!** *Hahahahahaha!*

The scattergun. Twelve gauge pump. As it beats the bejeezus outta your shoulder, every round fired is an orgasm. Cheap, powerful and louder than shit. No better home defense weapon exists. Ask any felon what his worst nightmare sounds like, and he'll tell you that it's a round being jacked into the chamber of a law-abiding taxpayer's fuckin' shotgun.

When I bought my Mossberg 500, I was actually in the market for a Remington 870 Express, which is a fine shotgun indeed, but after Uncle Shithead gets finished with my paycheck, there's not much left. So I settled on the Mossberg, which was on sale at the local sporting goods store for $199. Included were two barrels - an 18" barrel for scumbags, and a vent-ribbed 28" barrel for ducks and geese. Switching barrels is a simple procedure, taking only a few seconds.

This is a great shotgun, made even greater by a little home-gunsmithing which I'll describe later. The day I picked it up, Red and I took it down to the duck blind we keep in the L.A. River near where the Glendale freeway meets Interstate 5. There was a homeless geek making camp in the blind, and when he saw us coming he nearly crapped his pants. Red sent him on his way with a couple of 3" magnum loads of rock salt that we keep handy for just such occasions. This of course scared the ducks away for a while, but entertainment always has a price. We opened a case of Hamm's and waited.

Eventually enough ducks returned to give the Mossberg a run for its money. With a full magazine and a round in the chamber (six all together) Red and I took aim at the closest ones, counted to three and opened up. Instantly, ducks were flying crazily in all directions, and the Mossberg brought down four of them. Four from the sky and one in the water meant I only missed once. Not a record, but impressive nonetheless. Red downed three of them with his Sears Ted Williams Special; equally impressive. As dead and dying ducks pitifully floated down stream, and as we exchanged high-fives and victory whoops, I felt an affinity for the smoking shotgun in my hand that was stronger than love. I knew it was the start of a beautiful friendship.

We swilled the last of the beer and staggered up the mud and concrete bank toward the truck, blasting away at old car parts and discarded appliances as we went. Since Jimmy won't let us clean guns in his bar anymore (he said it scared customers away, but who would want chicken-shit customers like that in the first place?), we decided to pick up another case of beer and clean the guns at my place.

Field-stripping the Mossberg is a breeze. First remove the barrel. Next, push out the pin just above the rear of the trigger guard, and the whole trigger assembly comes out as a unit. Pull out the cartridge interrupter and cartridge stop. After that, move the slide about halfway back, and the bolt slide can be lifted out of the receiver. Lift out the bolt and the elevator, then pull the slide completely off the magazine tube. Now clean it!

After cleaning, I took a standard foam-core emery board - fine grit on one side and super-fine grit on the other side - which is available at most supermarkets in the women's cosmetic section, and using the super-fine side smoothed out the bearing surfaces on the bolt and bolt slide. The surface inside the receiver doesn't need this treatment, as it is finely machined aluminum. After a light oiling and reassembly, the

EXPLODED VIEW

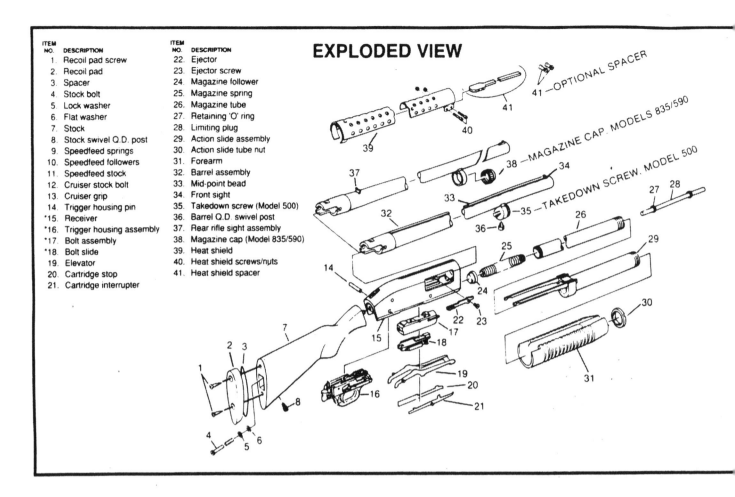

ITEM NO.	DESCRIPTION	ITEM NO.	DESCRIPTION
1.	Recoil pad screw	22.	Ejector
2.	Recoil pad	23.	Ejector screw
3.	Spacer	24.	Magazine follower
4.	Stock bolt	25.	Magazine spring
5.	Lock washer	26.	Magazine tube
6.	Flat washer	27.	Retaining 'O' ring
7.	Stock	28.	Limiting plug
8.	Stock swivel Q.D. post	29.	Action slide assembly
9.	Speedfeed springs	30.	Action slide tube nut
10.	Speedfeed followers	31.	Forearm
11.	Speedfeed stock	32.	Barrel assembly
12.	Cruiser stock bolt	33.	Mid-point bead
13.	Cruiser grip	34.	Front sight
14.	Trigger housing pin	35.	Takedown screw (Model 500)
*15.	Receiver	36.	Barrel Q.D. swivel post
*16.	Trigger housing assembly	37.	Rear rifle sight assembly
*17.	Bolt assembly	38.	Magazine cap (Model 835/590)
*18.	Bolt slide	39.	Heat shield
19.	Elevator	40.	Heat shield screws/nuts
20.	Cartridge stop	41.	Heat shield spacer
21.	Cartridge interrupter		

MOSSBERG MODEL 500 SPORTING

Gauge: 12, 20, .410. **Barrel:** 20/22/24/26/28" with Accu-II (IC/M/F) choke tubes, or fixed. **Weight:** 7-1/4 (12), 6-3/4 (20), 6-1/4 (.410). **Stocks:** Checkered walnut-stained hardwood with recoil pad or synthetic. **Sights:** Bead front and mid bead with or without ventilated rib, except Slugster, with adjustable rifle sights. **Features:** Pump action, blue finish 3" chamber (12/20) 2-1/2" (.410), double slide bar action ensures positive feed/ejection, tang safety, high strength alloy receiver, shoots steel shot, 5-shot (3") capacity plugged to two. **Price:** $246 to $274, 2-barrel combos in 12/20GA $281 to $359.

MOSSBERG MODEL 500 SLUGSTER

Gauge: 12, 20. **Barrel:** 24". **Weight:** 7-1/4 lbs. **Stocks:** Walnut-stained hardwood with raised comb and recoil pad. **Sights:** Rifle or scope base "Trophy." **Features:** Available with smooth bore or rifled barrel, designed for use with special Ballistics Research Institute (BR) slug. **Price:** Rifled barrel $294 to $320; smooth bore $261.

MOSSBERG MODEL 500/590 MARINER

Gauge: 12. **Barrel:** M500 18-1/2", M590 20". **Weight:** 6-1/2 lbs. M500. **Stocks:** Black synthetic field, Speedfeed or pistol grip. **Sights:** Bead front. **Features:** Made for salt water environment, all metal is treated with Marinecote, a Teflon and nickel coating, M500 holds 6 shots (3"), M590 holds 9 shots (3"), pistol grip models have heat shield Mini Combo set includes pistol grip and heat shield. **Price:** From $336 to $401.

action was as smooth as 12 year-old Kentucky bourbon.

As stated above, a shotgun is ideal for home defense. Even super-cheap target loads are deadly at close range, but the best all around man-stopper is buck shot; #4 giving a good wide pattern with decent-sized shot pellets, and #00 extremely fuck-em-up serious with bigger and fewer shot, but with a correspondingly narrower pattern (just aim better). Slugs will definitely rip a man to shreds, but overpenetration becomes a problem, especially with magnum loads. If you use slugs for indoor purposes, make sure to use hollowpoints. They expand to the size of baseballs upon entering the target, which serves the dual purpose of positively stopping said target and, due to the expansion, are less likely to go through too many walls. You'll have a lot of explaining to do if your 12 gauge slug rips through a couple of walls and inadvertently caps the neighbor's sleeping kid. Also intriguing are different types of specialty ammo for shotguns, most of them illegal in the People's Republic of California. *Flechette* rounds look particularly nasty - originally designed for military applications, each shell contains 20 finned steel darts. Yeouch! The *Strung Buck* consists of two .54 caliber balls connected by six inches of steel wire. A well-placed shot will act like a high-speed garrote, instantly decapitating the target. *Blockbuster Slugs* are aerodynamically shaped (like little bombs) and have an internal cavity which allows you to fill the thing up with whatever you feel is necessary: explosives come immediately to mind, but the possibilities for creativity are limitless (gasoline, battery acid, dog poop - use your imagination!). And don't forget the *Flame Thrower*. Each round throws a shower of fire and burning sparks out to 300 feet. That is *art!*

I prefer just a plain ol' shotgun, but there are accessories galore out there if you want to turn yours into some kind of exotic, space-age, Star Trek-looking death machine. For practical accessorizing, a good place to start would be the replacement of the butt-stock in favor of a pistol grip. Mossberg offers them, but Pachmayr makes better ones. Pistol grip-equipped shotguns offer unbeatable maneuverability in tight situations, such as a firefight in a staircase or on a fire escape, but they take getting used to; I've tried the darned things and can't hit diddly with them. Another accessory worth considering is a bayonet lug. A shotgun's deadly firepower coupled with the violent possibilities of an added bayonet conjures up a chilling image. Another practical addition would be a sling, which is a common find at gun shows. The only thing I've added to my Mossberg so far is a heat shield to the short barrel. I don't know if it does any good, but it sure looks bitchin'.

Like all shotguns, firing the Mossberg is an experience bordering on the divine. To wield that kind of power is to be God. I know from experience that a 3" magnum round of #00 buck shot will knock a 1989 Kawasaki Ninja right off its kickstand at 20 paces. Fuckin' Jap bike. I also know that cops all over the country would rather rely on their standard-issue shotguns than batons and candy-assed tear gas for putting down "civil unrest." Three days of rioting in Los Angeles could have been trimmed down to about three minutes, had the LAPD been allowed to show some spine.

The legendary Mossberg 500. Exquisite and lethal. Distinguished and brutal. I love my Mossberg, and it loves me. It sleeps beside me at night, its cool blackness sweetly gleaming reflections of the streetlights outside my window. Outside my window there seethes a violent, barbarous world. A world that had better not fuck with me and my Mossberg.

FRANCHI SPAS-12 DUAL ACTION SHOTGUN
A POLITICALLY INCORRECT SLAUGHTERMEISTER
By James Steinbach

Ah yes, another infamous weapon of the VID-BEK arsenal. The SPAS is arguably the most enjoyable and most lethal gun I've ever owned or fired. Unfortunately our Canadian federal government does not trust its law-abiding citizens to own certain types of sporting firearms and has deemed the SPAS illegal to possess.

About two years ago then-Minister of Justice Kim Campbell rammed new and entirely unnecessary gun legislation down the throats of the sheep-like public. I know it's a cliche, but people kill people, inanimate objects don't. And government, no matter how much they'd like to, cannot legislate morality or behaviour. (Kim went on to become our P.M. for about two months before suffering the worst defeat in Canadian history; the Tory party was annihilated, with something like two M.P.'s left in the House. Kim has disappeared, sinking back into obscurity where I hope she rots, never to enter politics again.)

Logic does not enter their anti-gun argument at any stage. This is clearly illustrated by what weapons the gov't decided to ban and others that were not even mentioned. The most glaring example of this is the Mini-14 .223 cal. rifle made by Ruger. This is the weapon which Marc Lepine used to shoot 14 women at a university in Montreal back in 1990, igniting the anti-gun movement. The Mini-14, which started the whole debate was not affected at all.

"Shooting this devastating arm is hilarious..."

Give me $400 and I can have a shiny new example of the Mini in your hands inside of twenty minutes. Another example is the banning of the Intra-Tec 9mm and H&K MP5 K while the Cobray MAC-11 9mm is still OK. There is absolutely no difference between the ability of these three firearms. The same applies to shotguns: all semi-auto "military style" (whatever the fuck that means) were prohibited. Yet anyone can still purchase a detachable magazine-fed pump-action 12 gauge, which is actually more lethal than the SPAS because of the speed in which it can be reloaded.

Rather than handing my SPAS over to the local authorities with an ignorant, shit-eating grin on my face, I put it on consignment in Washington State before the federal legislation was implemented. At least I'll see a little return on my purchase price, unlike a friend who was forced into surrendering his banned $1500 (!) H&K MP5 K to his local RCMP without so much as a *dollar* in compensation. Think about that - one thousand five hundred dollars plus the price of all his accessories down the shitter for no good reason (helluva lot of cashish for those in our socioeconomic group!).

The SPAS is an Italian manufactured 12 gauge shotgun designed to accept 2 3/4" shells only. It can be operated in pump-action or gas operated semi-automatic and has a capacity of eight plus one, for a total of nine uninterrupted shots. It weighs about ten pounds unloaded making for a rather heavy package with a full magazine. Single-handed pistol firing is out of the question (although 'roidmonger Schwartzenegger accomplished this in the police station slaughter in *Terminator*).

Shooting this devastating arm is hilarious; imagine nine rounds of #00 buck as fast as you can pull the trigger - about two or three seconds - delivered into your target. That could be equated to shooting something about *45 times* with a .32 auto. Whatever the item targeted down range, not much of it will remain after the fact. In semi-auto mode the shooter must lean into the SPAS giving a stiff and tight grip. Shooting the gun in this manner will guarantee smooth functioning. The SPAS will fail to chamber sometimes if shot with a loose grip or from the hip, especially when using the lightly-loaded, $4.00-a-box ammo we buy from our local Canadian Tire outlet.

The SPAS has appeared in many films, including the highest grossing film of all time, *Jurassic Park.* I was hoping to see some serious dino carnage at the hands of the SPAS, but it was wasted; it wasn't fired once during the entire film. The best use of the SPAS was in the Oliver Gruner Actioner *Nemesis,* in which the hero squeezes endless rounds of semi-auto and even caps a few bad guys in the process. If you would like to add an assault shotgun to your collection I would highly recommend the Franchi SPAS, although if your funds permit I would spring for a USAS-12 instead. The USAS is a detachable mag-fed semi-auto 12 gauge that utilizes either a ten-round box magazine or a 20-round drum magazine. This item is probably even more fun than the SPAS. The downside is the price; the USAS is around $1200 while the Franchi can be had for about half that. I picked up my piece for $500 used, and got back $480 when I was forced to sell it.

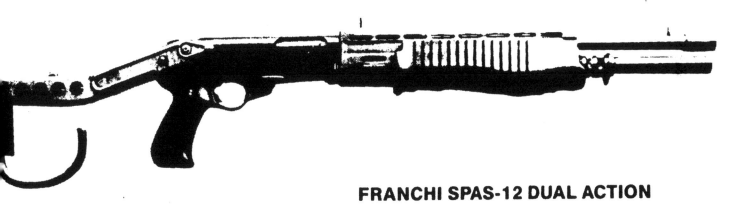

FRANCHI SPAS-12 DUAL ACTION

Gauge: 12 with 2-3/4″ chamber. **Barrel:** 21-1/2″. **Weight:** 9.6 lbs. **Stocks:** Forearm and pistol grip, nylon, folding metal butt. **Sights:** Blade front, reer peep, optional scope and mount. **Features:** Gas operated semi-automatic with slide action backup, 8-shot magazine, matte black finish, folding carrying handle, cylinder choke, optional full and modified, optional shot diverter. **Price:** $713. From American Arms.

James Steinbach puts together an amazing zine called GOKE. It's dedicated to cool stuff and cool stuff only: gun tests, porno video reviews, topless bar reviews, motorcycle racing, social commentary from the point of view of someone unaffected by trendy "sensitivity" crap. I recommend it. Send $2.00 American to

948 Madison Street, Victoria, BC V8S 4C5, Canada.

James pointed out an embarrassing gaffe in issue #1 of GFM. In the Norinco .45 article I mention a scene in a film called *Fingered* starring Lydia Lunch, where a guy gives her pleasure with a .45. Well, James is an authority on such films, and points out that the gun/phallus was actually a .357 magnum revolver. I haven't seen the film in a few years, and I recall being drunk at the time of the viewing, but there is no excuse for factual error and bad research on the pages of GFM. I sincerely apologize to you readers, and promise to be more vigilant in this and future issues. For my punishment I'm going to shoot myself in the foot with a Ruger Mark II Target .22LR pistol. I'm not going to use exotic ammo, as I'm sure a plain lead bullet will inflict sufficient pain. In issue #3 I'll describe to you how it feels, as well as the resulting hospital procedures and mandatory police report. - HK

A COUPLE O' RUGER WHEELGUNS
SINGLE-ACTION VS DOUBLE-ACTION .357 MAGNUM REVOLVERS

Sturm, Ruger & Co. have proven themselves over the years to be godlike gun manufacturers. They don't make a single product that isn't of outstanding quality. First known for their .22 caliber single-action Colt lookalikes in the '50s, they soon branched out with a version chambered for the "new" .357 magnum cartridge (basically a super-hot .38 special) called the Blackhawk. It had the old-timey cowboy looks of the Colt Peacemaker, but was built on an enormously sturdy and rugged frame, making it nearly indestructible. It also featured modern adjustable sights, which were a welcome addition to an old design. The problem with the old design, however, was the fact that the thing would fire if you dropped it (not many modern men are in the habit of leaving the hammer resting on an empty chamber, as was the custom in the days when the mighty Colt reigned supreme). So the early '70s saw the unveiling of the New Model Blackhawk, which features Ruger's patented and ingenious transfer-bar safety system. This system ensures that the gun will *under no circumstances fire unless the trigger is pulled.* Way to go, Ruger! Now even idiots can enjoy the thrill of single-action shooting.

The Security Six .357 magnum represents Ruger's foray into the *double-action* category, and incorporates the same high standards you'd expect from this wonderful company.

Editor's note: this is where some readers new to the world of firearms terminology will ask what the difference is between single and double-action. Have patience, gun fags, for these are our potential allies in the war against the gun-grabbers and the hysterical multiculturalist traitors in the controlled news media. The difference between single and double-action revolvers, dear readers, is thus: *with a double-action revolver it is possible - and a good habit to get into - to leave the hammer at rest (down) and just pull the trigger to fire. The trigger mechanism pulls the hammer back, and then lets it fall to strike the primer, igniting the round (the hammer goes back and forth - "double" action). To fire a single-action revolver, you must manually pull the hammer back to cock it before pulling the trigger. The same logic applies to semi-automatic pistols, except that with a single-action (like the Colt Government .45) you only have to cock the hammer for the first shot. Thereafter, the slide action ejects the spent casing, cocks the hammer and pops a fresh round into the chamber in one cycle of the slide.* There. Does that clear some things up? Good.

About the double-action Security Six: great gun, but no longer produced. Don't panic; they've just incorporated the design with a few improvements (such as a heavy barrel) into the GP series revolvers. Even greater guns, but I don't have access to one right at this moment, so I can't very well review it, can I? I hate being poor.

The Security Six used in this test belongs to your favorite society columnist (Red) and is in pretty decent shape, considering the fact that he built a dog house using the gun as a hammer. It was even loaded (don't try this at home!) with Federal 158 grain jacketed hollowpoints. The butt was dinged up a little, but everything functioned without a hitch. It is constructed of stainless steel and sports a 6" barrel.

This is a really smooth shooter, and recoil isn't all that bad due to the long barrel (a heavier barrel would help, though) and is extremely accurate with everything from cheap .38 special semi-wadcutters to full-power jacketed softpoints and hollowpoints. Red gave me a box of his own handloads, which - even though he swears by them - I refuse to fire. Read his column and then imagine yourself firing something that that crazy fucker loaded!

My old friend Skip (who rides a Harley and plays in a band with a bunch of longhairs) loaned me his New Model Blackhawk for this article. Skip's a good man, even though he associates with hippies. This gun has a blued finish, hardwood grip and 4 5/8" barrel, the shortest they make, as the muzzle is flush with the end of the ejector-rod housing.

Now this gun is a real hoot to fire. It's not the most punishing gun I've ever fired, but with stiff magnum loads, its recoil could wake the dead. Don't get me wrong - I *like* guns that kick the shit out of you, but it gets a little old after a hundred rounds or so. The clasically curved single-action style grip lets the gun rock back in your hand, soaking up some of the kick, but the bottom edge of the grip digs in to the heel of your hand, causing *pain*. Here's how to fix that: while at a cowboy action shoot a couple of months ago, a guy showed me how he swapped the grip frame on his New Model Blackhawk with one from a Super Blackhawk .44 magnum. No modification is necessary; all you need is a screwdriver. At first glance they look identical, but the Super Blackhawk grip is bigger and *much* more comfortable. I recommend this operation.

Even for bouncing around so much, the accuracy is great, which is something to be expected from any gun made by such a fine company. The gun performed flawlessly (also to be expected) and the spent casings ejected easily; the ejector rod only having to be used after the gun started getting dirty. I had a pretty hard time giving it back to Skip, so I guess I've got to go out and buy one of my own. I'm taking donations, if you want to send me some dough.

The only thing that these two guns have in common is the cartridge they fire and the company that made them. Yet for some reason they're amazingly similar in feel and function. They have similar *personalities*, if that's possible. I would have to be more in touch with my sensitive, caring side to really explain it well. It's a Ruger thing, I guess. I would highly recommend either one of these babies.

You can't buy a *new* Security Six of course, but really nice used ones usually go for around two bills. The New Model Blackhawks are priced anywhere from about $350 to $450 (new), depending on your choice of barrel length, caliber, stainless versus blue, etc. Like the Security Six, they can be found used for a couple hundred bucks.

If you're using a revolver for strictly self-defense purposes, stick with double-action unless you've been firing single-action for a lot of years. When a bunch of crack-crazed animals start shaking you down, you don't want to have to think, even if it's something as natural as cocking a gun. Your brain will not be functioning as normal, and you'll be peeing your pants and making weird noises from your throat. Nothing to be ashamed of, **JUST POINT THE GUN AND START KILLING.**

I can't think of a happier ending.

On the left is a single-action job with a 5½" barrel. On the right is a Security Six with fixed sights and 4" barrel.

CHINESE SKS
WHAT THE HELL! IT WORKS!

Red recently bought a Norinco SKS caliber 7.62 x 39mm sporting rifle, and the world is not a safer place. I went to his house to take a look at it, and I no sooner got out of my truck when he hurled the thing at me from across the front yard. I had to run to catch it, and I dropped my beer in the process. The bastard. I barely caught the damned rifle before it skittered out into the street, and found that it had a full magazine, a round in the chamber and the safety was off. Off as in *removed altogether*. Hey, I enjoy danger as much as the next guy, but...

I called him an asshole and he babbled something incoherent. He had apparently been drinking Gatorade margaritas all day and was pretty well bent. I left him there and took the SKS out to my secret shooting range, but the fucker found me before I got ten rounds off. For a moment I thought I'd have to shoot him, but by that time he seemed relatively sane. We settled down for some serious shooting.

I'll admit that I was pretty skeptical about this rifle, what with all the horror stories and urban legends surrounding it, and the ridiculously low price of $150 (only a month ago they sold for half that). And while some - maybe even most - of the stories are true (see *"The President and His Cronies..."* article in this issue) I still think this weapon is a bargain. The fact that tens of thousands of them are now in the hands of patriotic Americans and functioning flawlessly should attest to its desirability. With the addition of an accessory or two (namely a detachable 30-round magazine) this thing is capable of mowing down scores of deserving slimebuckets in a very short time, which is what we all look for in a rifle.

One of the media-inspired urban legends has it that if you let the bolt slam forward with a full magazine, it'll go full-auto. *I wish!* Shit, we tried and tried, and couldn't get it to do it. I've heard from reliable sources, however, that the SKS is pretty easy to convert to a fully automatic machine gun. The method seems to be a closely guarded secret, but as soon as I find out how to do it, it'll be a secret no longer,*and the readers of *Gun Fag Manifesto* will all have the potential to be armed with cheap automatic weapons.* By God, we'll be an army!

The SKS has a 21" barrel, and its overall length is just over 40". Muzzle velocity is a zippy 2,440 feet per second. It weighs approximately seven pounds, and has a politically correct magazine capacity of ten rounds. The magazine is supposedly non-detachable, but detach it anyway and throw it in the trash where it belongs. Magazines with a capacity of 30 and even 40 rounds are common, and I suggest that if you decide to get an SKS, you should go out and buy plenty of high-capacity magazines while they're still legal, and before there's a run on them (which *will* happen) making them scarce and expensive.

Firing the SKS is a lot of fun (even though we couldn't get it to go full-auto) and ammo is really cheap, for now. We probably burned up 2,000 rounds before it got too dark to see the targets, and another 500 or so after dark, just for the noise and the flames. The only problem encountered the whole day was when the bolt didn't lock up one time, resulting in a misfire. Red jammed the bolt handle forward and it fired, all right, but without the trigger being pulled! Red's hand was still in the way of the bolt when it went off, and it chewed his finger up a little, but by that time we were too drunk to care. Besides, a bloody gunstock looks cool.

Field-stripping is easy, as the whole thing is pretty much held together by one pin. There is a compartment in the buttstock for cleaning supplies, and a cleaning rod is affixed to the underside of the barrel.

My advice? Buy one **NOW WHILE THEY'RE STILL CHEAP** and wait for instructions for full-auto conversion,*which will hopefully be in the next issue.

* For entertainment purposes only, of course.

RAVEN .25 ACP
WHATAFUCKINPIECEASHIT!

My initial attraction to this piece of shit was, of course, the price (I bought it at a local pawn shop for $40). I thought it might be nice to have a small, cheap sidearm to pack around during the hot summer months when my clothing is not bulky enough to hide a .45, and I also thought that if the cops confiscated a $40 pistol, well, so be it.

This is absolutely the worst handgun I have ever had the misfortune of firing. It jammed on virtually every other shot. At ten yards, the few shots that actually made it out of the barrel landed all over the target. The grip is so small that I could barely get two fingers around it, thus crowding the web of my hand up too close to the slide, which repeatedly bit like a sonofabitch, actually drawing blood. This chintzy piece of trash has no redeeming quality whatsoever. It is inaccurate, unreliable, poorly constructed and butt-ass ugly. For self defense, you'd be better off carrying a rolled-up newspaper!

The only genuine steel in this "gun" is the barrel itself. Other parts (the frame, slide, etc.), are made of the same die-cast metal that toy guns are made of. In fact, when holding this thing in your hand, it's hard to tell at first whether or not it *is* a toy. The cheesy plastic grip panels fit so poorly that they look like they were made for a different gun. It disgusts me to admit that this dingle-berry was made in the U.S. of A.

I don't know what the hell I was thinking when I bought this tawdry cockroach of a pistol. The niggardly .25 ACP round is not likely to stop a little old lady, let alone a shrieking crack-head. It scares me to think that some poor dumb shitheads rely on something like this for personal defense. It ain't gonna work, fools! First, you have to coax the wretched thing to fire, and if you do get it to fire, and if by some miracle you happen to hit the punk you're shooting at, *and if he notices that he's been hit,* he's going be mighty pissed off, and

you're just going to look stupid.

I'm always hearing arguments by fellow gun enthusiasts in defense of these so-called "Saturday Night Specials," which are being targeted by the usual cretins in Washington. We *have* to defend these guns, simply because they're *guns,* and I have no problem with that. The position our side is taking on this subject disturbs me, however, and that is that "poor people have the right to defend themselves." Well, ain't that precious? **FUCK POOR PEOPLE!** If they choose to depend on the state for their housing, their dope money and their goddamned food stamps, then they can fucking well depend on the state for their protection! *Fuck 'em!*

After painstakingly firing one whole box of ammo, I sat the offensive little fly-speck upon a rock and executed the fucker with my .45. One shot from a *real* gun sent the thing flying in a thousand directions.

May its cheap soul rot in Hell.

BUT, ON THE OTHER HAND...

My experience with cheap, small-caliber handguns is limited to the Raven .25, and that experience pretty much soured me on the little buggers. Maybe I haven't given them a fair shake, as Chet Antonini points out in the following article. I wrote the Raven piece before Mr. Antonini sent me his article, and while I've never been a fan of small caliber handguns (I must confess that I like really loud guns that kick like bastards) he raises some interesting points. I like his idea of causing immense pain before eventual death, which is something I hadn't considered. This being a (supposedly) free country, a country in which free men can make decisions based upon information gleaned from a free press, read both of these articles and come to your own conclusions. If you're in the market for one of these little poppers, I recommend spending the extra cash for a name-brand piece such as a Beretta or Colt; they've got to be more reliable than the cursed Raven. Read on, gun fags:

DEATH DIRT CHEAP

IN DEFENSE OF SATURDAY NIGHT SPECIALS
BY CHET ANTONINI

The biggest obstacle to buying the coolest handguns is your ego. A lot of people just don't have the courage to buy one of those ultra-concealable, small caliber handguns sometimes called "saturday night

specials."

Too bad.

First-time buyers, especially, get jeered at when they (quite naturally) move away from the hand-held cannons like the Desert Eagle

toward smaller, more reasonable-looking guns. Little do they know they've identified themselves to the store clerks as rubes, queers and possibly niggers - by even looking at those palm-sized, small caliber weapons.

"Hell, if you shoot somebody with that thing," the cretin behind the counter snorts, "you're just liable to make 'em mad...that's all."

Red-faced and stammering, the customer gets led back over to the big guns, the expensive guns, guns that fire enormous bullets with "stopping power," guns so powerful the recoil dislocates your wrist bones. Soon the customer learns that's the most important thing - stopping power. Looky here, this .45 slug'll goddamn shoot a man in half if it so much as grazes his shoulder. Anything less than a nine millimeter is of no use, see? Gettin' hit with a .22 is like, well, it's like maybe it stings a little. You'd be better off just to hit the guy over the head with one of them guns than to fire it.

(Editor's note - a lot of gun stores are staffed with barely-educated geeks making five bucks an hour who claim to be the omniscient authority on firearms. This is particularly true with the younger salesmen. Always remember that when you're the customer, you're the boss).

Their disdain for "belly guns" or "nigger guns" makes you wonder why the hell they display the things in the first place. I've heard gun store clerks tell people that gang members *want* to be shot by someone pointing a .32 at them. Particularly stupid is their oft-expressed viewpoint that .22 or .25 caliber bullets are practically harmless.

Right. I'm sure Bobby Kennedy would agree that such bullets don't do much damage at all - except he got his head blown off by one. No wait. Ask Jim Brady. See what he has to drool on the subject. The .22 long round that broke into his skull traveled a few laps around the inside of his head before it ran out of steam. Not only did the tiny round "stop" him, it did a neat job of removing or damaging most of

his neocortex.

Clerks also tell people that the little guns are so inaccurate you'd be lucky to hit someone with such a pea-shooter anyway. That's another lie.

Let's get real here!

Entirely too much emphasis is placed on a handgun with the magical power to disintegrate someone with a single shot. Any study of bullet wounds will show that what a bullet does once it hits the body is not predictable. Caliber, velocity, foot-fucking-pounds of energy are so much hee-hawing. Small caliber guns have a lot to recommend them, not the least of them being the kinds of ammo they fire.

AMMO

Small caliber bullets will bust into a human body just as well as any other bullet, then, unlike more powerful ammunition, it loses a lot of energy, gets deflected off bones or even solid tissue and from there it's anybody's guess where it will end up. While a larger caliber might punch right through causing a beautifully scientific "wound channel," the .25 caliber might tunnel around a person's innards, chopping up an intestine here, fragmenting into a lung there before lodging itself alarmingly close to a vital organ.

Such a wound does more than sting a person - though it might not kill him. Not outright.

Such wounds might be exactly the type you want to inflict. Why limit yourself to fatal wounds only? It's not always necessary or desirable to kill someone after all.

Even if not instantly dead, the person stands a good chance of dying unless he gets immediate medical care. In many ways you, the shooter, are the one who decides how fast that medical care will be coming. A few .22 slugs roto-tilling the abdomen have caused serious internal bleeding. And it hurts a lot. It is agony. Such

a sight might be even more pleasing than a corpse depending on who you shoot.

And so what if the guy lives? He ain't ever going to be the same again. Perforated intestines, chopped up pancreases and the like cause pain and debilitation for years, probably for the rest of the dude's life. There are going to be operations to remove the slugs and slug fragments from him, more operations to sew up all the rips and tears and to piece together all the severed veins and arteries. Hell, they might have to give the guy a colostomy!

One last comment on the Holy Doctrine of Stopping Power: the ability to instantly kill or incapacitate a person with a single shot depends mostly on placement of the bullet - not the bullet itself. Cop files are full of instances of guys soaking up many rounds of "one shot stoppers" and carrying on.

Extremely angry or scared people have a natural immunity to shock. So do drunks and people on other kinds of drugs. Very determined people too, can be unstoppable.

At the same time, some people are felled by the mere *sound* of gunfire. I know of one guy who was hit in the leg by an ejected shell from a blank cartridge, fell writhing in the street and had to be helped to his car by his buddies, although no damage had occurred at all. Shit, some people will faint if you just point a gun at them. Imminent mayhem and death can have profound psychological and/or physiological effects.

ACCURACY

Once again, what's the goal here? Is it really the one-shot stop? Who fires just one shot? The fact that these big-ass .40 caliber guns have magazines holding more than 15 rounds suggests that at least someone was thinking about pulling the trigger more than once. Same goes for the little belly gun. You've

\VIS P-32

\\iber: .32ACP. **Barrel:** 2.8". **Weight:** 22 oz.
cks: Polished wood. **Sights:** Fixed. **Fea-\ns:** Single action, 6-shot magazine, bright
ome or black teflon finish. **Price:** $87.60.

DAVIS P-380

Caliber: .380. **Barrel:** 2.8". **Weight:** 22
oz. **Stocks:** Polished wood. **Sights:** Fixed. **Fea-tures:** Single action, 5-shot magazine, black or
chrome finish. **Price:** $98.

JENNINGS FIREARMS J-25

Caliber: .25ACP. **Barrel:** 2-1/2". **Weight:** 13 oz.
Stocks: Ivory, black combat, walnut **Sights:**
Fixed. **Features:** Single action, alloy frame,
satin nickel, bright chrome or black teflon
finish, 6-shot magazine. **Price:** $65. From
Jennings Firearms, Irving, CA.

\CU-TEK AT-32

\\iber: 32ACP. **Barrel:** 2.75". **Weight:** 16 oz.
\cks: Combat rubber or wood. **Sights:**
\d post front, rear drift adjustable. **Fea-\s:** Single action, manual safety with firing
\block and trigger disconnect, 5-shot maga-
\e with finger extension. stainless steel or
\k finish, exposed hammer, lifetime war-
\ty. Price: stainless $164, black $169.

**RAVEN ARMS
MODEL P-25/MP-25**

Caliber: .25ACP. **Barrel:** 2-7/16". **Weight:** 15
oz. **Stocks:** Walnut, ivory plastic on slotted
plastic. **Sights:** Fixed. **Features:** Single
action, nickel, blue, chrome finish, surfaces
hand-polished, 6-shot magazine. **Price:** Any
finish $69.95. Available from Raven Arms, In-
dustry, CA.

**BERETTA
MODEL 21**

Caliber: .25ACP, .22LR. **Barrel:** 2-1/2".
Weight: 11-1/2 oz./.25ACP, 11.8 oz./.22LR.
Stocks: Walnut or plastic. **Sights:** Fixed. **Fea-tures:** Double action, 8-shot magazine
(.25ACP) 7-shot (.22LR), blue, matte, nickel or
engraved. **Price:** Blue $235, matte $185,
nickel $260, engraved $285.

RATEC PROTEC-25

\oer: 25ACP. **Barrel:** 2-1/2". **Weight:** 13 oz.
\ks: Wraparound plastic, black, grey or
\wood. Sights: Fixed. **Features:** Double
\n only, black, satin or Tec-kote finish. 8-
\magazine. Price: Black $99.95, other fin-
\104.95.

PHOENIX ARMS RAVEN

Caliber: .25ACP. **Barrel:** 2.5". **Weight:** 15 oz.
Stocks: Ivory, pink Pearl or black slotted.
Sights: Fixed. **Features:** Single action,
chrome, nickel or blue finish, 6-shot magazine.
Price: $69.95. From Phoenix Arms, Ontario,
CA.

LORCIN L-22

Caliber: .22LR. **Barrel:** 2.55". **Weight:** 16 oz.
Stocks: High impact plastic, pink, black or
pearl. **Sights:** Fixed. **Features:** Single action,
9-shot magazine, chrome or black. **Price:**
$89.95.

got your 6, 7, 8, or 9-shots. Squeeze 'em off! One hit is sufficient.

In fact, in my experience these little guns are plenty accurate - for a couple of reasons. First, most gun battles take place within ten or fifteen feet. At ten feet almost anybody can group shots closely enough to hit the face or heart every time. The smallness of the weapon just makes this more likely. Since the barrels of these guns extend out to about as far as the index finger would, it is easy to use the "point & shoot" method of aiming. You can also shoot one-handed and without taking a karate stance before firing.

The gun's lack of serious recoil means the shooter is less likely to flinch when pulling the trigger, thus missing the target. In short, a person can feel more comfortable more quickly with a belly gun than with other weapons. This means less practice and more loafing around, less money wasted on practice ammo fired into some indoor range's backstop.

Small caliber guns are far more concealable than other guns. In that they win hands down. An ace bandage will hold one so close to your stomach you can wear a T-shirt and not be noticed. You can even "palm" one in your hand and just stand there. When your opponent takes a swing (or goes for his big bad .45) you shoot him.

Small caliber guns are cheaper, too (and so is the ammo). That means for the price of your Dirty Harry gun you can buy a few of these little guys and hide 'em around the house, throw one in your car, leave one at work, etc. This just increases the chances you'll be armed when you need it most.

Finally, if the barrel is just an inch or so longer than normal, a belly gun can be silenced by one of many homemade methods. Usually it's enough to duct-tape a two liter soft drink bottle over the muzzle to silence a sub-sonic gun. of course your precious accuracy might suffer with such a rig, but there are advantages to a silenced weapon.

So fuck the snoots who tell you not to buy the "pea-shooters" and if you really must have something in the one-shot stop category, buy a .32 and use Winchester Silvertip ammo. This round has been proven to have just as much fucking stopping power as a 9mm.

Chet Antonini writes for Loompanics and is co-author of a book entitled YOU ARE GOING TO PRISON. He also publishes an excellent zine in Seattle called PILLS-A-GO-GO. For a copy, send two bucks to 1202 E. Pike St., #849, Seattle, WA 98122-3934.

1891 MOSIN-NAGANT RIFLE

By E. J. Hoffschmidt

IN spite of its age, this turnbolt military rifle is still in use in Russia and her satellites. It has outlived at least three Russian semiautomatic rifles.

Adopted in 1891 by the Imperial Russian Army, the Mosin-Nagant was Russia's first modern smokeless powder rifle. It was designed by Colonel Serge I. Mosin of the Imperial Russian Army in collaboration with Emile Nagant, famous Belgian arms designer and manufacturer. It might be pointed out that Mosin's name is also encountered in

E. J. HOFFSCHMIDT *is an artist-illustrator.*

arms literature as Mossin, Mouzin, Moisin, Mossine. etc., depending upon nationality of the writer. The term "3-line" often used in describing this rifle indicates the nominal caliber of .300 inch, based upon a Russian unit of measurement equal to .1 inch.

Mosin-Nagant rifles have been manufactured in Russia, Switzerland, France, and in the U. S. by Remington Arms Co. and New England Westinghouse.

The U. S.-made Mosin rifles were better finished than those of present-day Soviet manufacture. The Director of Civilian Marksmanship disposed of a quantity of these rifles to NRA mem-

bers after World War I.

Original Model 1891 rifles had octagon-shaped receivers whereas subsequent versions have round receivers. Numerous models exist, including both carbines and rifles. (Specimen in photo is Model 1891/30.) Telescope-sighted rifles were furnished for use by snipers.

This rifle is not too suitable for conversion to sporting type because of the split receiver bridge which complicates the mounting of receiver and scope sights. From a design standpoint, the bolt handle is too far forward and the safety mechanism is stiff and awkward to operate.

1 To apply safety catch, pull back cocking piece (1) far enough to allow it to be rotated as shown, over back edge of receiver

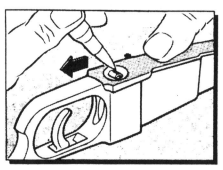

2 This rifle has a simple magazine floorplate release. Using a cartridge or finger, pull back floorplate latch (30). Then swing magazine floorplate (29) open

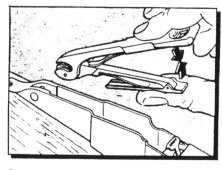

3 To remove magazine floorplate (29) and magazine follower (24), squeeze floorplate and follower together as shown. This will open hinge at end of floorplate and allow it to be pulled free of hinge pin riveted through magazine

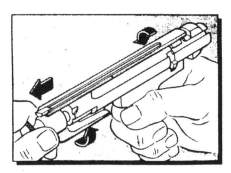

4 To strip bolt (8), grasp as shown. Pull back cocking piece (1) far enough to disengage it from end of bolt. Rotate it as shown, allowing it to go forward. Now slide bolt head (6) and bolt connector and guide bar (5) off bolt body (2)

5 Since firing pin (4) is screwed into cocking piece (1), they sometimes bind. End of bolt connector and guide bar (5) can be used as a wrench to screw out firing pin (4). When reassembling bolt, be sure marks on firing pin and cocking piece line up

6 To reassemble bolt, screw firing pin (4), firing pin spring (3), bolt (2), and cocking piece (1) together. Line up open end of guide bar with lug on cocking piece, then rotate bolt head until it lines up as shown. Push it all together and rotate cocking piece back to cocked position

The bolt release is simple in that it is only necessary to hold back on the trigger to remove the bolt from the receiver. Bolt takedown is simple and can be done without tools. Floorplate and magazine follower can be removed in an instant for cleaning. The magazine feed system is clever in that only one cartridge can enter the feedway at a time. A cartridge feed interrupter is actuated by the pressure of the bolt as it rides over the ejector. The interrupter separates the incoming round from other cartridges in the magazine, relieving it of the pressure of the rounds below, thus preventing rim over rim jams. ———————————————————— ∎

Parts Legend

1	Cocking piece	18	Trigger
2	Bolt	19	Trigger hinge pin
3	Firing pin spring	20	Trigger spring and bolt stop
4	Firing pin	21	Bolt stop retaining screw
5	Bolt connector and guide bar	22	Magazine and trigger guard
6	Bolt head	23	Front guard screw
7	Extractor	24	Magazine follower
8	Bolt (assembled)	25	Magazine follower spring assembly
9	Rear guard screw	26	Follower hinge pin
10	Ejector spring retaining screw	27	Lower magazine follower spring
11	Ejector spring and feed interrupter	28	Spring retaining screw
12	Ejector	29	Magazine floorplate
13	Receiver	30	Floorplate latch
14	Barrel assembly	31	Floorplate latch screw
15	Handguard	32	Follower hinge pin (upper)
16	Front and rear barrel bands	33	Stock
17	Front sight	34	Buttplate

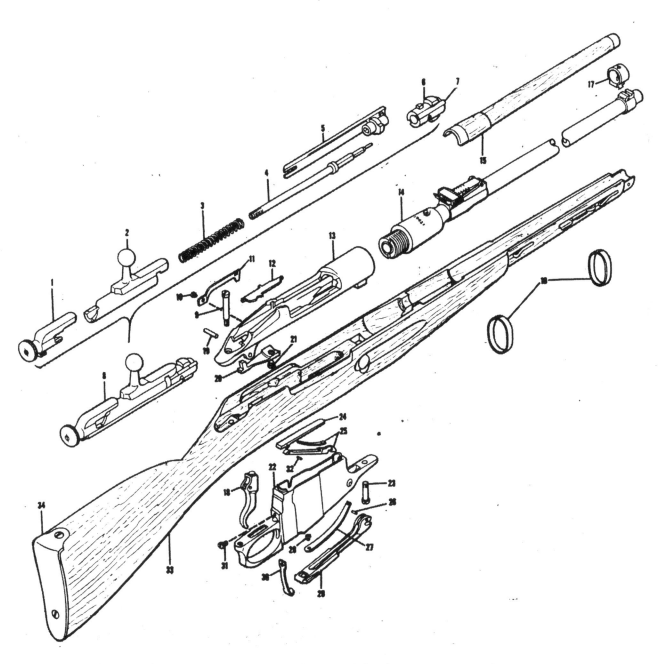

EDITOR'S NOTE: When putting this issue together, I discovered that I was going to end up with two blank pages. Bad planning and too much beer. So I stole this article from an old magazine. So what? So I'm lazy! You can still find these rifles at gun stores for less than a hundred bucks, and they're a real hoot to fire. So the article is worth a read.

MEAT IS GOOD FOOD

KILL IT AND EAT IT!

After our society collapses under the weight of the treasonous First Couple's communism, the few remaining stores which haven't been looted and/or burned to the ground are going to be hard-pressed to come up with any food with which to stock their barren shelves. And after waiting all day in line for your mouldy little hunk of bread, you're going to need a wheel barrow load of twenties to pay for the wretched thing! This is no way for a gun fag to live.

Don't stand in line for anything. There is food everywhere; you just have to have the means with which to kill it (hopefully, you will have been smart enough to hide some guns and ammo before the shit hit the fan). Every animal on the North American continent is edible. You can eat anything that walks, swims or takes to the sky. Furthermore, you can gobble up almost every part of a North American animal - even deer antlers, when in velvet, are not bad slow-roasted in a bed of coals. Really the only things you should *not* eat are the livers of polar bears and seals, as they are so rich in vitamin A as to make them poisonous. And I wouldn't recommend eating crackheads, as they're probably poisonous, too.

Meat is everywhere

Even the city offers a plentiful harvest of game. Skunks, raccoons and possums abound in L.A., to say nothing of the millions of dogs and cats. For the smaller city game, a good .22 pistol is ideal; it's not too loud, it's concealable, cheap to shoot and in an urban environment you're not likely to have to deal with long ranges. Easier yet it to simply coax a friendly dog or cat along, pet it some, call it a good little poochie-woochie or whatever, and smack it in the head with a hammer.

You'll probably not want to stay in the city after the Great Fall, however (for one thing, there won't be any safe drinking water), in which case you'll need to be a little better armed. For bigger game your assault rifle will work fine. I like the M1 Garand (.30-06) for hunting deer, elk, etc., but you should have no problem using a 7.62 x 39mm (AK-47, SKS) or .223 Rem (M16, AR-15, Mini-14). These military rounds are fully jacketed and don't expand too much. You only want to poke a hole in your meal, not splatter it into the next county. A shotgun is best for shooting birds, of course. Now, remember all that ammo you've been stockpiling? Pretty darned heavy, isn't it? I'd hate to have to carry it very far. You need to load it into your vehicle and get out of town, which takes gasoline. Along with the ammo, you should also have stashed four or five jerry cans of gas (it's still pretty cheap - what are you waiting for?).

But this article is about food, not common-sense survival equipment. Specifically, this is about *meat*. Man may not be able to live on bread alone, but he *can* live on meat alone. Don't listen to the skinny vegetarian punk liberals who claim to know how to eat. One look at their oily pallor and bony, humorless faces ought to tell you that they *do not* know how to eat. Many societies throughout history have thrived on diets of meat, meat, meat. The Mongolian army kept herds of cattle on their adventures, and that's all they ate. Beef. They proceeded to kick the shit out of the Chinese, which is what finally inspired the construction of the Great Wall. It's the only way the Chinese could keep the vicious sonsabitches at bay.

Skin and blood

When you've just killed something and don't know when the next meal will make itself available, don't bleed the thing any more than can be helped. Blood is rich in easily-absorbed vitamins and minerals, and can be stored and carried in a plastic bag, or more traditionally, in the entrails (if you're going to do this, clean the entrails well - especially if the animal was not a vegetarian). Blood is especially delicious when used in soups or stews.

Skin is nutritious as well, but not nearly as tasty. It's not bad, it's just not that great. A lot of sportsmen will roast an animal in its skin, which is a delectable and handy way to prepare a meal at camp, but it can be wasteful. Even rawhide is perfectly edible, as it's just untanned skin. Go ahead and slice a chunk off, chew it until you're tired, and swallow the slimy lump. It ain't T-bone & taters, but it'll keep you afloat for the next kill.

Rules for cooking

Don't cook anything longer than is absolutely necessary. Heat destroys nutritive value in all foods, and meat is no exception. Heat especially ruins vitamin C, and no matter what the bunny-huggers tell you, meat is high in this important vitamin. It'll keep you from getting scurvy, which is akin to getting kicked in the 'nads every 30 seconds or so, along with getting your teeth ripped out. Every mucous membrane - use your imagination - will bleed, and in advanced cases, blood comes out of your very pores, as well as your ears, your eyeballs, etc. It's a hideous disease, and only vitamin C keeps you from getting it. So unless you suspect parasites, eat your meat rare, and the fresher the better.

A nice plump sizzling steak will supply you with every ingredient necessary for good health. Add a couple of beers while times are still good, and you've got a delicious, well-balanced feast suitable for breakfast, lunch and dinner. There is absolutely no reason for a gun fag to go hungry on this continent. Shoot, cook, eat and drink. Is there really anything more to life than that?

HOLLISTER KOPP'S ROCKABILLY BAND!

RED'S

A World of Peace

LAST WORD

JAKE JOSEPH L.Z. KILROY KOWALSKI IV AKA RED

240 SPEER
24-296
1⅛"

0748 HRS IN SOME TRASH-STREWN LOT 12 MINUTES NORTHEAST OF BURBANK.. FULL OF WELFARE FUCKING MONEY BY-PRODUCTS...THERE SHOULD BE NO WELFARE FUCKING BY-PRODUCTS AS THERE SHOULD BE NO WELFARE...I'LL GET TO THAT ANOTHER TIME...I AWOKE IN THE BACK OF MY '62 CHEVY TRUCK WITH THE HATEFUL STEAMING FUCKING SMOGGY SUN THAT WAS AS FULL OF HATE FOR THE FUCKING L.A. LIBERAL SCUM AS I WAS... BEATING DOWN INTO MY HUNGOVER EYES...A CAMEL BURNT TO THE FILTER STUCK IN MY CHAPPED AND CRACKED LIPS WHICH I ALMOST SWALLOWED WHEN I SAW THE CARNAGE OF THE PREVIOUS NIGHT...A HALF-EATEN TRIPLE CHEESE TOMMYBURGER ROLLED UP IN ONE OF MY HOLY SOCKS...I GUESS I'LL BE TAKING IT HOME FOR MY DOG...MY COLT .45 WAS STUFFED IN THE WAISTBAND OF MY SEARS BIG FUCKING WHITE AMERICAN MADE FUCKING BAGGY BOXER SHORTS...I DON'T WEAR FAG SKIVIES...FUCKING RIPPED WHITE TIGHTIES...AND MY SKEET-N-TRAP LAUNCHER ATTACHED TO THE EDGE OF OF THE TAILGATE AND MY 12 GAUGE SEARS TED WILLIAMS SPECIAL NOWHERE TO BE SEEN...FUCKING HOLY FUCKING FUCK...ABOUT THIS TIME I DECIDED TO FUCKING BAIL BECAUSE I WAS GETTING REALLY SICK TO MY STOMACH...I SAW A PACK OF DESEASE-RIDDEN MEXICAN CHIHUAHUAS DIGGING UP OLD DIAPERS WITH LITTLE MONTE CARLOS AND COORS LIGHT LOGOS ON THEM...THERE WERE THREE SPENT SHELLS IN THE BED OF MY TRUCK AND TWO LIVE ROUNDS IN THE GUN...NOT ENOUGH SHOULD THE NATIVES BECOME RESTLESS...TOO STUPID AND FUCKING LAZY ANYWAY...WHAT HAPPENED TO THE OTHER THREE ROUNDS WAS A MYSTERY...I CRAWLED THROUGH THE SLIDING GLASS REAR WINDOW SALUTING THE NRA STICKER AND PLANTED MY GRIZZLED FACE INTO SPANKY THE DANCER'S TITS...I ACHIEVED MORNING WOOD...SHE SCREAMED HYSTERICALLY...BETTER LIVING THROUGH CHEMICALS IN MORE WAYS THAN ONE...THINGS WERE STARTING TO COME BACK TO ME AS SPANKY WAS HOLLERING GIBBERISH...LIKE ALL THE REST...FRANTICALLY TRYING TO COVER HERSELF WITH MY GREASY BOILERMAKERS CONCERT TEE...I FIRED UP THE RIG AND LAID RUBBER ACROSS THE DIRTY FUCKING WELFARE LOT...GOT THREE OF THE FILTHY LITTLE SHITS...BOUNCED MY TRUCK OFF THE CURB AND DRAGGED 300 FEET OF CHAIN-LINK FENCE...IT COULD HAVE BEEN USED TO BUILD A PRISON RIGHT THERE IN THAT LOT...AND SLAMMED INTO A GRAFFITIED BUS BENCH...SPANISH FUCKING SHIT ABOUT GETTING MONEY FROM FUCKING UNCLE BILL AND THE 1994 DODGERS HOME SCHEDULE...I GAVE SPANKY $12.00 AND CHANGE IN CAMEL CASH AND PROPOSED TO HER...SHE SLAPPED ME ACROSS THE FACE AND PULLED A CHEAP FUCKING DAVIS .380 AUTO ON ME AS SHE JUMPED OUT OF THE TRUCK...IT WAS LOVE AT LAST SIGHT...

I HIT LAUREL CANYON BLVD DOING 90 MPH SWERVING OVER THE DOUBLE YELLOWS...POPPED IN A ZZ TOP CD...ANY ZZ TOP CD FUCKING WORKS...OPENED A HOT TALLBOY OF PBR AND LIT ANOTHER CAMEL...LIGHTS AND SIRENS IN THE CRACKED MIRROR AS I WAS GRINDING METAL TO METAL WITH A PROBABLY STOLEN '67 LINCOLN HEARSE WHICH REMINDED ME THAT FOUR BALLS TOMMY'S FUNERAL WAS THAT DAY...I WAS GOING AS SOON AS I FINISHED DUCK HUNTING WITH HOLLISTER KOPP WHO I WAS SUPPOSED TO MEET A FUCKING HOUR AND A FUCKING HALF AGO...I PULLED OVER AFTER THE HEARSE DID A FUCKING ONE-EIGHTY THAT WOULD HAVE MADE JIMMY G. ROCKFORD ACHIEVE WOOD...THE FUCKING CASKET FELL OUT OF THE FUCKING HEARSE...IT HAD A BOISE CASCADE STAMP ON IT...BREAKING OPEN WITH A FUCKING DEAD MIDGET IN IT...DEAD MIDGET GETTING RUN OVER BY A DODGE TRUCK FULL OF FUCKING DAY LABORERS...FUCKING HOLY FUCKING FUCK...I SAW THEN THAT THE LIGHTS AND SIRENS WERE FROM FUCKING FAG FUNERAL COPS...FUCKING METER-MAID REJECTS...I COULD TAKE CARE OF THEM WITH NO PROBLEM WITH THE TWO ROUNDS I HAD LEFT IN MY .45 AND A MASON JAR OF MY BROTHER'S FUCKING HOME MADE PEPPER SPRAY...THE FUCKING BEST IN THE LOWER 48 FUCKING STATES...NOT CURRENTLY APPROVED BY THE F.D.A. AND THE E.P.A. AND CERTAINLY NOT APPROVED BY THE A. FUCKING C. FUCKING L.U...UNOFFICIALLY ENDORSED BY RED-BLOODED FUCKING PATRIOTIC AMERICANS BLACKLISTED BY FUCKING COMMIE AMNESTY INTERNATIONAL AND FUCKING FAG WILLIE FROM PHILLY RUNNING THE LAPD...I SLAPPED IT INTO R FOR REVENGE AND SLAMMED MY I-BEAM BUMPER INTO THEIR FUCKING HONDA REBELS AND SENT THEM FLYING 40 FEET NORTH OF THE HEARSE...I GOT OUT WEARING ONLY MY SEARS FUCKING BOXER SHORTS MY NRA CAP AND MY CALTRANS DAY-GLO ORANGE VEST...FROM GLORY DAYS AND CHERRY PICKERS PAST...I LAID DOWN MY LAST TWO ROUDS AS COVER FIRE AS THEY CAME SKIPPING AT ME HOLDING HANDS WITH THEIR .38'S DRAWN...I DOUSED THEM WITH HALF THE JAR OF PEPPER SPRAY WHICH MADE THEM DROP FASTER THAN CLINTON'S POPULARITY DOWN TO THE HOT OILY ASPHALT...SCREAMING IN UNBEARABLE PAIN LIKE FUCKING MICHAEL FAY OR A FUCKING UGLY NEWBORN BABY WITH DOWN'S SYNDROME...

FOUR FUCKING HOURS LATER HOLLISTER AND I WERE ENJOYING THE BEAUTIFUL BEEF DOUBLE-DIP SANDWICHES AT PHILLIPE'S IN DOWNTOWN FUCKING WELFARE L.A. AND TOASTING A DUCK HUNTING JOB WELL DONE...NOT TO MENTION ROCK-SALTING BUMS ALONG THE FUCKING WELFARE L.A. RIVER...WE DIDN'T TALK MUCH AFTER HE HANDED ME THREE SPENT SHELL CASINGS FROM MY FUCKING .45...THERE WAS SILENCE BEERS   SILENCE   HEAD NODDING MORE BEERS...I DIDN'T WANT TO KNOW ABOUT THOSE THREE ROUNDS AND IT WAS TIME TO BAIL...WE WENT OUR SEPARATE WAYS WITH AN UNDERSTANDING BUILT ON BEER, BULL-GARAGE-SHIT, GUNS AND FEAR...I PISTOL-WHIPPED HIM JUST FOR THE FUCK OF IT...

12 PBR TALLBOYS AN IN-N-OUT BURGER GUT-ACHE AND 25 MILES NORTH OF THE SALTON SEA AS THE SUN WAS GOING DOWN ON THE GREATEST MAN-MADE FUCKUP IN THE WESTERN HEMISPHERE...SINCE THE SOUTH DIDN'T IMPORT ENOUGH LEMATTS...THE ONLY GOOD THING THE SHOWERLESS FROGS INVENTED BESIDES FRENCH BORDELLOS...I STOPPED AT MY GIRLFRIEND KASEY'S TRAILER BECAUSE I KNEW SHE WAS IN HACKETTSTOWN NJ ON A MODELING ASSIGNMENT FOR THE NEW CRAFTSMAN TOOL CALENDAR...MISS JULY WITH A CHOPSAW AND MISS OCTOBER WITH A TORQUE WRENCH...I TOOK A MUCH NEEDED SHOWER DRANK SOME WINE AND RELOADED SOME .45 AMMO TO RELAX WHILE LISTENING TO TOM WAITS AND WATCHING THE TRACTOR PULL NATIONALS ON ESPN...I WAS GETTING READY FOR OLD FOUR BALLS' FUCKING WAKE WHEN THEY ANNOUNCED ON THE NEWS THAT FUCKING EX-CON RODNEY GLEN KING WAS SOAKING THE FUCKING HONEST AND LAW-ABIDING TAXPAYERS FOR THREE POINT EIGHT MILLION FUCKING DOLLARS FOR HIS WELL-DESERVED BEATING ADMINISTERED BY HIGHLY TRAINED AND PATRIOTIC CIVIL SERVANTS...FUCKING HOLY FUCKING FUCK...

I HAD ON MY BEST CAMOUFLAGE FUCKING SEERSUCKER SUIT...FOUR BALLS TOMMY'S
FUNERAL WASN'T MUCH TO TALK ABOUT...ONLY TEN OR SO OF US FOOLS...HIS BODYBAG
ON THE BACK OF MY FRIEND BLACKIE'S '74 ONE-TON FLATBED CHEVY STRAPPED DOWN
WITH ABOUT 600 FEET OF DUCT TAPE...WE DIDN'T WANT THE FUCKING BODY TO MOVE
WHEN WE OPENED FIRE...WE RECITED THE PLEDGE OF ALLEGIANCE DRANK SCOTCH SMOKED
CUBAN CIGARS LISTENED TO MOTORHEAD AND TALKED ABOUT WHO WAS GOING TO WIN THE
NBA CHAMPIONSHIP...DIDN'T TALK TOO MUCH ABOUT FOUR BALLS TOMMY...NOT MUCH TO
TALK ABOUT...HE WAS THREE NUTS NEGATIVE OF A FULL STRAIGHT ANYWAY...I
REMEMBERED THE TRIPLE CHEESE BURGER AND FED IT TO MY DOG...HE WAS HAPPY...AT
2300 HRS I LIT A STRING OF FUCKING 1500 MEXICAN BOTTLE ROCKETS WITH MY VIETNAM
BUDDY WESTMORELAND'S HOME MADE FLAME THROWER WHILE TED NUGENT'S LIVE VERSION
OF STRANGLEHOLD PLAYED...FUCKING 26 MINUTES LATER IT WAS TIME FOR THE
FINALE...WE OPENED FIRE ON FOUR BALLS TOMMY'S CORPSE FOR SIX GLORIOUS
MINUTES...I PERSONALLY RELOADED 28 TIMES AND DRANK SIX SHOTS OF GOOD
SCOTCH...TOMMY'S SIXTH ILLEGITIMATE FUCKING WELFARE BASTARD SON BILLY HOPPED
INTO THE TRUCK AND SLAMMED IT INTO REVERSE...HIT THE BRAKES AT ABOUT SEVENTY
AND SENT WHAT WAS LEFT OF TOMMY'S BULLET-RIDDLED BODY INTO THE SOUTH CANAL TO
FLOAT TO DESTINATIONS UNKNOWN...OR JUST FEED THE FUCKING FISH...WE DRANK BEER
AND TALKED ABOUT GOLF PUSSY GOD FARTS CHEAP TRICK DEODORANT DIRTY CHILDREN
JAY'S J-DOG PHONE BILLS AND STRAWBERRY POP TARTS...

I HEARD THAT I WAS GOING TO BE INDICTED BY THE IMPERIAL COUNTY GRAND JURY
WITHIN THE NEXT FEW DAYS...FUCKING HOLY FUCKING FUCK...BUT AT 0545
UNDERSHERIFF BILLY BILLYBOB CALLED ME FROM THE WRECKING BALL SISTERS'
WHOREHOUSE AND SAID SHIT WAS COOL 'CAUSE FUCKING DEAD JARED AND CALEB WERE ON
THE TAKE RUNNING ILLEGALS AND HAVING SOMETHING TO DO WITH THE ASSASSINATION OF
THE FUCKING ESE TACOHEAD RUNNING FOR PRESIDENT OF MEXICO...FINE THEN...AT
LEAST I WASN'T GOING TO FUCKING CHILIHOLE FOLSOM...I GUESS I'LL PAY THE WIDOWS
A VISIT AND TELL THEIR KIDS THE FUCKING TRUTH...NOT THAT POLITICALLY CORRECT
BULLSHIT FUCKING EVERYTHING-IS-ALL-RIGHT COVER STORY ABOUT THEM SAVING A
BUSLOAD OF TRIPLE A BASEBALL PLAYERS FROM YUMA...A FUCKING FUCKED UP
PERCEPTION OF FUCKING CLINTON REALITY...

THE NEXT DAY WAS
THE BORDER
PATROL'S 33RD
ANNUAL TURKEY
SHOOT...IT WAS TO
LAST 16 HOURS...WE
WON THE SHOOTOUT
26 TO FUCKING 12
AND THEN THEM DAMN
FUCKING FEDERALES
SHOWED UP WITH
THEIR OFFSPRING
AND
WIRECUTTERS...I
GOT TWO TACOHEADS
IN THE LEGS...AND
TOMORROW IS MY SON
RALPH L.Z. JAKE 12
PACK BILLY'S
INITIATION INTO
THE JUNIOR NRA
SHARPSHOOTER'S
HALL OF
FAME...HOPEFULLY
NEXT YEAR HE'LL
MAKE JUNIOR
S.W.A.T...THEN OFF
TO THE MOJAVE
DESERT FOR THE
BUDWEISER SHOOTING
TEAM'S ANNUAL
FUCKING GOOD
TIME...

P.S. Hollister... by the time the 2nd
issue of GFM goes to press... the shit will
really be hitting the liberal ass fucking shitting
fan... I'll be totally underground by this time
... with true gun fags in our national parks ...but
making it a better place for families and fucking
USA to go camping ... my next few
correspondts will touch heavilly on the un-
constitutionality and fucking holy fucking fuck
illegality ~~~~~~~~~~~~~ of ~~~~~~ killing
public officials at the highest level ...legally
converting Gramp's old 1911 to fully autos...
not paying your taxes cause your are
pissed off ... and the recipes of Tommy's
chile and Duponts C.4. Also send
money, beer, ammo ... feed my dog if
you can and don't forget to pickup
my new SKS for me... may you ~~~~
have plenty of cold beer, lots of
cheap ~~~~ and a babe on the back
of your hog for the summer.

J.J. LZAR IV

82

S.KIDWILER '11 '94

GADFLY GUN FAGS

The swine are gaining momentum. Their cowardly attacks on you and me and on American culture in general have reached fever pitch. Can you believe that the fuckers are going to start suing the manufacturers of firearms whenever someone gets hurt? Since when do you sue the manufacturer of a product *because it worked perfectly?* (The wife of one of the lawyers shot by patriot and gun fag supermartyr Gian-Luigi Ferri is behind this hare-brained scheme.) We're living in a weird world. What can you do?

Aside from a violent overthrow of the United States government (a tough job, but someone *has* to do it), there really doesn't seem to be much we can do. An assassination here and there is good for keeping our spirits up, but it's illegal, and like a lizard losing its tail, the media-government just regenerates another politician, and the pathetic zombie constituents vote him or her into office.

**WE MUST AT EVERY TURN BE A THORN IN THEIR SIDES.
BE AS IRRITATING TO THEM AS POSSIBLE.**

Call your congressman on a daily basis. They hate that. The 29th district (California) congressman is the geek Henry Waxman, and his number is **(202) 225-3976.** Or send him a polaroid of yourself standing naked with your gun collection (it's a good idea to blank out your face). If you're shy or feeling "inadequate," just draw a swastika over your private parts:

**REP. HENRY R. WAXMAN
2408 RAYBURN HOUSE OFFICE BLDG.
WASHINGTON, DC 20515**

Senators are particularly loathsome creatures, and need to be harassed frequently. Outside the People's Republic of California, call the capitol switchboard at **(202) 224-3121** and have them patch you through to your target, or send hate mail c/o said target to **U.S. SENATE, WASHINGTON, DC 20510.** Two sworn enemies of our culture are the tawdry strumpets Diane Feinstein and Barbara Boxer. If you're a stalker or are interested in becoming one, they'll make perfect victims. Here are their specific addresses:

**DIANE FEINSTEIN
720 HART SENATE BLDG.
WASHINGTON, DC 20510
(202) 224-3841 or (415) 457-7272**

**BARBARA BOXER
112 HART SENATE BLDG.
WASHINGTON, DC 20510
(202) 224-3553 or (310) 915-7300**

Another fun thing to do is call the toll-free number for the repugnant anti-gun organization curiously called Gun Fighters of America. If you ever meet anyone involved with this group, *shoot them immediately.* Call them at **1-800-949-4867.** After listening to 15 seconds or so of their treasonous drivel, leave any name and address on their message tape. The beauty of this trick is that it *costs them 80 cents per call!* This is the same tactic that the queers used to bankrupt Jerry Falwell's Moral Majority. He ended up with a *$2 million phone bill!* I personally have already cost the "Gun Fighters of America" hundreds of dollars. You can only call three times on one phone before they cut you off, so make a habit out of calling three times on every phone you can find.

Stand up and defend yourselves, gun fags! We may have to start shooting them at some point, but for now we can call & write. It's the American way, and it makes them miserable.

Eine Bewaffnete Bevolkerung
ist eine Freie Bevolkerung

GUN FAG

MANIFESTO

③ $4

inside:

Hunting Boar
...
Russian SKS

Pollyanne's Dream Gun

MOLLY KIELY 1995

GUN FAG MANIFESTO
ENTERTAINMENT FOR THE ARMED SOCIOPATH

ISSUE #3, MARCH OR APRIL 1995. **GUN FAG MANIFESTO** IS PUBLISHED WHENEVER THE PUBLISHER FEELS THAT THERE IS ENOUGH MATERIAL TO ASSEMBLE AN ISSUE. THIS COULD BE WEEKS, MONTHS, YEARS OR NEVER.

LET THIS BE UNDERSTOOD RIGHT NOW: THE TERM *GUN FAG* IS USED - USUALLY DEROGATORILY - BY VARIOUS BRANCHES OF LAW ENFORCEMENT, AND REFERS TO JUST ABOUT ANYONE WITH A KEEN INTEREST IN FIREARMS, PARTICULARLY THOSE WHO TAKE THE U.S. CONSTITUTION SERIOUSLY AND HAVE MORE GUNS IN THEIR HOUSES THAN WINDOWS. MOST PEOPLE DIRECTLY AND INDIRECTLY ASSOCIATED WITH **GUN FAG MANIFESTO** FALL INTO THIS CATEGORY.

NEW ADDRESS: ███████████████████████ **MEMORIZE IT.**

STAFF:

HOLLISTER KOPP
Editor & Publisher
JAKE JOSEPH L.Z. KILROY KOWALSKI
(AKA RED) Society Columnist
POLLYANNE
Featured Gunwriter & Cover Model
MOLLY KEILY
Artiste par Excellence
PENNY TRATION
Mistress of the Macintosh
JOHN BERGSTROM
Attack Cartoonist

CONTRIBUTORS:

REVEREND SMITTY
KEITH ROBB
RUFUS T; ALLIGATOR
REP. HENRY R. WAXMAN
SEN. DIANNE FEINSTEIN
KJARTAN "KARNO" ARNORSSON

NEW!

LISTEN UP

TRENDY DISCLAIMER

We at **GUN FAG MANIFESTO** stand by the right to free speech under the First Amendment and the right - nay, the *duty* to keep and bear arms in accordance with the Second Amendment of the Bill of Rights, U.S. Constitution. We accept responsibility for nothing, and do not advocate violence except when provoked by criminal dirtbags.

HOLLISTER KOPP
EDITOR & PUBLISHER

Independence Day, 1995

Okay, here goes. Another issue of firearms-related blather by a man with mud on his boots and hate in his heart. This was supposedly going to be a holiday special (yeah, those holidays that happened a half-year ago) but it came together a little late. I believe there's a disclaimer around here somewhere that covers me in this respect.

So, how 'bout that bombing in Oklahoma, eh? There are some theories and some speculation floating around as to who actually did it (aside from the accused) but none of that matters. The reality of the thing is a bonanza for the geeks running the mainstream media. It has allowed them to focus sharply on the segment of society which they hate more than anyone else - us. Gun fags. Second Amendment aficionados. Constitutionalists. Real Americans. *As if it were indeed a GUN that blew up the friggin' federal building!* The bastards are gleefully portraying firearms enthusiasts as foul-mouthed, beer drinking, paranoid, government hating bigots. Which is mostly true, but we're a *diverse* crowd of foul mouthed beer drinking paranoid government hating bigots, and they never give us credit for that. We don't always fit the Billybob stereotype (ball cap, camo pants, combat boots, beer belly out to there, still live in parents' basement, etc.) which is invariably invoked upon us. Hell, there are a lot more of us than those pinko pansies would like to admit.

Gun fags are everywhere. Pick any office building, and you'll easily find a dozen Glock-totin' yuppies. Visit the barrio and try to find a house that *doesn't* contain a pistola or two. Middle-class suburbs are armed to the teeth. Bikers carry guns as casually as pocket change. Kids with orange mohawks and pierced noses are heavily into firepower. Mild-mannered CPAs, grocery clerks, milkmen, secretaries, dishwashers, bicycle messengers and (especially) mail carriers are at this moment fondling all manner of weaponry, and the creeps operating the American information machine have the gall to insult and belittle them daily. Amazing.

And our gov't sees the bombing as a wonderful and timely opportunity to further chip away at what's left of our God-given rights. They've strapped the Bill of Rights into a dentist's chair and are indelicately extracting its teeth. The House of Representatives has given us the appropriately entitled H.R. 666, which is designed to allow illegally obtained evidence to stand up in court. S. 54 is the Senate's version of the same sinister plot. They both add up to a kick in the balls to the Fourth Amendment, which until now has remained relatively unmolested. I called Representative Little Henry Waxman's office and requested a copy of the former, and Senator Dianne "I was never in a porno movie" Feinstein sent me the latter. I included them both in this issue, with the text completely unaltered.

The bombing of the federal building in Oklahoma City turned out to be a good deal for everybody but us (and the folks who were in the building at the time of the blast, naturally). The media meatheads are merrily spewing vitriol at patriots (remember when that was a *good* word?), and the powerheads in Washington are slickly putting together the finishing touches on the final solution we all know is coming. So the next time your front door is kicked in, it might not be a crack-addled cretin bent on larceny and feelin' bullet proof, it just might be Clinton's Federal Police, bent on something far more ominous than larceny, and they won't even need a search warrant.

If they come for your guns, give 'em your ammo first.

INCOMING

Kopp,

I pen this communique from a vile and treacherous place. A town in which the exercise of ones natural right to keep and bear the firearms which the Lord on high has given us is regulated by local ordinance. The requisite permits are available only to the rich and powerful. I am forced to live amongst the lawless as one of them.

You are truly a courageous man. It is a rare thing indeed to find a patriot with the strength of character to place himself so resolutely on the "short list" of our oppressor. Fear not sir, we have your back.

The die is cast, let them come.

Burl Iver-Johnson
Chicago, Illinois

Hollister

GFM #2 is great. My commendations on a job well done. It's always good to see someone willing to stand up to the PC army and stand up for gun owners and their rights.

James Steinbach's observations on the SPAS-12 were right on. I've had mine 5 years and it's given me many hours of happy shooting. What's more- IT SCARES THE SHIT OUT OF MY DIRTBAG NEIGHBORS!! Not to mention the yuppie scum that seemed to have invaded my fave gun range (they're just pissed because I "accidentally" shot out the tires of one of their brethren. Oh well. Don't park so fuckin' close.)

On the subject of burying weapons I'll leave you with this warning. You can take it with as many grains of salt as you wish. In my native N Ireland the RUC and the British Army have airborne surveillance devices capable of detecting metal objects buried up to 10 FEET underground. I know this because one of the Army's choppers crashed in a swampy area near Londonderry. IRA allies seized the offending device (after dusting the surviving crew members) and turned it in to the IRA. Analysis show it to be a sort of combination of metal detector, infrared scanner, and radar. Burying your stash under the house seems to be the best way to thwart this device. Just thought you'd like to know.

THE FIRING LINE

OFFICIAL PUBLICATION OF THE CALIFORNIA RIFLE & PISTOL ASSOCIATION, Inc

271 East Imperial Highway, Suite 620 • Fullerton, CA 92635 • (714) 992-C,R,P,A,

Have a cold one on me

March 13, 1995

Hollister Kopp
P.O. Box 480728
Los Angeles, CA 90048

Dear Mr. Kopp:

This is to acknowledge the receipt of your recent submission to The Firing Line titled "The City Council Knows What's Best For Us." We appreciate your fine work in preparing this article, and we are holding onto it for the proper moment to use it in our magazine. Meanwhile, we encourage you to send us any further submissions that your creative urges produce.

The California Rifle and Pistol Association is here to serve you. We thank you for your opinions which are vital to us.

Firearms Forever,

James H. Erdman
Executive Director

hey thar mr. kopp-

i just saw a review of your zine GUN FAG MANIFESTO in factsheet 5. after reading the description, i've come to the conclusion that i am a gun fag. i've got 4 windows in my apartment, and i own 5 firearms. i'm enclosing $4 for issue 2 if they are still available.

ya know i saw something really funny on 60 minutes last night. they had a report about guns and an interview with diane franken-stien. in the report they said that the expert manufacturers of the banned 19 weapons are now changing the cosmetics of their weapons to get by the ban. one example was of the tec-22, they have changed the name to the AB-10 and have removed the threading on the barel, and POOF! it's legal. and when leslie stall asked mrs. frankenstien about this, she said it is not right. she seemed really perturbed that this was being done. well seeing as teh crime bill was a joke to begin with, the joke was on her, and we are having the last laugh at her expense.

on that note i'll seal this up nice and tight and stick it in the mail.

thanx,

jeff skipski
po box ████
phoenix, az 85005

>35FSDOW@emh.kunsan.af.mil (Kunsan Weapons)
>
>Date: 95-06-08 19:32:48 EDT
>
>(8 Jun 95)
>To all my Viper buds and other Shit Hot Fighter Gods on the net -
>
>   It was a good day at Aviano! As you guys have no doubt heard, we
>rescued Scott "Zulu" O'Grady today after 6 days of E&Eing in the Bosnian
>countryside. We had an idea that he was still out there but hadn't had
>positive radio contact until about 0000Z this morning whe. Capt T.O. Hanford
>had some extra gas so he stayed in his CAP a little longer and tried to reach
>Zulu on the SAR A (PRC-112) freq from the day of the shoot down.
> After about 40 minutes of calls in the blind, T.O. started getting some
>suspect clicks on the mike. Finally, Zulu came up voice. T.O. didn't have
>all the info from Zulu's ISOPREP so he came up with
>a quick way to verify it was indeed Zulu, although it sounded like Zulu
>recognized T.O.'s voice and called him by name (although the comm was weak
>since T.O. (Basher 11) was about 70 miles away). The comm went something
>like this.
>
>"Basher 52 this is Basher 11"
>click
>"Basher 52, this is Basher 11, are you up on this freq"
>"This is Basher 52"
>"Say again, understand this is Basher 52"
>"This is Basher 52...I'm alive"
>"Say again, Basher 52, you are weak and unreadable, this is Basher 11"
>"This is Basher 52!"
>
>pause
>
>"Basher 52, what squadron were you in at Kunsan?"
>"Juvats! Juvats! I'm alive!"
>"Copy that, you're alive! Basher 52, sit tight and come back up at 15 past
>the hour"
>
>   T.O. then started coordinating with Magic to pass words to the Deny
>Flight CAOC (command center) that he had positive radio contact with Basher
>52. They replied that T.O. should pass the word "manana" to Basher 52.
> When he did, Zulu replied "I want to get picked up tonight!" (imagine
>that). So T.O. passed that to the CAOC and the decision was made to press
>with a rescue. We were 2 hours before sunrise so it would be daylight but
>there was concern (rightly so) that word would get out to the press and
>every SA-6 in the AOR would be mobile and spiking us and the rest of the
>rescue package. So they went ASAP.
>
>   T.O. stayed airborne (now at about the 4 hour point in his sortie -
>one note here: T.O. got high marks for wingman consideration for advising
>his wingman that it was a good time to take a piss on the way to the tanker!
> That video clip probably won't make CNN) and the 510 FS Buzzards scrambled
>our alert guys (I was #2). Unfortunately, Vaughn "Slot" Littlejohn and I
>had just gone from 60 minute alert to 180 minute alert and I had headed home
>to get some sleep. The phone rang at about 0255L (after about 10 minutes of
>sleep) telling me to get in there ASAP. I was back at the SQ in 15 minutes.
> Before I was even in the door, our ADO, Phil "Psycho" Sever told me we had
>positive radio contact, get dressed, step, crank, and taxi ASAP - I would
>meet SLOT in EOR whenever he made it in. We were in the air at about 0400L
>(1+05 from a dead sleep at home) loaded with 2xGBU-12s, 2 slammers, 2 9Ms, a
>131 pod, and 2 tanks (Standard DF SCL). We swapped out with T.O. manning
>the cap and staying in touch with Zulu every 15 minutes. A SEAD package was
>getting airborne as T.O. started his RTB. We had a plan with the F-18Ds
>(Harm shooters (kind of), with NVGs and a WSO), EFs, and EA-6Bs to try to
>establish contact. But since we already had contact, the F-18s just did a
>recce run to get a good fix on him and to check the weather.
>
>   Meanwhile, Zobe the hero, callsign Rock 42, was hanging on Slot's
>wing 70 miles away listening to the whole thing, ensuring my tape was on. I
>can't wait to tell my grandkids about the day I put all my Weapons School
>training to use - "No shit, kids, there I was - tape on, tape off, tape on,
>tape off. The pressure was incredible!" Seriously, although I didn't do
>shit, it was shit hot to listen to the entire mission unfolding. The helos
>were inbound, authenicating Zulu (they asked him what he was called in high
>school when he got drunk!) With a good ID they moved in, had Zulu pop some
>smoke, and picked him up. The whole thing from the authentication to the
>pick-up was about 10 minutes (seemed like an eternity). To hear comm like,
>"Basher 52, got you in sight", was pretty moving, especially after thinking
>for most of the week that Zulu was a mort ("Wilbur" Wright didn't see a
>chute, no radio contact, etc.) I've
>never been choked up in the jet before, but I was this morning.
>
>   Unfortunately, they weren't out of danger yet. We hit the tanker
>and when we came back up to Magic freq the helos were about 13 miles from
>feet wet. Then I heard the escort chopper, c/s Bull, say, "Bud, impacts
>underneath
>you. SAMS IN THE AIR! SAMS IN THE AIR! FUCK!!" Luckily, they missed,
>although they took some small arms fire and apparently the gunner from Bull
>silenced that. About 10 minutes later, we heard the call that they were
>feet wet, then shortly after that that they had "mother in sight" (the ship), two
>more bits of comm that I will never forget.
>
>   So we got one of our own back. What a day. I wish we could have
>done more in the rescue but it was almost entirely a Navy and Marine show
>(we and the mud-eagles were in the cap) and they kicked ass. So don't bad
>mouth the squids and jarheads too loudly - they put on a good act today and
>we've got a Viper driver back because of it.
>
>   I thought you might enjoy hearing the story straight from the CSAR
>Commander of VTR Ops! Hope it wasn't too mushy, but after all, I did cry
>when I watched Old Yeller. That's just the emotional type of guy I am!
> Hope all is well with you guys at your various bases. Drop me a line and
>let me know what's up. Fly safe, check six, and pray for the UN leadership
>to get a clue and let us blow these bastards back into the stone age!
>
>Zobe
>

THE REAL REASON FOR GUN OWNERSHIP

By The Company of Freemen

The State Creates its Own Enemies

Ghoulishly capitalizing on the tragedy of a mass murder, the anti-gun forces are surging forward with their plans for total gun confiscation. If law-abiding citizens were disarmed, they claim, criminals and crazies would be unable to kill and maim. That's an obvious lie - criminals, by definition - disobey laws, and madmen can kill with knives, cars or champagne bottles as easily and as senselessly as they can with guns. The not-so-secret agenda of the State and its apologists is clear: disarm peaceful citizens to render them powerless. Turn law-abiding Americans into criminals with the stroke of a legislative pen. Anyone who refuses to surrender his or her weapons would become an Enemy of the state, much the same as any armed citizen is right now in the (former) Soviet Union, or communist China, or socialist Nicaragua, or fascist El Salvador, or monarchist Great Britain. Gun confiscation is non-partisan - it is always and forever aimed at anyone disliked by the current gang in power.

Gun Seizure Sparked 1776 Revolution

The American Revolution began in a dispute over gun control when British Redcoats marched toward Lexington and Concord to disarm farmers there. London *claimed* to be the "legitimate" government ruling America, just as Washington or Sacramento or Albany *claims* to be today. And their attempt to disarm us stems from the same powerlust that drove King George. We must therefore hold onto our guns - *legally or illegally* - for the very same reason the colonists did.

The Truth About Gun Ownership

The anti-gunners, certain that the role of government is to grant privileges and dictate behavior, shout that citizens have no reason to be "allowed" to own assault rifles, which have no "legitimate sporting use." The constitution, though, says nothing about "a well-regulated hunting club" being necessary. We do not own handguns, assault rifles, shotguns and other powerful weapons because we are hunters or plinkers or collectors. We do not even own guns because the constitution "allows" us to. The constitution does not *grant* rights, it *recognizes* rights already and irrevocably held forever by the people themselves (individuals), and *forbids* government from trampling on them. We have a right to keep and bear arms *regardless* of whether the Second Amendment exists or not! All Article Two guarantees is that we shouldn't have to defend that right against "our" federal government. We've seen that simple guarantee erode though, haven't we?

The real reason for gun ownership is to protect the individual from the state, whether it be an invading state from across the seas or a domestic state grown tyrannical and oppressive. The goal of total, repressive confiscation is clear in the subtle, shifting arguments of the anti-gun forces. when handguns were the target, they clamored for prohibition because handguns were not militia-type weapons protected by the Second Amendment. Now they cry for assault rifle bans because "mere citizens" have no business possessing "military style" weapons!

These eager confiscators rightly point out that assault rifles, handguns, and indeed all weapons have only one purpose: to kill. Again they speak a truth, but only partially. The unasked question is, *to kill whom? And under what circumstances?* The answer is, *to kill any who attempt to rob, maim, rape or kill us.* Even that answer, though, does not fully express the most important reason for gun ownership. Only a small number of people are actually touched by criminal violence. The state, however, touches each and every one of us every hour of every day. People in government seek to tax our earnings to pay for their whims, to draft our children to fight wars they star, to regulate and interfere with our lives out of pure love of power and their desire to wield it. They have become as tyrannical as any Tory Redcoat, Soviet Commissar or Nazi Gestapo. And they are coming to steal your last line of defense against them.

WILL YOU MEEKLY OBEY?

When any law against guns is passed, how is it backed up? How will the state remove banned weapons from private hands? How will agents of the state disarm the citizenry? Why, by the use of guns, of course! This contradiction has never bothered statists. Why are assault rifles and

handguns evil and wicked in the hands of private citizens, yet perfectly fine in the hands of employees of the state? If this truly is "government by the people," why do we see servants

disarming their masters by force? What do they fear from us, if theirs is a legitimate, benevolent government? If the state does not seek to control us, why does it want us disarmed?

The usual answer - stripped of equivocation - is that "mere citizens" are like half-witted children, incapable of safely handling "dangerous" commodities such as weapons or explosives or medicines or information. And only when some half-witted children pass some civil-service exam or are elected by other half-wits to work for the wise and benevolent state do they magically become smart and honest and trustworthy enough to carry weapons and decide whom shall be allowed to possess guns and what sort of design, shape or weight such weapons shall be.

Sounds pretty condescending and paternalistic, doesn't it? That's how they view us. Sheep for the shearing at tax time, cannon fodder during war time, and dangerous idiots the rest of the time.

And they ask us to obey their decrees?

Government Creates Crime

What many gun owners refuse to face, usually by saying, "it can't happen in America," is that the government can and does create new classes of criminals with the mere stroke of a pen. In 1919, Prohibition turned millions of people overnight from sociable drinkers to Enemies of the State. The victimless crime of ingesting alcohol turned neighborly, peaceful people into fair game for imprisonment, fines and seizure of property. Some fought back, often with simple shotguns against "revenuers" armed with assault weapons (the Thompson

submachinegun) in a modern version of the Whiskey Rebellion. The Prohibition amendment created crime by definition. If, tomorrow, smoking or drinking coffee were declared illegal, the state would suddenly point to a new "criminal underworld" of massive proportions. In the eyes of the state they would become a "new breed of criminal" to be weeded out of society and thrown into prisons. So it is with any prohibition of popular activities, *including gun ownership.*

Gun Prohibition is Racist

The gun Control Act of 1968 was rammed down the throats of the American public, blatantly exploiting then-current fears of gun-toting black rioters by implying that the law would help to disarm American blacks, other minorities and all dissenters at a time of civil upheaval. To paraphrase a popular slogan, "If the government does not trust minorities with guns, minorities cannot trust government." Ask any Native American.

In a mirror-image case 25 years later, assault rifle bans are being ramrodded through legislatures by appealing to fears that gun-toting *white racists* are on the loose.

The real and only purpose of gun control is to disarm the innocent and the peaceful of whatever race, creed or social status.

Gun Prohibition is Sexist

The same goes for women. Police and purported feminists urge women to resist rape with fists, fingernails, key rings and screams. But why should *any* woman allow an assailant to get within arm's reach of her? Why don't women's rights activists in or out of government reveal the most effective way for a woman to defend herself: to buy a gun and learn how to use it? The truth is, they *want* women to feel weak and perpetually threatened so that they will beg the state for protection. A woman standing proud, armed and fearless is the last thing most self-proclaimed "feminists" want (since that would undercut their perverse longing for a huge *paternalistic* government!).

Governments Kill More Than Any Mass Murderer

How can people who work for or worship the state - *statists* - point to the murder of five children in a schoolyard or twenty people in a restaurant and claim that as sufficient reason to disarm tens of millions of Americans? Are they so presumptuous to suggest that we are capable of such violent madness? Perhaps there is a degree psychological projection going on here: statists feel within themselves the urge to kill and project it onto people they fear the most - us, the victims of the state. For while tens of millions of people own guns, only a minuscule fraction ever use those guns to aggress against others. Every state, however, has guns and even more powerful and terrifying weapons in its clutches and every state has used them, will use them and are using them to murder hundreds, thousands and millions of innocent, unarmed people.

How can the insane mind of Patrick Purdy even dream of matching the death toll of the most minor skirmish in the smallest of wars or "police actions?" The murder of five innocent children is heart-rendingly tragic, but how many thousands of innocent children were roasted in Hiroshima and Nagasaki? How many unarmed, peaceful young people were murdered at Tien An Men Square? How many women, children and old people have been shot with the bullets of their own government in Vietnam, Cambodia, Angola, Nicaragua, El Salvador, India, Israel, Afghanistan, Tibet, Argentina, Libya, Ireland, Russia, South Africa, Chile, Pakistan, Zimbabwe, Iran, and on and on and on for every state you can name, even "our" United States. For statists who use "mass murder" of a few people as an excuse to disarm Americans when the state is the largest, bloodiest, longest-lived institution of mass murder in all of history is appallingly hypocritical. Do we owe allegiance to the apologists for such atrocities? *NEVER!*

Private ownership of weaponry is the last defense against all tyranny, foreign and domestic. The thought that there might come a time when peaceable gun owners (even members of the patriotic NRA) must

take arms against an American Li Peng commanding the local police and the U.S. military is anathema to nearly everyone. The possibility, however, must be faced. A lot of American colonists were horrified at the thought of defending themselves against "their" king's army, too.

Civilian-Based Defense Preferred to Standing Army

Some say that the Constitution "granted" the right to keep and bear arms to provide for a "well-regulated militia." Since we have a standing army, the argument goes, civilians no longer need to own guns. Yet that amendment was written precisely because the British used *that exact argument* in their attempts (from 1768 to 1777) to disarm the colonists.

Americans *detested* the standing armies of the British government and knew that civilian-based was the ultimate, perhaps the *only* protection against *any* threat to liberty, whether from London, Moscow or Washington DC.

Defying Unjust Laws is Right and Proper!

When the day comes (and it will, if we don't raise our voices in protest now) that the Imperial State commands its subjects (that's how they view you and me, regardless of what they say) to turn in our weapons, what will we do? Make no mistake - if people refuse to surrender or destroy their weapons, they will be dealt with by heavily-armed police; they will be imprisoned, fine, perhaps even shot if they try to defend their Constitutional - their human - rights.

Of whom should we be more wary - invading foreign troops whose rule we would never sanction, or "our own" government, to which most of us grant some legitimacy and which is *right here, right now*, all around us? Perhaps paraphrasing a parent's question will provide the answer: If the state passed a law telling you to jump off a cliff, would you? No fair answering that "good, pure, sober politicians wouldn't let that happen." With guns, it is happening *right now*.

And when that friendly cop on the beat (whom most gun owners exalt as a good man just doing his job and who may even be a fellow NRA member!) comes around to your house, he will be armed with "good government" handguns and assault rifles. "Sorry, pal," he'll say, "but the law is the law."

That possibility is something many gun owners - staunch defenders of law and order and supporters of local police - refuse to face. They blank out the fact that even - perhaps especially - in America, they may have to choose between owning their guns and facing the full implication of the declaration of Independence,

"...that, whenever any form of government becomes destructive of these ends, it is the right of the people to alter or abolish it..."

Some would rather surrender meekly to the state, giving up their last shred of defense against tyranny, rather than face that choice. But if they do surrender their firepower, the choice will have been made. And it won't matter whether our new masters speak Russian, Chinese, Japanese, English or American Bureaucratese. They will be our masters nonetheless.

What To Do

First of all, *keep your guns!* Do not turn them in just because some law is passed ordering you to do so. That's just what they want - sheeplike compliance. You are not a criminal. Don't let the state declare you one or treat you

like one. The colonists who turned in their weapons to their Tory town governments soon learned the folly of their actions. **Any government that outlaws gun ownership is an outlaw government!** It is no more necessary to obey an oppressive, tyrannical state than it is to obey any thief who demands that you turn over your property under threat of death. We know the free person's answer to such a demand. So does the state. that is why statists seek to browbeat us into disarming without a fight. They need the sanction of the victim. They cannot hope to disarm us by force. That would tip their hand and guarantee a revolution. But by stealth, instilled guilt and appeals to our peaceful, law-abiding natures will they attempt to expropriate our only defense against their continued and increasing predations.

Resist the urge to obey the edicts of self-proclaimed rulers. Don't walk timidly into a concentration camp filled with once-free men and women. Decry with every fiber of your being this trampling of our fundamental human rights!

THE RIGHT TO OWN GUNS IS A CIVIL RIGHT, WITHOUT WHICH ALL OTHER CIVIL RIGHTS ARE IMPOSSIBLE TO DEFEND.
THE RIGHT TO OWN GUNS IS THE RIGHT TO OWN - AND PROTECT - YOUR BODY AND YOUR PROPERTY.
THE RIGHT TO OWN GUNS IS THE RIGHT TO RESIST TYRANNY.
ANY WHO SEIZE GUNS ARE THIEVES OR TYRANTS.

Every law restricting free, immediate access to firearms is a direct attack on individual freedom. The course of action is up to you. Demand the repeal of all such laws or ignore them with impunity. But never accept them as legitimate restraints upon your liberty. Nothing legitimate can issue from the pen of tyrants.

Permission is explicitly granted to reproduce this article by photocopy, computer bulletin board or any other method.

The Company of Freemen
Contributed by Rufus T. Alligator

Eulogy for the Tank Guy

On May 17, 1995, there arose from the bleak tract-home glutted suburbs of San Diego, the methamphetamine capitol of the world, a martyr of the highest caliber. A man not afraid to throw some weight around - 53 tons, in fact - and take his many grievances to the streets, to tell the world in no uncertain terms that he was PISSED OFF. Things had not been going well for Shawn Nelson. He was a plumber by trade, and not only was business slow, but a trusted buddy had done two of the most cowardly and despicable things to Shawn that can be done to any man: the bastard stole Shawn's truck AND his tools. This alone could have pushed even the most well-adjusted of men over the edge, but Shawn persevered.

His wife left him and both his parents died shortly after. He got a girlfriend and she left him too. People were constantly following him, monitoring his phone, watching him. He couldn't be sure which agency they were from, but they were feds, no question about it, probably under orders from the U.N. He was, as are many individualists, frequently harassed by black helicopters.

The sons of bitches shut off his electricity, forcing him to covertly string extention cords around the neighborhood, poaching power from people's back patios in order to provide light for his mine. There was gold in his back yard - lots of gold - and they were all gonna eat their words when he became an instant zillionaire. He was out there faithfully night after night, sweating and digging and doing enough crystal meth to kill ten lesser men. At the time of his death his mine was twenty feet deep, all dug by hand.

One dreary day when it seemed the whole world was against him, *even laughing at him*, he received his final insult. They shut off his water. Goddamn! He was a plumber, and they shut off his WATER! Of course he knew how to turn it back on, but that would miss the point, wouldn't it? They still wouldn't get it, would they? Well, to show his cruel oppressors a little perfect irony (with emphasis on iron), his next move was only possible through government training. Something they forgot to take from him was his memory, and he remembered well bopping around *Der Fatherland* in an M-60 tank during his brief stint in the Army.

Reinforced with a case of beer and a snootful of speed, he drove down to the local National Guard motor pool, ripped off his shirt, jumped into a fuckin' tank and fired 'er up.

What followed was twenty-two minutes of pure joy as Shawn flattened over 50 cars, snapped power poles like pencils, smashed bridges, knocked down signal lights and crushed fire hydrants with a glee unknown to him in years. He demolished everything in his path. Helpless cops just followed along, hoping the monstrosity would run out of fuel or break down or *something*. How in the hell do you stop a tank? They called one of their off-duty buddies who was in an armored unit of the Marine Reserves. He laughed and said the only way you're gonna stop him is to climb aboard, pry open the hatch and shoot the fucker. He then jumped into his own car and joined the pursuit.

Then Shawn made his last mistake. It had been fifteen years since he drove a tank, so he was understandably a little rusty. He tried to cross a three-foot concrete divider in the middle of Highway 163 and threw a tread. Dozens of cops surrounded the roaring, pitiful tank as it struggled and teetered helplessly atop the concrete. Four of them jumped up onto the behemoth and unlocked the hatch with bolt cutters. Shawn Timothy Nelson looked up toward the Heavens and saw Glock. The black helicopters had landed.

Shawn's generous legacy far exceeds a mere six miles of devastation and 5,100 homes and businesses without electricity. His gift to society is one of hope, a reminder that the uniquely American spirit of individualism which made this country great has not yet been beaten down by the forces of mediocrity. The personalized license plate on his Chevy van read **KAN FIX**.

I can't think of a more perfect inscription for his tombstone.

THE CITY COUNCIL KNOWS WHAT'S BEST FOR US!

"Tonight, it is easier to buy nine-millimeter ammunition than it is to buy a can of spray paint."

So began the February 27, 1995 Pasadena City Council meeting, in an introductory speech by Pasadena's castrato Chief of Police Jerry Oliver. Above the speaker's podium was a huge red, white & black banner disturbingly reminiscent of a Nazi flag with the words *Save Our Children* and the outline of a dead little whippersnapper. Chief Oliver's statement is in fact a lie, but never mind that.

The purpose of the meeting was to debate a proposed law requiring anyone buying ammo to provide identification (supposedly for age verification) and complete a registration form listing the amount, brand and type of ammo purchased. The records would be monitored by the police. The law, according to its proponents, is designed primarily to keep juveniles from gunning each other down over dope or parking spaces or whatever they're gunning each other down over these days. The law passed on a 5-2 vote. Did someone forget to tell the esteemed Pasadena Councilpeople that there is already a law barring minors from purchasing ammo? Nope.

The Councilcommies are not stupid, although they're doing everything possible to have us believe it. The real reason behind this new law is the same real reason behind every other gun law. Control. Good old fashioned jackboot-to-the-teeth, pledge-your-allegiance-or-die CONTROL. Yo ho ho and a bottle of castor oil, motherfucker. You even think about stepping out of line, especially when it comes to gun laws, and we'll send the goddamn BATF in to kill your family. So just settle down, we know what's best for you. Just fill out and sign the registration forms. It's for the good of the people, comrade.

Not to be outdone, the Los Angeles City Council has been as busy as a one-legged man at an ass-kicking contest trying to come up with an even more socialistic proposal than that of Pasadena's. Already, *eight* of them (a majority on the 15-member coven) have indicated that they would support such a measure. The council's Orwellianly-titled Public Safety Committee has requested that the City Attorney's office draft up an ordinance. Mayor Richard Riordan, L.A.'s

disappointment of the decade, has of course lent his support. Whatta creep.

L.A. Councilman Marvin Braude is the weasel who got the ball rolling. He attended the Pasadena meeting and was divinely inspired. In a rare display of English-speaking, Marv blurted that "It's an extraordinary thing for the city of Pasadena to take this action." Indeed. After a brief pause in which he scratched his nuts through his pants pocket (like no one can tell!) he stated that "It's a courageous thing for them to do this." No, Marvin, courage has nothing to do with it. Again, laws like this (as anyone who cares to look beyond the saccharine rhetoric knows), are to keep the politicians in control. The fact that we're armed scares the living shit out of bastards like itchy ol' Marvin Braude. A couple of other dingbats lending their support to this crap are Councilwoman and "recovering" dope-fiend Laura Chick and the spectacularly moronic Councilgeek Mark Ridley-Thomas. By the way, does anyone know his maiden name? Is it Ridley, or is it Thomas?

And I can't wait 'til Councilwoman Jackie Goldberg opens her blow-hole on this subject. THAT will be entertainment. She is quite possibly the most vindictive, humorless and mean-spirited human being on earth. And ugly! She claims to be a lesbian, but it would seem that even the skankiest fat, smelly and toothless bull-dyke would have second thoughts about being intimate with Jackie the Pachy.

Worse even than the bellicose carpet-muncher Jackie Goldberg is the criminally insane Councilwoman Rita Walters. Her fellow cretins on the Council actually give serious consideration to her nutty ideas! Maybe it's because to disagree with Rita Walters is to be a racist or a sexist or both. I don't know. But the subject of gun control makes Rita swoon like a trailer-park harlot at a Tom Jones concert, and the new law in Pasadena has got her so horny she can't sit still. She could barely contain herself as she threw her obligatory two cents in the other day, suggesting that the city take it a step further by requiring a *background check and a permit* to buy ammo. Fear this horrible woman, for she is dangerous.

Every time I hear mention of L.A. City Council President John Ferraro,

the vomit is so close to erupting that I start goose-necking and my eyes water. The foul bastard should be taken to the town square, stocked and beaten with rubber hoses before the cheering crowd until he loses consciousness, then unlocked and tossed into the mob. Without even being asked to speak, Ferraro said, "Maybe we've waited too long, but I think anything we can do to slow up the use of guns we should do." Well, fuck you, John Ferraro, I hope you die of a crack overdose.

Gun control freaks are predicting that Pasadena will initiate a domino effect, and God help us if they're right. If L.A. passes such a measure - and it's becoming a very real possibility - it could become a sickening monument to the creeping fascism that liberals so adore. It'll be Sarah Brady's flagship city, Dianne Feinstein's communist brothel and Henry Waxman's depraved little wet-dream. Local governments across the country will be clamoring for the limelight with more and more crackpot ordinances to "Save Our Children," like they give two shits about children. The smarmy Los Angeles Times is of course eating this up, and in its typical greasy editorial style has called the law "the tiniest of steps," and "tepid, sensible restrictions on bullet sales..." They openly advocate the banning of all firearms, except for those in the possession of law enforcement and military personnel, and they have the nerve to bitch and whine whenever someone accuses the media of having a liberal bias!

The nightmarish scenario is unfolding so fast that by the time you read this the L.A. City Council may have already stormed the Constitution, looted the Declaration of Independence and raped the Bill of Rights. And while the bastards are celebrating with a sleazy bacchanal in their faux-ivory tower, somewhere in a bleak downtown office building there are constipated, irritable authorities with coffee & doughnut heartburn and **AUTOMATIC WEAPONS,** looking over your records...

Let's just hope that Burbank, Glendale, and their unkempt but well-meaning cousin Culver City can stand up to this fetid torrent of garbage and remain American.

Kids & Guns

WELL-ARMED YOUTH, BEING NECESSARY TO A FREE STATE...

Kids and guns are as inseparable as hops and barley. Kids *love* guns. It's a shame that our official policy makers haven't done more to encourage this natural relationship. If there's anything more American than apple pie, its the beaming face of a little boy or girl during that magic moment when they unwrap their first .22 rifle under the Christmas tree. It's a moment they'll always remember, a milestone in their lives that will rival the first time they get laid.

Every child in America should have a gun, and know how to use it. Hell, most kids already know how to use them. The average kid watches television every day, and sees people drawing weapons, loading them, reloading them, firing them, smacking punks upside the head with them, etc. Before the second grade, your average American whippersnapper has seen every conceivable way to use every conceivable firearm, as long as nudity is not involved.

And why not? Why not teach our youngsters early on how to properly defend themselves? Remember when Patrick Purdy hosed down all those little tykes with his AK-47 in Stockton, California? There was the predictable howling from the media geeks and liberal toe-jammers about the danger of semi-autos and how easy it is for psychos to obtain them. The NRA, as usual, went scurrying off like tormented puppies and hid behind their tired old arguments about the majority of gun owners being innocuous little vanilla meeklings.

But nobody spoke up for those bullet-riddled children. Properly trained and armed, those young-uns could have turned Purdy into blood sausage before he got two rounds off. They would have been hailed as local - maybe even national - heroes, and after making the rounds on the talk-show circuit, they could have socked away enough money to pay for their college educations. Our society's present attitude with respect to kids and guns is clearly very wrong.

Firearms are such an integral part of our social fabric that it seems unnatural - even criminal - to deny our youth the wondrous world of firepower. Toys R Us, probably the biggest toy seller in the country, recently decided to stop selling toy guns. This appalling insult to children is happening in the wake of several incidents of kids pointing toy guns at cops, with the predictable outcome (cop shoots kid). Aside from this phenomenon being strict natural selection - the culling of the herd, as it were - it doesn't happen often enough to justify such a knee-jerk reaction. To deny a little kid his right to keep and bear toy arms is nothing short of cruel.

How else are they going to become familiar with the feel of firearms, learn quick-draw skills, cover & concealment, modern techniques of urban combat, etc? Unfortunately, most parents won't let their kids play with *real* guns, so how do they expect them to become proficient shooters and upright Americans without the proper tools with which to practice? A natural open-mindedness and aptitude for learning make children the perfect recipients of indoctrination, especially on a subject so undeniably fascinating as GUNS. And depending upon the application, shooting can be either rewarding or punishing; two essential ingredients in child-rearing.

As a youngster, whenever I got into enough trouble to warrant physical punishment, I didn't get the whippin' out in the woodshed like so many of my contemporaries. No, my dad was a little more creative and thoughtful than that. If I got caught, say, spying on my aunt Eva in the shower (she was a *babe*) my dad would make me tack a 3" x 5" card to a tree some 200 yards out, then from the bench rest out behind the back porch I'd have to hit it three times with his .416 Weatherby. He'd stand behind me and cackle like some kind of twisted hillbilly General MacArthur, complete with binoculars and foul-smelling corncob pipe. This was a serious penalty; that rifle punched a damn sight harder than any schoolyard bully, I'm here to tell you.

After hitting the target three times (a feat that sometimes took upwards of 15 shots to accomplish) I'd have to take down the target, police up the empty brass and reload it, then clean & oil the Weatherby. When that was finished, I could regain possession of my Remington .22 rifle and go play.

Valuable lessons learned:

- To respect the authority of not only my father, but the .416 Weatherby
- To pretty near pick a hair off a gnat's ass at 200 yards with an elephant gun
- To secretly load the .416 cartridge with about two thirds the normal amount of powder, making future disciplinary action much more comfortable
- If you want to gawk at naked women, get a copy of Playboy and hide it under your mattress

This sort of discipline may seem excessive, even bizarre by the standards set by today's so-called experts. *They're commies, and they're wrong!* Look at kids today. For cryin' out loud, the only kids with guns are street punks in the ghetto! Precisely ass-backward, sociologically speaking. I had a subscription to Boys Life when I was a kid, and I remember gun articles being a common feature in that very wholesome magazine. Would any contemporary youth-oriented publication feature a single gun article? *Does Al Gore collect chain saws?*

Incredibly, today's "educators" have adopted a rigid agenda of namby-pamby crap, and are force-feeding this treasonous swill to our children. "Self esteem" and "empowerment" have replaced English skills and mathematics. The odious mantras of "tolerance" and "equality" are designed to make dumbfucks feel just as important as smart kids. "At-risk youth" (i.e., worthless punks) are receiving disproportionate attention in the classroom, thereby literally stealing valuable education from kids who might actually benefit from it. Paul Revere and Thomas Edison have been dropped from American history curriculum because they were (gasp) *white men.* Kids are now told that everything Europeans have accomplished over the centuries has been via theft and murder. They're told that the continent of Africa is home to the most sophisticated, noble and advanced societies to ever grace the planet...

Indeed. Some pretty awful people have constructed this environment for our kids, and it doesn't take a psychic to figure out where they stand on the subject of firearms. This is a positively heartbreaking tragedy, and I find that if I dwell too long on the subject, my mood turns from just plain bad to goddamn straight-up homicidal.

What this boils down to is that kids today are being feverishly pummeled with socialist anti-gun propaganda (with all its inherent satanic undertones), the result of which could be the collapse of civilization as we know it. We're creating a population of pansies, where the Star Spangled Banner will be replaced with a Hare Krishna chant, the Pledge of Allegiance will be considered the manifesto of bigots and tyrants (takes one to know one, I say) and our currency will feature the likes of "civil-rights pioneers" Barbra Streisand and Rodney King. All weapons will be illegal, and our system of public education will be ruled by an elite corps of fat lesbians.

Something needs to be done *soon* in order to re-arm our youth and reverse the terrible course which the despots of PC have set for these innocent and hapless youngsters. Until every child is familiar with the responsibility and joy of shooting, and until all normal children are encouraged to protect themselves and their families with deadly force, we, as a society, will suffer. We were once a great nation. To reclaim that lofty status we must start with our future, which is to say, our children.

Il faut cultiver notre jardin.

HIDE YOUR GUNS!
BIG BROTHER IS INDEED WATCHING

By Keith Robb

First off I would like to say here at the outset that these are not hard and fast rules, but merely guidelines to help you keep your stash safe and sound during these troubled times, as well as the even worse times that are sure to come in the future. Some of these tips come from a number of defunct Libertarian journals and some come from personal experience. All are valid and useful.

When I speak of personal experience I mean this: I was born and raised in Northern Ireland (Belfast to be exact) and we Catholics have been dealing with an intrusive British presence in our midst for some time. We have gleaned a certain knowledge from this that I will attempt to pass along to you, the reader.

METAL DETECTION

There are three basic types of metal detection methods available to the common police department:

1. A fluoroscope - used most often to locate metal objects in the human body, such as bullets
2. A magnometer - used to detect iron, steel and other magnetic materials
3. A mine detector - will locate any electrically conductive metal

Metal detectors are at their poorest in loose, dry soil and are almost useless in soil rich in mineral deposits such as iron, copper and other ferrous metals. This can be used to your advantage by (a); simply burying your stash in a PLASTIC container buried in soil rich in naturally occurring metals, or (b); scattering nails, metal filings and old pieces of pipe in the soil all around where you have buried your loot. One caveat: this can also lead the authorities to your treasure, so in order to throw them off your trail I advise scattering the aforementioned junk in as many different areas as possible to serve as a red herring of sorts.

SOME USEFUL TIPS

🔫* Bury in dry, loose soil.

🔫* Pack metal loosely in a non-metallic container. Leave at least six inches of air space between object and container. DO NOT ALLOW METAL TO COME IN CONTACT WITH THE SURROUNDING SOIL!

🔫* Keep a low profile. This means bury the articles in such a way that the narrowest part is facing the detector.

🔫* Bury far from where people are or have been. For example, treasure hunters love to search in and around old buildings.

🔫* If you must bury in your back yard, make sure to fertilize with nitrates and scatter iron filings and nails to throw off metal detectors.

🔫* If at all possible, bury under reinforced concrete: the iron rebar supports will wreak havoc with metal detectors. Guaranteed to break the ice at parties.

🔫* If you have the moolah, stash your loot in a secret room in your house. If you do this, make sure to keep the offending objects in the center of the room.

🔫* Caves make good hiding places. Choose one that can be closed off while still looking natural. Avoid at all cost caves which are well-known, both because of the potential for treasure seekers and for the concern aroused in the public when their fave make-out spot has been blocked out.

I'll end off with another caveat: In my native Northern Ireland, the RUC and the British Army have at their disposal an airborne metal detector capable of detecting metal objects buried up to TEN FEET underground! If the Brits have these devices, then so do we.

Keith Robb is publisher of **The Real Deal,** ▬▬▬▬▬▬▬▬▬▬▬▬▬▬▬▬▬▬▬
His best friend is a S&W model 686 .357 magnum.

HELLO, ARMED CITIZENS! TODAY, WE'LL DISCUSS A PROBLEM THAT TRIPS UP MORE SHOOTISTS THAN ANY OTHER! NAMELY,

HOW TO GET RID OF THE BODY

AFTER YOU'VE SHOT SOME ONE (WHO NO DOUBT ASKED FOR IT.)

A NOTED PSYCOPATH.

FOR THE CARNIVORES AMONG YOU, THIS IS NO PROBLEM.

YOU HERBIVORES CAN TRY THE OLD MAFIA METHODS, LIKE DUMPING THE STIFF IN THE RIVER, OR BURY IT IN YOUR BACK YARD.

BUT A LOT OF SHOOTINGS HAPPEN IN URBAN AREAS WITH NO RIVERS OR BACK YARDS. IN THESE CASES, MORE CREATIVE METHODS MUST BE USED.

ONE OF MY FAVORITE DISPOSAL METHODS IS TO STUFFING THE CORPSE IN A BOX, AND MAILING IT TO SOMEONE I DISLIKE.

USING THE RETURN ADDRESS OF SOMEONE ELSE I DISLIKE, NATCH!

ANOTHER FUN METHOD IS TO GET A BAG OF CEMENT AN' CASTING THE STIFF INTO A CONCRETE STATUE. THEN SELL IT TO SOME ART SNOB!

DON'T WORRY IF YOU HAVE NO ART TALENT, AND THE STATUE COMES OUT HIDEOUSLY UGLY. THE UGLIER IT IS, THE BETTER THE ART FAGGOTS WILL LIKE IT!

YOU COULD ALSO DRESS THE STIFF IN BULKY CLOTHES, AND LEAVE IT IN THE WAITING ROOM OF YOUR LEAST FAVORITE DOCTOR.

THE WAY MOST CLINICS ARE UNDERSTAFFED & OVERCROWDED, IT COULD GO UNDISCOVERED FOR SEVERAL DAYS!

IF YOU HAVE A REALLY TALL SKYSCRAPER IN THE NEIGHBOURHOOD, YOU COULD TOSS THE STIFF OFF OF IT.

A BODY THAT FALLS A COUPLE THOUSAND FEET LIQUEFIES ON IMPACT. RENDERS IT UNIDENTIFIABLE!

CITIZENS WHO KILL IN SELF-DEFENSE ARE ROUTINELY PUT THRU HELL BY THE LEGAL SYSTEM. I HOPE THIS SHORT GUIDE WILL BE OF HELP TO YOU WHO WISH TO AVOID THIS, AND CLEAN UP YOUR OWN MESS. JUST USE A LITTLE IMAGINATION —AND DON'T GET TOO COCKY!

GUN.

ARIZONA LAW ALLOWS YOU TO CARRY A HANDGUN AS LONG AS IT IS NOT CONCEALED. YOU MUST CARRY IT OPENLY ON YOUR HIP - SO I DO.

DO I CARRY A GUN BECAUSE IT MAKES ME FEEL MORE MACHO? IS IT MY TICKET TO ACTION AND ADVENTURE?

DRAW!

NOPE. QUITE THE OPPOSITE, IN FACT.

MY GUN HAS MADE MY LIFE QUIETER. FOR EXAMPLE, ME AND MY ROOMATE, STEVE, BOTH GET AROUND BY BIKE.

HAW HAW!

WHROOOM

STEVE HAS OFTEN BEEN HASSLED BY DRUNKS AND PUNKS IN CARS - THINGS THROWN AT HIM, NEAR-MISSES....

I, HOWEVER, HAVE NEVER BEEN HASSLED WHILE RIDING OR WALKING ARMED. VERY FEW THINGS SEND OUT A STRONGER "DON'T-FUCK-WITH" SIGNAL THAN A GUN.

AN ARMED SOCIETY TENDS TO BE A MORE POLITE SOCIETY.

SO... DO I CARRY THE GUN PURELY AS A STREET PUNK DETERRENT? WOULD I NEVER USE IT?

I hope I'll never need my gun - but if I ever do, I'm liable to need it VERY BADLY!!

OF COURSE I'LL USE IT. MY SURVIVAL INSTINCT IS QUITE STRONG. IF I AM ATTACKED - IF MY LIFE IS THREATENED - I WILL SHOOT. THAT'S WHAT A GUN'S FOR.

BAM! BLAM!

BESIDES TARGET PRACTICE, I HAVE PREPARED MYSELF FOR IT BY STUDYING FIREARMS LAWS AND RUNNING MENTAL SCENARIOS.

IF I WITNESS A MUGGING OR A RAPE, MY GUN GIVES ME THE POWER TO INTERVENE DECISIVELY. A GUN IN THE HANDS OF A RESPONSIBLE PERSON MAKES THE NEIGHBOURHOOD SAFER.

BLAM!

BECAUSE I HAVE A GUN, AND KNOW HOW AND WHEN TO USE IT, I FACE THE OUTSIDE WORLD WITH LESS DREAD. MY GUN IMPROVES MY QUALITY OF LIFE!

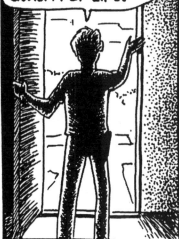

ALL TOO FEW THINGS IN OUR MODERN WORLD IMPROVE OUR QUALITY OF LIFE. BEING ARMED MAY NOT MAKE EVERYBODY MORE SERENE, BUT IT WORKS FOR ME!

STOP RAPE. BUY A GUN.

END

HATE

THE REV. SMITTY DOESN'T

LOVE YOU ANYMORE
By Rev. Smitty

First off let me say this: chances are, I hate you and want to kill you. Hold on, do not get flattered, I hate and want to kill just about everyone. I have a basic rule about people; about eighty percent of them are rotten assholes, stupid fucks or worthless whores. And that goes for just about any subgroup of the human race as well. Thus you take any group: firemen, hairdressers, Americans, Europeans, people who wear white shoes, longhairs, punks, liberals, conservatives, any grouping imaginable and eighty percent should be tossed in the ocean. Certainly there are some variants; some groups would have a higher percentage (attorneys, cops, people who listen to pop music, Middle Easterners, people in the film or music biz, etc.) and some would have a lower percentage (I just cannot think of any right now but I'm sure there are some). Given that, one might say that my trust in the human race is very low. I am not politically correct, affiliated with either major political party, or a "feel good" kind of guy in any way (something that coincidentally is exuded by nearly every man or woman who has ever run for office in the last 50 or 60 years). Yes, I am a curmudgeon, a misanthrope, but mostly I am a realist. And there, folks, is the point of my pontificating.

I do not own a gun. But wait, don't throw this article in the garbage disposal yet! I am friends with gun fags almost exclusively, including Hollister Kopp and the enigmatic, Infamous Red, and have become convinced in recent years that I must become a gun fag. I have just not got around to it yet (if any of you readers have any suggestions, let me know what kind of piece I can purchase that will scare the bejeesus out of the "eighty percent"). So you ask, what can I possibly have to say, what can I offer, what bit of enlightenment would I have for readers of this publication? I offer this: **VIOLENCE**.

I know little about firearms, ammo, weapons, gun laws and the like, but I do know about violence and anger and fear and hate. Christ, whaddya want, I live in L.A.! If there is an uglier place in this country (aside from perhaps Florida) I would certainly like to know where it is so I could move there and be even angrier and more depressed. What I have to offer friends is not what kind of weapons to purchase or how to hang onto them in an ever-increasing "feel good," rights-taking society. What I offer is why we want firearms, why we absolutely must

have them to survive not only personally but as a society.

As I stated before, for years we have become more and more of a feel good, PC country. Let us not deal with the true issues or even the problem, let us come up with a temporary solution that will make us all happy. Bullshit! I am sick of people sweeping everything under the rug; the rug is about to blow up, it so full of ignored problems. Look at the recent passing of Proposition 187 (for those of you outside of California, 187 was an initiative that was to deny health care, social services, public education, etc. to illegal aliens who do not pay taxes for these services). Basically it was trying to treat a huge sucking, festering wound in the California economy. What an uproar it created! The ACLU, judges around the state and country, Latino rights groups, conservative and liberal politicians and even the president spoke out against this "cruel and racist" measure. It was just another part of our feel good society. Yes, it would deny schooling to innocent children who perhaps do not even want to be here in the first place; yes, it could even *cost* rather than save California money in the short term. But sometimes that is what must be done heal a problem rather than just make it *feel* better. If I had my toe cut off I would not want to be put in bed with a

105

super pain killer, sew my fucking toe back on! I do not give a shit how much it hurts or how much better the temporary solution of morphine would feel. I want my gawddamn toe on no matter what the cost!

I know what you are saying; what about guns? Okay, finally, here it is. What we are facing with firearms in this country is a case of temporary versus long term solutions. Boy what a wonderful world it would be if there were no guns. Violent crime would be cut drastically, our streets would be safe to walk night and day, children would not be gunned down in school and at parties, everyone would be happy all the time, angels and fairies would fly around and give us presents, everyone would run naked through fields of flowers and be drunk and fat and have sex twenty times a day. Gimme a break! There is no way in hell that guns are going to be eradicated from the planet. Sorry to break it to you. You make laws against owning guns and only one thing is going to happen; a good chunk of the rotten eighty percent out there are going to have protection and decent twenty percent of us are going to be sitting ducks.

I work in hollywood. I have had jerks flash guns at me, I've been threatened by little pipsqueaks packing iron, I've had many friends mugged, and I myself have even been shot at in my own neighborhood. I do not want to kill anybody...well, OK, there are a lot of people I would like to kill, but I would never do it unless my life or the life of someone close to me was threatened. I have a news flash for you: that is just not the case with a good chunk of the population. There are more people than not who would put six clean holes in your back for the most minor of reasons, especially if they thought there was half a chance they could get away with it. And let me tell you, most of these moronic hunks of meat think they can get away with just about anything. Every day I walk past two ape-like security guards on the way to work. These guys are so vacant you can look into their eyes and see other galaxies. A sack of hammers has greater intelligence. I have seen insects with more purpose. And yes, both of these muscle-bound amoebas carry guns. Like they need them! Either one could punch me in the *hand* and kill me. But that is not the point.

These individuals do not have the intelligence, foresight, restraint or social acumen to carry deadly weapons. If you do not believe me, check it out: security guard "accidental" shootings are much more common than you might think. I once worked with an ex-security guard who bragged about shooting someone by mistake. Not only was he not charged with a crime, but had his permit to carry restored in a matter of months. This is a guy who also bragged about trying to impress a girl by putting his gun to her head.

This type of story is so common to me now that I don't even bat an eye when I hear one. Cops are even worse; they know they can get away with more. I have seen cops lie in court, threaten to beat kids up for not kowtowing to them, give tickets and even haul people in just because they do not like the civilian's clothing or hair, and on and on. Cops are the most sinister egomaniacs on the planet, and the average IQ for a cop is probably well under 80. The smartest cops in this country are German Shepherds, and they are the only ones who *don't* carry guns.

Am I saying we have to take guns away from these vegetables? Absolutely not! All I want is a fighting chance. Not just from "legal" gun carriers, either. They certainly are frightening, but they are nothing compared with the other gun carriers. In California, as in most parts of the country, carrying a loaded handgun is illegal,which means that decent, hard-working intelligent people do not carry guns and psychotic, slacker morons do. At least twice a week I see some crazy hip-hop kid with the attention span of a humming bird ride by on a skateboard with a gun stuck in his belt. I was out to dinner a few months ago and saw two kids who could not have been more than 14 or 15 run by the window of the restaurant, one chasing the other with a pistol. My brother has had at least two motorists point guns at his car after *they* cut *him* off.

Ladies and gentlemen of the jury (the twenty percent), the screwballs are loose. The eighty percent are armed to the teeth. And I reiterate, *we are sitting ducks!* How is this for a beautiful scenario: Your faithful narrator is walking to his car after a hard day's work. A car pulls up next to him on the dark side street. In a flash

a baggy-pants character jumps out of the passenger side and before you know it our hero has a muzzle in his side. "You know what's happenin,'" a young voice blurts out. Yours Truly slowly and reluctantly takes out his wallet and hands it over pleading, "Can I at least have my driver's license back?" to which he is answered with a hard shove to the back. Our hero now hears his wallet running back to the getaway car. The blood boils in his face. In an instant he whirls toward the car pulling his .357 out of its shoulder holster. BLAMMO! Our hero separates his wallet from the filthy assailant's hand while in turn giving Mr. Mugger a severe case of hole-in-the-back. Then, before the driver knows what's going on, our friend gives the rear tire of the car some ventilation before turning the hand of the driver into Swiss cheese as a message. Finally, Yours Truly picks up his wallet, drives home and sleeps like a gawddamn baby that night! Ha! There's your justice.

I would like to go to a party where there are no idiots. That is just not going to happen. When I go to a party and some hip-hop moron starts waving a gun around because he's drunk and thinks he's tough I'd like to feel secure. I do not need to put a gun to his head and tell him to make himself scarce. Oh, sure, I'd love to do that, but I have something that the eighty percent does not - restraint. I would just like to know that if it came right down to it I could air condition some jerk before he air conditioned me. As my best friend likes to say, "I'm not afraid of anyone, can always run." But it's tough to run from a bullet. There are too many loose cannons out there. It is time for the odds to be evened up. That's as good as it gets.

You want there to be no guns around? You want there to be no crime? You want justice and equality and fairness for all? **KILL YOURSELF!** Cuz that's the only way you're gonna get it. In the mean time protect yourself. And by all means do something **REALLY EXTRAORDINARY** and conduct yourself with restraint. There is nothing wrong with security; security guards, yes, but not security. I don't like the odds. I'm going to get me an insurance policy **RIGHT NOW.**

BIG BUSINESS RULES AMERICA

YOU GOT A PROBLEM WITH THAT?

Big hoopla lately over a federal health panel's decision to allow research on human embryos. Everyone screaming about moral concerns, precious human life, eugenics, etc. fuckin' etc. Well, they can all just shut their putrid traps, because this is just the beginning of a scientific renaissance. Real human vivisection could be just around the corner!

Where are we going to get live humans for this important work? Simple. There are millions of human lab rats in our prison system right now who are ready and waiting for all kinds of heinous experiments. They may not agree that this is a good idea, but who cares? They owe something to the society that they helped wreck, and in furthering science and technology, we could see to it that their debt is paid in full.

Since our government doesn't have what it takes to pull off a program that makes this much sense, we'll have to look elsewhere. Now who, besides the commie news media, are more efficient and powerful than the government? What segment of our society is capable of attacking problems, eliminating waste and showing solid results? The answer, horror of horrors, is Big Business, and one of their biggest obstacles to real productivity lies with governmental restrictions in the area of research & development. The bigger companies would gladly pay good coin to have unrestricted access to a pool of "volunteers" on which to perform experiments, and this could be a great boon to weary taxpayers: cost-free prisons.

Major corporations could more than make up for the financial burden of jailing scumbags, if their research teams were allowed to experiment at will on the inmates. This would also serve to placate the wacko animal-rights cultists who are at present waving around those well-known photographs of monkeys trussed up like S&M fags and cute lil' bunnies with stainless steel gizmos prying their eyeballs open for the next blast of hair spray. Substitute rapists and thieves for the animals in those photos and you won't elicit too much sympathy, except from maybe the ACLU, who should be simply ignored anyway.

General Electric, Kraft Foods and Proctor & Gamble, after all, are far more solvent institutions than any state government, and certainly better off and better-run than the *federal* government. Imagine the benefit to society if the prison system, instead of being an immense drain on the American taxpayer, would instead turn a neat profit! The present emphasis on keeping people out of jail (at no small cost) would vanish. There would be a huge incentive to jail as many punks as possible. The efficiency inherent in private enterprise and competition would ensure that our current crime problem would be ELIMINATED. Hell, they could eventually even hire their own police force, prosecuting attorneys and judges to railroad the sonsabitches into jail. Three Strikes, hell!

Once in the system, the inmates could be divvied up into categories based on age, height, weight, etc. and experiments could begin producing reliable, irrefutable data which would be invaluable to the continuation of science and industry. For example, what better (and cheaper) crash-test dummies could you possibly hope for? And the FDA could approve or prohibit experimental drugs and medicine in a fraction of the time it presently takes. A couple of drug companies could infect an entire prison with, say, tuberculosis. Administer all sorts of concoctions to see what works best, and voila! A cure for TB. Huge profits for the winning company. Dead and maimed criminals. A cost-free prison. Everybody wins!

Weapons testing, of course, would be extremely effective using the prison population. This is something I've advocated for some time. General Dynamics could sponsor a prison, as could Rockwell, Hughes and Lockheed. Now THAT would be competition! Or rival prison gangs could be armed on one side by Smith & Wesson and the other side by Ruger. A major war would ensue, which could be monitored closely for each weapon's relative effectiveness. When it was over, the company who sponsored the victors would have plenty to boast about in their advertising, and the losing team

would have important data to study back at the proverbial drawing board.

The prison population is only a problem now because as a society we've taken it upon ourselves to play wet-nurse to a bunch of worthless maggots who, if given the chance, would return the favor by burglarizing our homes and sodomizing our children. This is a vastly unhealthy policy, which is draining us of vital resources. How can we hope to properly educate our children when we're coddling dirtbags to the tune of billions of dollars? The solution is - and has been - staring us in the face, and our elected officials lack the spine to implement anything even remotely positive. I only hope that I'll live to see the day when every bastard geek politician JOINS the prison population! Hell, jail 'em all and let Big Business officially run this country! Why not? AT&T or IBM could certainly do a more efficient job of running things than the graft-guzzlers now in power. They have better foreign policy, they respond to their constituents and they always operate on a balanced budget.

Yeah, I know, a lot of you independent types are wondering what the hell I've been smoking. *Big business being entrusted with governing powers? How could you possibly advocate such blasphemy? Are you queer for that slobbering old vegetable known as Ronald Reagan? How could society stay alive if Big Business ran the government?*

It's already that way, ya rubes! Why not cut the crap? Admit it! Politicians are nothing more than stooges for major corporations (foreign *and* domestic), and they're damned expensive stooges at that. Let's get real! All they do is pass laws designed to limit our freedoms, and now and then throw a couple of restrictive rules toward Big Business, just to make us think they're watching out for our best interest. That weak, symbolic gesture known as VOTING has become nothing more than a sick joke.

Open, honest and straightforward corporate totalitarianism. Hell, it just might get us somewhere.

SO A GUY SHOOTS AT THE WHITE HOUSE.
BIG DEAL!

There are only two things I find incredible about this story: first is the inexcusable bumbling and incompetence displayed by the perpetrator, and second is the fact that it doesn't happen a lot more often!

This man, like many before him, felt the call to patriotic duty. He loved his assault rifle more than his wife and kid, which would be understandable if it were an M1-A or an M14 - *but an SKS for cryin' out loud?* (this is our first clue that the guy may be a couple rounds short of a full clip). Nevertheless, a sense of destiny and the spirit of America welled up inside him like his first schoolboy crush. By God, he was going to do something for his people.

On Saturday, October 29, 1994, fledgling gun fag and constitutionalist zealot Francisco Martin Duran stood fuming with righteous indignation on the sidewalk along Pennsylvania Avenue, right in front of the Evil Empire's very nucleus, the White House. *This is it,* he's thinking. *Somebody's gonna fuggin' pay for the desecration of My America. The fuckers are asking for it.* Under his raincoat he's got a sweaty grip on his new baby, the Chinese SKS which he bought the day the President signed the infamous crime bill. He's equipped it with a folding stock and 30-round detachable magazine, and it snuggles reassuringly under his coat, unnoticed by the dozen or so tourists in the area. Who can blame him? So far so good.

Standing tall with the wave of calm that comes with a sense of conviction and finality, Francisco plants his feet, yanks back his coat Clint Eastwood-like and the SKS comes out a-roaring. Thirty rounds downrange as fast as the trigger can be pulled. My hat goes off to Mr. Duran. People scramble for cover behind the concrete barricades designed to keep people like myself from spinning doughnuts on the White House lawn. Spent shell casings are flying in all directions. Another nutcase is on the loose.

This is beautiful, man. Sonsabitches ain't NEVER gonna forget me now! Jesus this thing is loud. Reload, goddammit! Got some fuckin' adrenaline goin' now, boy! Go go go go go!

Our man pops out the empty mag and sprints down the sidewalk trying to stick another one into the well. The SKS wasn't designed to accept a detachable magazine; it's kind of a mickey-mouse arrangement, and to quickly slap in a fresh one takes some practice. So before he's locked and loaded, a couple of goody-goody spoilsports tackle him and hold him down (they were probably hall monitors in high school). This is where Francisco Martin Duran starts to disappoint me.

Along come the Secret Service goons. One of them kicks Francisco in the teeth, another one grabs him by the hair and kneels down hard on his neck. Stiff thumbs find pressure points which cause paralyzing pain, and dig in. He's cuffed, searched and indelicately shoved into a waiting car. They take him into a stark interrogation room and cuss him up one side and down the other for being the second guy in as many months to goddamn MISS THE TARGET (if you'll remember, the last guy crashed his Cessna in the lawn, killing only himself). I have it on good authority that the Secret Service would rather work for Saddam Hussein than Bill Clinton.

Patriot and Gun Fag Francisco Martin Duran

Francisco m'boy, ya fucked up. Let me spell a couple of things out for you:

1). Training: Practice, practice, practice! You knew you were going to swap magazines at least once, and you knew it would be under stressful circumstances. Before you attempted the mission, you should have been able to perform this very basic task in your sleep, and quickly. And you certainly could have exercised better aim. All you managed to accomplish was a couple of pock-marks in three-foot thick walls, and you managed to knock out one window pane in the press briefing room. This paltry damage hardly seems worth 20 years to life in the federal pen and a $1 million fine. Besides, you should have known that except for the briefing room, all the windows in the White House are bullet proof, which brings us to

2). The Plan: Before you dive gung-ho into your mission, even if you don't foresee living through it, at least study the target and define your objective. I assume you at least fantasized about a bullet finding the President, since you left that infantile note in your truck. How were you supposed to manage that? Your target was safely and comfortably watching a football game with one hand stuffed in his boxer shorts, a can of Coors at his side and a mouth full of Chee-tos. Not only did you not kill him, you didn't even *scare* him.

3). Equipment: Where was your sidearm? When those two brown-nosers ran up to tackle you, you could have effortlessly made examples of them and gone about your business. This would have given you time to reload and fire the SKS until the sharpshooters stationed on the roof of the White House finally took you out. You could conceivably have sent hundreds of rounds across that lawn before dying a spectacular and heroic death. This still would not have affected your target, but at least in this way you could have made a statement!

There's plenty more you could have done to make this a grandly more successful outing. You could have lit yourself on fire before pulling the trigger. You could have rigged your truck with explosives, just to give the feds a little surprise when they went to search it. For that matter, you could have rigged *yourself* with explosives. You could have left cryptic notes about Jodie Foster (that oughta throw 'em for a loop). You could have had a copy of *ANSWER Me!* in your pocket. At the very least you could have put up some kind of a fight when they nabbed you, ya pansy!

Got one word for ya, Francisco: **DUH**. What kind of "patriot" are you, anyway? Sorry, man, but that was a pretty pathetic excuse for an attack. You *should* be jailed, if just for being lame. At least the guy with the Cessna showed some style.

109

H. R. 666

IN THE SENATE OF THE UNITED STATES

FEBRUARY 9 (legislative day, JANUARY 30), 1995

Received; read twice and referred to the Committee on the Judiciary

AN ACT

To control crime by exclusionary rule reform.

1 *Be it enacted by the Senate and House of Representa-*

2 *tives of the United States of America in Congress assembled,*

3 **SECTION 1. SHORT TITLE.**

4 This Act may be cited as the "Exclusionary Rule Re-

5 form Act of 1995".

6 **SEC. 2. ADMISSIBILITY OF CERTAIN EVIDENCE.**

7 (a) IN GENERAL.—Chapter 223 of title 18, United

8 States Code, is amended by adding at the end the follow-

9 ing:

2

1 "§ 3510. Admissibility of evidence obtained by search

2 or seizure

3 "(a) EVIDENCE OBTAINED BY OBJECTIVELY REA-

4 SONABLE SEARCH OR SEIZURE.—Evidence which is ob-

5 tained as a result of a search or seizure shall not be ex-

6 cluded in a proceeding in a court of the United States

7 on the ground that the search or seizure was in violation

8 of the fourth amendment to the Constitution of the United

9 States, if the search or seizure was carried out in cir-

10 cumstances justifying an objectively reasonable belief that

11 it was in conformity with the fourth amendment. The fact

12 that evidence was obtained pursuant to and within the

13 scope of a warrant constitutes prima facie evidence of the

14 existence of such circumstances.

15 "(b) EVIDENCE NOT EXCLUDABLE BY STATUTE OR

16 RULE.—

17 "(1) GENERALLY.—Evidence shall not be ex-

18 cluded in a proceeding in a court of the United

19 States on the ground that it was obtained in viola-

20 tion of a statute, an administrative rule or regula-

21 tion, or a rule of procedure unless exclusion is ex-

22 pressly authorized by statute or by a rule prescribed

23 by the Supreme Court pursuant to statutory author-

24 ity.

25 "(2) SPECIAL RULE RELATING TO OBJECTIVELY

26 REASONABLE SEARCHES AND SEIZURES.—Evidence

HR 666 RFS

3

1 which is otherwise excludable under paragraph (1)

2 shall not be excluded if the search or seizure was

3 carried out in circumstances justifying an objectively

4 reasonable belief that the search or seizure was in

5 conformity with the statute, administrative rule or

6 regulation, or rule of procedure, the violation of

7 which occasioned its being excludable.

8 "(c) RULES OF CONSTRUCTION.—This section shall

9 not be construed to require or authorize the exclusion of

10 evidence in any proceeding. Nothing in this section shall

11 be construed so as to violate the fourth article of amend-

12 ments to the Constitution of the United States.

13 "(d) LIMITATION.—This section shall not apply with

14 respect to a search or seizure carried out by, or under

15 the authority of, the Bureau of Alcohol, Tobacco and Fire-

16 arms.

17 "(e) LIMITATION.—This section shall not apply with

18 respect to a search or seizure carried out by, or under

19 the authority of, the Internal Revenue Service.".

20 (b) CLERICAL AMENDMENT.—The table of sections

21 at the beginning of chapter 223 of title 18, United States

22 Code, is amended by adding at the end the following:

"3510. Admissibility of evidence obtained by search or seizure.".

4

Passed the House of Representatives February 8,

1995.

Attest:

ROBIN H. CARLE,

Clerk.

104TH CONGRESS
1ST SESSION

S. 54

To amend title 18 to limit the application of the exclusionary rule.

IN THE SENATE OF THE UNITED STATES

JANUARY 4, 1995

Mr. THURMOND introduced the following bill; which was read twice and referred to the Committee on the Judiciary

---

A BILL

To amend title 18 to limit the application of the exclusionary rule.

1 *Be it enacted by the Senate and House of Representa-*
2 *tives of the United States of America in Congress assembled,*
3 That this Act may be cited as the "Exclusionary Rule
4 Limitation Act of 1995".

5 SEC. 2. (a) Chapter 223 of title 18, United States
6 Code, is amended by adding the following two sections:

"§ 3508. Limitation of the fourth amendment exclusionary rule

"Evidence which is obtained as a result of a search or seizure shall not be excluded in a proceeding in a court of the United States on the ground that the search or sei-

2

1 zure was in violation of the fourth amendment to the Con-
2 stitution of the United States, if the search or seizure was
3 undertaken in an objectively reasonable belief that it was
4 in conformity with the fourth amendment. A showing that
5 evidence was obtained pursuant to and within the scope
6 of a warrant constitutes prima facie evidence of such a
7 reasonable belief, unless the warrant was obtained through
8 intentional and material misrepresentation.

9 **"§ 3509. General limitation of the exclusionary rule**

10 "Except as specifically provided by statute or rule of
11 procedure, evidence which is otherwise admissible shall not
12 be excluded in a proceeding in a court of the United States
13 on the ground that the evidence was obtained in violation
14 of a statute or rule of procedure, or of a regulation issued
15 pursuant thereto.".

16 (b) The table of sections of chapter 223 of title 18,
17 United States Code, is amended by adding at the end
18 thereof:

"3508. Limitation of the fourth amendment exclusionary rule.
"3509. General limitation of the exclusionary rule.

O

Pull up an ammo box, my good man, and please be seated. There's a new and delightful arm in the Gun Fag arsenal, and the story needs to be divulged. It's an SKS, chum, and not just a common, emasculated Chinese jobbie. No, this elegant unit comes from Mother Russia. It comes with a bayonet. It comes with a distinctive and fashionable eastern-bloc ammo pouch, perfect for any occasion. It comes in a box adorned with a big red hammer & sickle. But lo, you will hear the naysayers and perfidious pundits of patriotism slight this underappreciated weapon with allegations of unreliability and inaccuracy. Let us now disprove this defamation of character. I've had this noble weapon now for nearly a month, and have sent over 5,000 rounds hither and yon with nary a hitch. Any misgivings I've had about this rifle in the past have now completely vanished.

RUSSIAN SKS

This rifle came into my life almost by accident, and has put a spring in my step and a happy tune on my lips. I spied the rugged Russkie down at Retting's gun store and on the price tag was hand-scrawled "Russian SKS - $214.00 - C&R." Hmmm. C&R. Curio & Relic. According to federal law, this thing isn't even a firearm. No waiting period, no background check, no DROS fee. God bless America! Rent's gonna be a little late this month, and I'll be a beerless vegetarian for a week or so, but I got me a piece o' .30 caliber, semi-auto commie history complete with a bayonet and a Russian star stamped into the top of the receiver. Yeeehaw!

During the latter part of the Big Deuce, Russian weapons designers were understandably envious of German military hardware. Of particular interest was the Sturmgewehr assault rifle. The natty National Socialists had already beat the crap out of the commies in the graphics department, to say nothing of those snazzy German uniforms. In this vicious cycle of one-upmanship the reds needed something with which to show up those snooty krauts. They decided to improve upon the Sturmgewehr. It was a fast-handling, easily manufactured weapon which delivered firepower that was nothing short of awesome. The cartridge it so voraciously consumed was a 7.62 X 33mm "intermediate" round which didn't quite have the velocity of a high-powered rifle round, but it was a light recoiler and far, far more deadly than the 9mm Luger and .45 ACP ammo being used in submachine guns. The concept was good, and a new era of firearms was unleashed with the birth of the Samozaryadni Karabin Simonova, caliber 7.62 X 39mm. The goddanged SKS.

With the bolt and locking concept borrowed from the Russian PRTS antitank (!) rifle, the prideful and austere vodkaheads came up with a simple, durable and reliable infantry weapon which was accurate and easy to maintain. It saw service with the Russkies toward the end of the war, then was replaced by the AK-47 in the fifties. Pinko governments the world over have adopted the SKS as the primary weapon of their frontline bullet-stoppers, most notably China and its minion countries. A lot of our boys found themselves on the business end of the SKS during the Vietnam "conflict" (actually a highly successful American weapons testing program, according to the esteemed Raoul Duke), with expectedly grim results. This rifle was also produced in huge quantities in East Germany, Yugoslavia and North Korea.

My Russian SKS is operationally the same as Red's Chinese SKS reviewed in GFM #2, with its 20 ½" barrel and overall length of just over 40 inches. It weighs about eight pounds with sling and bayonet attached, and can be loaded a round at a time, or with the much quicker 10-round stripper clip. The similarities end with the price (the Russian costs about fifty bucks more) and the quality of manufacture. The borscht-belchers really know how to make a gun. Close inspection reveals some fine work, and it's interesting to compare this baby to its Chinese counterpart. The first thing you notice is the handsome laminated wood stock. It seems a bit heavier than the Chinese stock, which is hewn from a solid piece of pine, or something (what kind of trees grow in China? - I really don't know). The stock is fine, but it looks as if the rest of the weapon has been *painted*, rather than blued or parkerized (the Chinese is parkerized). This strikes me as being a little weird, but so far it's been durable enough. I'll let you know if it starts peeling off or chipping excessively. The bolt & carrier are made of stainless steel, which contrasts nicely with the deep black finish of the housing. The receiver and barrel are machined out of a single section, rather than two pieces pressed together as with the Chinese SKS, and it appears to be a heavy-duty arrangement. All parts are apparently made of good steel, machined and fitted properly and professionally.

Like the Chinese SKS, it comes stock with that irritating non-detachable ten round magazine. I installed a non-detachable 30 round U.S.A. magazine (you can still find detachable mags, but in California they'll get you six months in the pokey - be careful!), and have encountered some trouble with it. For reasons I can't seem to pinpoint, the bolt stop doesn't always work with this magazine in place, which means the plastic follower in the mag gets badly chewed up by the bolt on the last shot. Then the thing gets stuck in such a way that you need to hold the bolt open, and with a violent stabbing motion, beat the follower back down into the magazine with a screwdriver or similar instrument. It makes people really nervous to see you doing this, so if you have to apply this method, be sure to make it obvious. It's good for a chuckle. And while this magazine looks cool (like an AK-47's), it can only be unloaded by racking the bolt back and forth, tossing live ammo all over the place. This also makes people nervous, especially if you whistle or talk to yourself while doing it.

The alternative I've found is a 20 shot magazine which works on the same concept as the stock one: the follower is attached to a spring-loaded arm inside the magazine assembly, and its housing is secured to the bottom of the rifle via a latch in the rear and a hinge up front. Pulling the latch frees the magazine, and it swings forward and dumps out all the unexpended ammo. It's made in China and costs about $25. It's a sweet system, and it won't land you in the hoosegow, at least as of this writing. It's also got a large surface area, perfect for stickers, etc. I'm currently looking for a hammer & sickle or a red star for it.

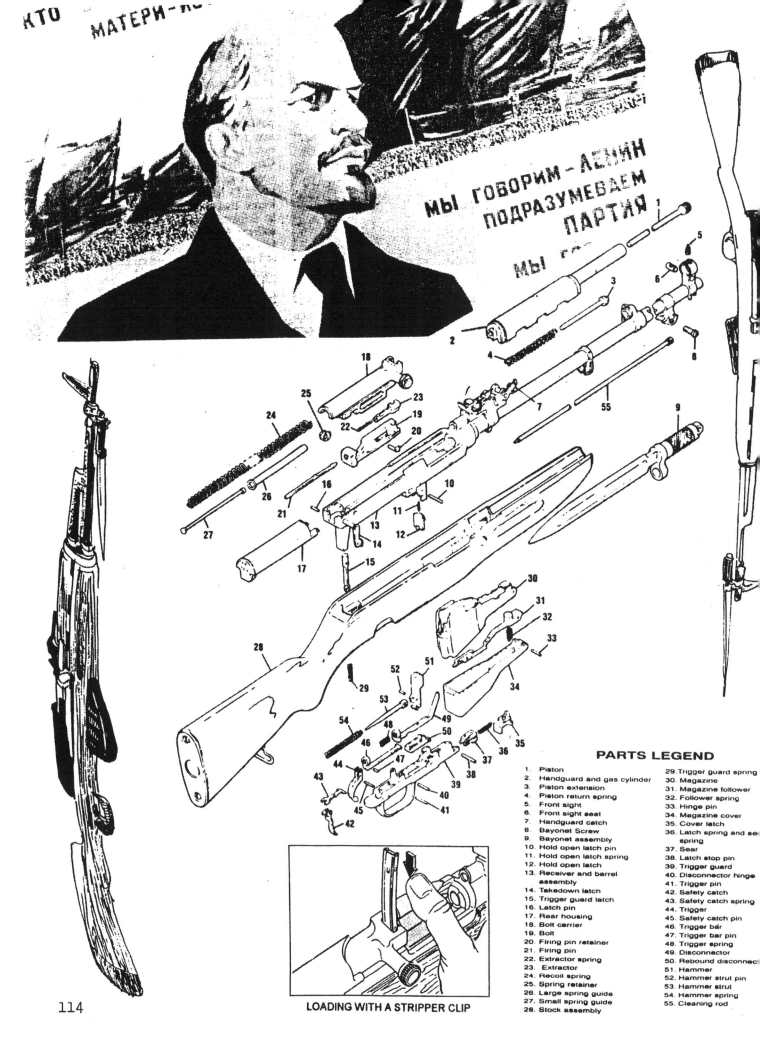

КТО   МАТЕРИ-

МЫ ГОВОРИМ – ЛЕНИН
ПОДРАЗУМЕВАЕМ
ПАРТИЯ
МЫ

LOADING WITH A STRIPPER CLIP

PARTS LEGEND

1. Piston
2. Handguard and gas cylinder
3. Piston extension
4. Piston return spring
5. Front sight
6. Front sight seat
7. Handguard catch
8. Bayonet Screw
9. Bayonet assembly
10. Hold open latch pin
11. Hold open latch spring
12. Hold open latch
13. Receiver and barrel assembly
14. Takedown latch
15. Trigger guard latch
16. Latch pin
17. Rear housing
18. Bolt carrier
19. Bolt
20. Firing pin retainer
21. Firing pin
22. Extractor spring
23. Extractor
24. Recoil spring
25. Spring retainer
26. Large spring guide
27. Small spring guide
28. Stock assembly
29. Trigger guard spring
30. Magazine
31. Magazine follower
32. Follower spring
33. Hinge pin
34. Magazine cover
35. Cover latch
36. Latch spring and se spring
37. Sear
38. Latch stop pin
39. Trigger guard
40. Disconnector hinge
41. Trigger pin
42. Safety catch
43. Safety catch spring
44. Trigger
45. Safety catch pin
46. Trigger bar
47. Trigger bar pin
48. Trigger spring
49. Disconnector
50. Rebound disconnec
51. Hammer
52. Hammer strut pin
53. Hammer strut
54. Hammer spring
55. Cleaning rod

114

As with most military weapons, field-stripping is a snap. Bad weather, high stress and low I.Q. were factored into the design of the rifle, making cleaning and maintenance easy & quick. Flip the rifle upside down, flip the safety on, and using the tip of a live round (it won't blow up - stop watching so much tv) press hard on the little button behind the trigger guard. The trigger assembly will pop out slightly, and you can then just pull it out. This procedure has also freed the magazine assembly, so pull it out too. The barrel/receiver group can now be separated from the stock, although you may have to smack it around a bit. Lift the lever on the starboard side of the rear sight and lift the handguard up and away from the barrel. Pull the piston out of the gas cylinder. Now locate the takedown lever on the rear housing (also on the starboard side), flip it up a quarter turn and pull it out. The housing can now be removed, along with the recoil spring assembly, bolt & bolt carrier. Take the recoil spring assembly in your left hand, and with the right hand compress the spring and then let it snap forward. HA! After you find the little spring retainer that just sailed across the room and disappeared into the heating vent, compress the spring and try to put it back on. HA HA! Clean & oil your SKS and reassemble it in reverse order.

When you've filled the magazine to capacity, be sure to let the bolt slam forward with its entire force. If you don't, it'll stop about a half inch before locking into full battery, and your first reaction is to help it along a little by pushing it forward. DON'T! Trust me. You'll be in for a loud and painful surprise, and your friends will humiliate you ceaselessly. If the bolt stops short of lockup, yank the handle back, letting the cartridge land where it may, and then let the bolt slam forward again. By the way, I've only seen this happen when chambering the first round of a full mag (Red has had this happen to him *four times* now - each time while under the influence of Gatorade margaritas).

Firing the SKS is pure joy. Mine's got an exceptionally smooth trigger which breaks predictably and smartly with every shot. Recoil is next to nothing, and I haven't experienced a single failure to feed. Spent cartridges fly consistently about ten feet up, forward and to the right of the shooter. Velocity is a peppy 2,400 feet per second, and the destructive power of this beast is worthy of a Rudyard Kipling poem. We bought a '72 Ford Maverick with a seized engine and no tranny for 60 bucks, towed it out to the desert and ripped it to pieces with our SKS's. There were geysers of shattered glass. Shreds of interior vinyl and seat stuffing billowed out like chicken feathers at a cock fight. A huge cloud of dust. Metal was actually torn from the body. It reminded me of the sacrificial ox in Apocalypse Now, how it just kind of settled to the ground in expressionless defeat, its life draining fast, forming in a pool beneath it. It was beautiful.

And oh, the noise. Hellish and exquisite. Few sounds are as viscerally pleasing to the ear as the CRACK CRACK CRACK of a real assault rifle doin' its stuff. A cammed-up Chevy big block with headers and Purple Hornies maybe comes close, or Louis Jordan's band at the height of their drunken savagery. But nothing I can think of sends the spirit soaring like the sound of an *assault rifle*, so I recommend not wearing ear protection while firing the SKS. You should embrace undiluted the full sensual charm of this weapon. It'll give ya goose bumps, baby.

For years the sinister Soviets have been supplying corrupt governments and despotic dictators with weaponry (so have we, for that matter), and the demise of the cold war has done nothing to stop the export of fine Russian guns. Only the customers have changed. Prost!

Mrs. Kopp's Little Spokesman
SMITH & WESSON MODEL 15 COMBAT MASTERPIECE

I presented Mrs. Kopp with her Smith & Wesson Model 15 on the first anniversary of our first date. Well, actually, I presented her with a copy of the receipt. There's nothing like a fifteen-day waiting period to kill a romantic moment. Regardless, she was thrilled, and to this day very happy with the gun.

The L.A. Times is, as we all know, always bellyaching about guns, and at the time I bought this one, their whine of the week was the subject of police weaponry being sold to the public. When police departments upgrade their officers with newer guns (usually replacing revolvers with autos) they end up with an armory full of orphans needing caring homes. The economically sound solution is to sell them wholesale to gun dealers. Why not? The Times made it sound like the cops were giving Stinger missiles to gangbangers.

This gun was a police trade-in. If you're in the market for a bargain revolver, this is a great way to go, as they're always top brands, always well cared for and come with exciting histories at no extra charge. This one used to belong to the Los Angeles County Sheriff's Department, an elite cadre of muscleheads so renowned for their well-documented brutality that they make the L.A.P.D. look like meter maids. The gun has definitely been upside a few heads during its gallant life, and it might have even plugged a few deserving punks along the way. It is a cherished member of the Kopp family.

The Model 15 is a .38 Special revolver with a 4" barrel. Very basic, very functional, very deadly. Its adjustable rear sight is its only luxury. We gave it a Pachmyr rubber grip, which fills the hand nicely and makes the gun quite comfortable and controllable, even with zesty +P rounds, which are nearly as hot as .357 magnums. It makes a great carry gun; it's a lot cheaper than a snubbie, and only 2" longer. Easily concealable. Besides, when Mrs. Kopp walks down the street, the last thing you're going to look for is the signature of a concealed weapon, I'm tellin' ya right now.

This gat is a real honey. It functions flawlessly and smoothly with even the cheesiest low-rent reloads. Mrs. Kopp routinely drills postage stamps at 25 yards with cheap lead semi-wadcutters. This is something I wish I could do with my S&W 586! There's nothing sexier... Well, I've said all that before.

A couple of things ain't perfect about this gun: one was its tiny wood grip, which as stated above was immediately replaced with a Pachmyr, and another is some slight holster wear around the muzzle and cylinder. No big deal. The purpose of this gun is not to impress street punks and various *üntermenschen* with a flawless blueing job. Besides, by the time some dumb bastard gets close enough to admire Mrs. Kopp's gun, he will have scored himself a blind date with a body bag. As far as design goes, my only beef with the gun is the unshrouded ejector rod. It's right out in the open, which leaves it vulnerable and likely to get bent if the gun is used as a blunt instrument. For this reason, if the Model 15 is used in a robust pistol-whipping session, it's best to restrict the blows to a sideways motion, shattering eye sockets, cheek bones, teeth, etc. An uppercut to the chin or nose with the front sight will establish pleasing results as well. Unfortunately, the celebrated Vertical Cranium-Crack is better left to full size autos and revolvers with shrouded ejector rods.

Now for the round: There is nothing wrong with a .38 special for defensive purposes. Cops have been gunning down geeks for decades with this round, even before hollowpoints and +P loads became *de rigeur*. I know about Evan Marshall's *Handgun Stopping Power* and the lofty status of the .357 magnum, and I agree that if you want somebody dead before they hit the floor, the .357 is the way to go. But try firing the monster indoors. Jesus, when the cops arrive to hose the mangled bastard out of your house, you'll have to communicate in sign language. Your ears will never be the same. Besides that, there's no telling when or where the .357 round will decide to stop. After passing through your uninvited guest, it's going to take a little tour of your neighborhood, and maybe visit the sweet old lady down the street. Explain that one to the cops in sign language.

I plan to get another Model 15 as soon as funds allow. There is, in my opinion, no better bargain out there on a superb sidearm. Go check 'em out. There's a pleasant .38 caliber surprise waiting for you right now, with a police department stamp of approval.

116

A SIDE-B'-SIDE TEST OF SIDE-B'-SIDE SHOTGUNS

"That sign back there sez No Tresspassin,' boy. I reckon you can read, can't ye?"

You're out on a peaceful bike ride in the hills, tooling up a gravel road enjoying the sights and smells of a beautiful spring day. You decide to take a little breather, so you amble off the road, settle down under a plush maple tree and take a sip from your water bottle. Out of nowhere pops this old codger with one tooth in his foul yap, wearing dirty overalls and sticking two huge, crusted barrels in your face. He asks you what'na hell you're doin' on his proppity, conks you over the head with that big goddamn scary gun and proceeds to blow your front tire in half. "Now GIT!" he yelps, splattering you with especially unsanitary spittle. You slink away, just having had a classic confrontation with the wrong end of a double-barreled shotgun.

Stereotypes aside, there is an undeniable mystique associated with the side-by-side. Graceful and sleek, yet primitive and brutal. The two-holer is as appreciated by a moonshine-chugging Mississippi Klansman as an Ivy League snob on a New Hampshire skeet range. You can spend many thousands of dollars on a hand-crafted European job with gold inlay and elaborate engraving, or pick up a rickety old Montgomery Ward Special at a garage sale for twenty or thirty bucks. They'll both go BLAM when you pull the trigger, which, after all, is the main idea. Falling somewhere between these two extremes is Red's Ithaca model 200SKG and my J.C. Higgins model 1017, both 12-gauge doubles with 2 3/4" chambers, and both the subjects of this here review.

Badly hung over, we left the Burbank headquarters at around 6:00 a.m. after loading Red's truck with targets (we cleaned his garage the day before and came up with plenty of stuff to shoot), a cooler full of baloney sandwiches, about a dozen boxes of cheap shotgun shells and, of course, the shotguns featured in this article. And as no desert trip would be complete without some pistol plinkin,' we brought Red's Colt .45 and my Ruger Blackhawk, as well as a gym bag full of handgun ammo. When we reached the town of Mojave we stopped at that wonderful little store that sells beer *and* ammo, and bought three or four boxes of game loads, two boxes of sporting clays and a case of Budweiser. Their ammo prices are on the steep side, but such a perfect establishment deserves patronage. After a quick breakfast at White's cafe we drove the five miles or so out of town to the usual shoot-em-up area, cracked open a couple of beers and opened fire. We warmed up by shredding a television, a car battery, a phone answering-machine and several aerosol cans. Where double-guns really shine is with sporting clays, and it is in this area that the guns displayed their true personalities. We commenced to laying bets and launching clays. Here's how the guns stacked up:

J.C. HIGGINS

The Higgins was a staple at Sears, Roebuck & Co. for years, and like another Sears legend - Craftsman tools - has a reputation for no-frills durability and swaggering, beer-bellied, cussin'-up-a-blue-streak manliness. Mine is equipped with 28" barrels, which is fine for long-range jobs like shooting geese, but for clays its length makes it a little slow to lock on target. 28" is a lot of pipe to swing into action when the target is launched. Perhaps a longer stock would help; I've got pretty long arms, and most gun stocks feel short to me anyway, but this one is short enough to make the gun feel slightly front-heavy, further slowing target acquisition. Also, with a short stock you have to hunker down onto the comb to get a proper sight picture, and when you fire the gun in such a position you get smacked hard on the cheekbone. This gets old.

Criminy, you'd think I didn't like this gun to hear me bitch and whine! This is a cool shotgun, and the above drawbacks are the *only* drawbacks as far as I'm concerned. The double triggers give it a cantankerous, old-timey look, making the gun eligible for entry in cowboy action shoots, which I don't do very often, but once in a while they're a real hoot. And with double triggers you don't have to fiddlefuck with a tiny button in the trigger housing to switch barrels (a real pain in the ass if you like to drink and shoot). Of course, the best aspect of having two triggers is obvious: you can fire both barrels at once. You want recoil? You got it! The gun is reliable as heck, too. Even smoking hot, the thing effortlessly ejects shells, hungry for more. Snap the action shut and savor that soul-warming hollow steel *thonk* sound, flick off the safety (like most side-by-sides, the safety on the Higgins comes on automatically as the action is closed) and fire away. Fun!

As far as I can tell, this baby was made sometime in the early 'fifties, back in the good old days when America was still America and any nutcase could purchase serious firepower through a mail-order catalog. The gun is about as plain-jane as you can get, which is something I appreciate. There is no decorative engraving on any steel parts, and no checkering on the stock. The sight plane is knurled to keep down glare, and all you get for a sight is a small brass bead up toward the end of the barrels. The receiver/trigger group is made of color case hardened steel, and the barrels are blued. The stock looks like it has been refurbished (and probably shortened) at some point in its life, and is finished in a natural strawberry blonde. The vented rubber recoil pad is so old that it doesn't act like rubber anymore. The J.C. Higgins shotgun is, all in all, a very groovy gun.

ITHACA

Ithaca shotguns are renowned for their beautiful workmanship and buttery-smooth functioning. While the company is based in New York, Red's gun was made in Japan, which, while not surprising, seems a bit odd for such an esteemed firearm. What this means - whether paranoid nationalists such as myself like it or not - is that Japan has made the grade as a first-world industrial power. I mean, cars are one thing, but the manufacture of really good GUNS says something about the status of a country and its people.

We have determined that the gun was made in the mid-1980s and is just about as sweet as can be. The tubes measure 26" and the stock is about an inch longer than that of the Higgins. The gun has perfect balance and almost aims itself. The sighting consists of a brass bead about halfway up the barrels and a V-notch sight up at the business end. Target acquisition is so quick as to be almost comical. Firing this shotgun nearly gives a guy a boner.

The stock is checkered at the grip areas and is beautifully finished in a glossy black cherry. While to me it doesn't matter, there is some fine scrollwork around the trigger housing and up on the breech end of the barrels. All steel parts are richly blued. Every aspect of the action is as smooth as a baby's butt, except that after twenty rounds or so the ejection gets a bit sticky. Nothing to worry about, but there's something about cracking open a shotgun's breech and having the smoking expended shells eagerly pop out at you that is just, well, *debonair*. My answer to sticky chambers (besides keeping them clean) is to take a standard brake cylinder hone (any auto parts store will sell you one for ten or twelve bucks) and using gun oil, extreme caution and patience, gently ream the chambers with a slow-to-medium speed setting on your drill. This method works if you're the careful type. If you're not, take it to a gunsmith.

The downside of this gun is the single trigger. Single triggers may be civilized and gentlemanly, but they're irritating as hell. This is a great gun, but dammit, *it needs two triggers!*

PRICE

Ah yes, the all-important price. I bought my Higgins from a cop for $125, which is probably a little less than what it's worth on the retail market. I'm happy with the deal. Red bought his Ithaca from a Korean War vet who was gassed during some particularly heinous U.S. Army tests, and has through litigation become quite well-off financially, considering his mental state. He probably has more guns than the FBI, and if plied with enough beer will sell you something on the cheap. Red paid exactly one hundred dollars for the Ithaca (it's worth nearly a thousand), and witnessed the guy selling a nearly-new Smith & Wesson Ladysmith .357 magnum to a girl for twenty bucks. I haven't yet had the pleasure of meeting this fellow, but mark my words, I'm gonna be his friend.

Thus concludes the side-b'-side test of the side-b'-side shotguns, and as you've probably gathered, Red's gun comes out the winner, especially when you consider the price. If it weren't for the cursed single trigger, it would have been the hands-down winner.

My recommendation? Just go buy a double-barreled shotgun. Spend less than a hundred-and-fifty bucks on one and have a blast. Ya can't go wrong.

THE BERETTA 92 FS 9MM PARABELLUM

By Pollyanne Hornbeck

This year for Christmas if you're a very good ghoul or boil Sandy Claws just may bring you your dream gun. So stop misbehaving right now. Stop lifting up your top and shaking your titties at Sin-a-matic and stop begging the girl in latex to dick clamp your penis at Club Vice. Stop trying to shoplift Glaser "Safety Slugs" because they're too fucking expensive to buy. Stop telling your girlfriend that you would break up with her except that you're afraid of being alone, and start recycling all those beer cans and bottles, you lazy bastards, or you're going to get a lump of coal in your fucking stocking!

You also better hope that Santa shops early since the Feinstein amendment was signed on Labor Day, and many goodies are disappearing on a first come first serve basis until whatever's left in the country is all gone. We're talking about anything that has a magazine capacity of over ten just for today. Never did the lovely Nazi anthem *Tomorrow Belongs Me* mean less than now as Big Brother is trying harder and harder to pat us down and cop a feel.

My dream gun is the Beretta 92 FS (besides a stainless .44 magnum Ruger Redhawk with a 7 1/4" barrel - but I have more time on this cuz it's a six-shooter revolver). But the Beretta is directly affected by the "Lamestein" amendment and has a magazine capacity of 15. If you're scared to wait until Xmas morn this is what you can do today. Retting and Sons still had a bunch in September and they were going for a little under $700. This is before any of the add-ons. If you haven't bought a handgun in a while you'll find an additional fee of ten clams for this piece of poo-poo test/certificate thingy called the BFSC - Basic Firearms Certificate. It's a thirty-question test that comes with a study booklet including "additional safety points" that state things such as: "guns are not clothing accessories - and should not be worn to impress or to appear 'cool.'" You can miss up to six or seven (I can't remember since I didn't miss any) and if you fail you can study the booklet and take the test again after waiting 24 hours. My advice is to just take the fucking test. Anyone with one brain cell of common sense will pass. take the booklet home anyway just to look over later for laughs. If you don't pass you shouldn't be messing with guns in the first place, so just put the barrel of a loaded gun into your mouth and pull the trigger until it goes Bang! and save the rest of us the trouble.

Now with the egg timer on, lots of places will be taking the pleasure of gouging you like a black-market Jew. A pal of mine got reamed for $900 in San Diego before I even got mine. Don't expect to haggle as they've got you where they want you. Go someplace respectable and where they know you and hope for the best. Beretta magazines were going for $60 a pop before the amendment passed and that was bad enough. Knockoffs could be found in the Sportsman's guide for a third of that price. They didn't fit as smoothly; sometimes you have to jimmie with the magazine release button to get it in, but after that it feeds just fine.

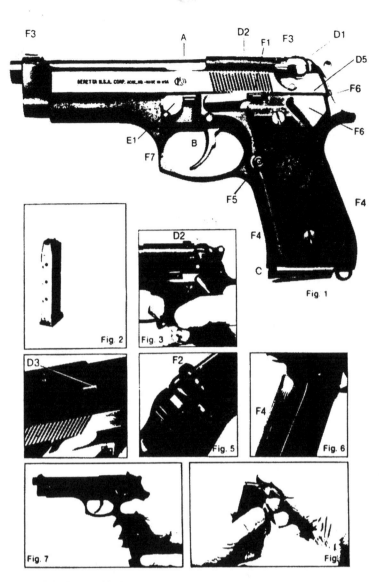

Fig. 1

Fig. 2

Fig. 3

Fig. 5

Fig. 6

Fig. 7

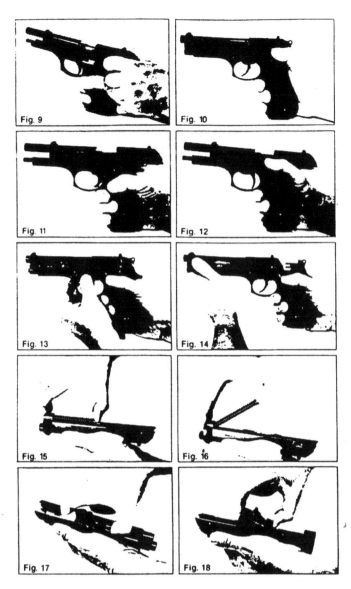

Fig. 9

Fig. 10

Fig. 11

Fig. 12

Fig. 13

Fig. 14

Fig. 15

Fig. 16

Fig. 17

Fig. 18

EXPLODED DRAWING

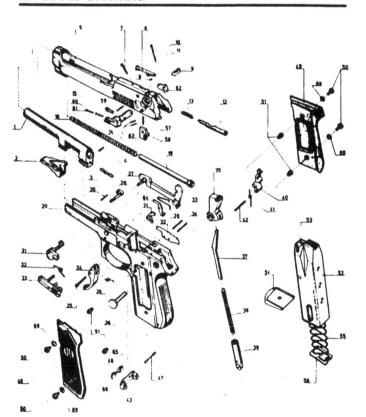

PARTS LIST   MODEL 92 F

Part #	Nomenclature	Part #	Nomenclature
1	Barrel (Factory Fitting Required)	34	Ejector Spring Pin
2	Locking Block	35	Hammer
3	Locking Block Plunger	36	Hammer Pin
4	Locking Block Plunger — Retaining Pin	37	Hammer Spring Guide
5	Slide (Factory Fitting Required)	38	Hammer Spring
6	Extractor	39	Hammer Spring Cap
7	Extractor Pin	40	Sear
8	Extractor Spring	41	Sear Spring
9	Rear Sight (Fitting Required)	42	Sear Pin
10	Trigger Bar Release Plunger	43	Magazine Release Button
11	Trigger Bar Release Plunger Spring	46	Magazine Release Button Spring
12	Firing Pin	47	Hammer Spring Cap Pin
13	Firing Pin Spring	48/49P	Grips (Plastic) Pair
14	Safety	48/49W	Grips (Wood) Pair
15	Firing Pin Plunger	50	Grip Screw
18	Recoil Spring	51	Grip Bush
19	Recoil Spring Guide	52	Magazine Box
20	Frame	53	Magazine Follower
21	Disassembling Latch	54	Magazine Bottom
22	Slide Catch Spring	55	Magazine Spring
23	Slide Catch	56	Magazine Lock Plate
24	Trigger	57	Firing Pin Catch Spring
25	Trigger Pin	58	Firing Pin Catch
26	Trigger Spring	59	Firing Pin Catch Retaining Spring
27	Trigger Bar	60	Safety Plunger Spring
28	Trigger Bar Spring	61	Safety Plunger
29	Disassembling Latch Release Button	62	Right Safety Lever
30	Disassembling Latch Release Button Spring	63	Right Safety Lever Spring Pin
31	Hammer Release Lever	64	Firing Pin Catch Lever
32	Ejector	65	Magazine Catch Spring Bush (Sh
33	Hammer Release Lever Pin	66	Magazine Catch Spring Bush (Lo
		69	Spring Washer

Basically I took liberties with Santa a few days before Labor Day. I found a store that still had a couple of Beretta 92 FS's, put every cent I had down on it and after the fifteen day waiting period acquired the money my boyfriend had been saving up for a new sofa to pay it off. The way I figure it, we're being controlled more and more about our rights and what we can and cannot have, and I think it will be quite a while before the government decides that Joe and Jane Public can make homemade nuclear terrorist equipment with couches. Obviously somebody's got to set priorities, and mine's got a time limit on it. And it's not like we don't have a chair or two around the house and dang, we even have carpet and that kinda makes the whole floor a couch, doesn't it? Besides, I'll pay him back someday, and he was only mad for a day or two and heck, I even let him shoot it on his birthday! But maybe if'n you play your cards right Santa will have shopped early for you and you'll find a bitchin' Beretta 92 FS 9mm under your tree yet. If so, let me tell you a little about what to expect.

Just imagine... Christmas morning, you've just untied the big red ribbon from your new Humvee, moved your new stockpile of 100,000 rounds of all your favorite ammo down into your survival bomb shelter and noticed that there is one last sparkling gift under the tree. The glistening silver foil is making your eyes twinkle and your honey says, "Sweetie, I've saved this special one for last, why don't you open it now." You crawl under the tree with your fuzzy reindeer slippers still on and pick up the box. You hoped but never dreamed... a Beretta 92 FS Caliber 9mm parabellum; three-dot sight; blue steel; fifteen capacity magazine; ambidextrous safety-decocking lever; fancy slim red "chamber loaded" indicator; V-grooved frame serration for good grip in wet, muddy or other yucky conditions; reversible magazine release button for picky southpaw shooters; and groovy serrated crosswise V-cut combat trigger guard for firm rest of your index finger when shooting in a two-hand hold. Shoot, bang! Who could ask for more?

Talk about a smooth slide, dreamy field stripping and just plain sexy smooth recoil. Forget the wedding - just get me to the range on time. Forget PMS, chocolate cravings or regular bowel movements, nothing makes me crankier than not shooting my Beretta on a consistent basis. The slide catch can be locked open manually and automatically stays open after the last round is fired. With a slick click of the catch it makes a sensuous steel-to-steel slam that just makes me quiver. Those swarthy Italians - do they know how to design a gun, or what?

So be good, be very good, or blow an elf, just be sure you get yours this Yuletide season. And if you run out of ammo don't forget the tasty option of cold-cocking. Season's Beatings!

Pollyanne's Dream Gun

121

The Villain's Gun

MAUSER C-96 9mm "BROOMHANDLE"

By John Bergstrom

I first saw the Mauser watching newsreels from pre-war China. A Koumintang officer walked behind a row of Maoist prisoners, shot each one in the back of the head and tumbled the bodies into a pit. That about sums up the Mauser's history. It is the villain's gun.

From 1896 through the 'forties it was the favorite of warlords, rebels, smugglers, thieves, opium traders, hit men, Nazis and Bolsheviks. Whatever else you might say of these types, they knew a great firearm when they saw it. The C-96 was the first semi-automatic to actually work, firing a good-sized slug reliably and accurately a decade ahead of its competitors. The Mauser reign was short lived; by 1920 Browning, Colt and Luger had it thoroughly outclassed. But sales to the core market of third-world death squads continued. I am convinced that this is because of its looks. A peasant would laugh at a Luger. He might respect the Colt, but put a Mauser to his temple and he'll know true fear. Production finally stopped in 1943 when a British bomber full of incendiaries did what the competition couldn't.

For half a century the Mauser drifted on the edge of memory. They sat in collections, too expensive and complex to shoot. Then China opened. Deng Xiao Peng began his desperate "sell our daughters for a nickel" bid to drag his country into the present. While political prisoners were merrily stamping out cheap AKs for the American sportsman, other little commie entrepreneurs were scouring the land for pre-revolution artifacts. Suitcases full of old weapons started appearing on the west coast. The renaissance had begun.

One of this magazine's stated purposes is the review of cheap, effective firearms. The Mauser falls outside this mandate. At eleven-and-a-half inches it is not concealable. Simply cocking the weapon is a three-step process. The insides are a jigsaw puzzle of razor-sharp pieces that must be cared for or the gun WILL FAIL. You do not order parts, you go on a safari for them. I recommend gun shows where you can try the part on. I've had a few bad experiences with mail order companies, especially Sarco. Lastly, these weapons are old. Things just happen. Last year the rear sight assembly came apart and almost took my ear off. The faint of heart need not apply.

The faint of heart should shoot themselves now and get it over with. Goddamn bunch of meeks. This is the price paid for having the coolest fucking gun on the range: people come to stare at the dinosaur. Curiosity becomes awe as they watch me cut the center out of a target at forty feet. A while back I stood shoulder to shoulder with this yuppie asswipe and his Glock. I didn't mean to shame him in front of his woman, but sphincter boy shouldn't have laughed at my "muzzle loader."

Honestly, this is not the gun I would bring on a bank robbery. But the Mauser is still very capable of tearing a new asshole in any who would dismiss it.

John Bergstrom is the villain responsible for *Attack Cartoons*

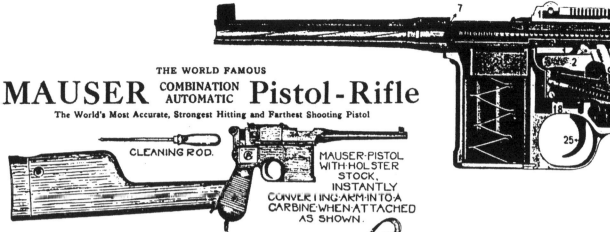

THE WORLD FAMOUS
MAUSER COMBINATION AUTOMATIC Pistol-Rifle
The World's Most Accurate, Strongest Hitting and Farthest Shooting Pistol

CLEANING ROD.

MAUSER PISTOL WITH HOLSTER STOCK, INSTANTLY CONVERTING ARM INTO A CARBINE WHEN ATTACHED AS SHOWN.

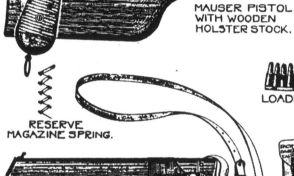

MAUSER PISTOL WITH WOODEN HOLSTER STOCK.

CLIP CARRIER FOR 40 7.63MM OR 9MM SHELLS 4 CLIPS.

LOADING CLIP.

RESERVE MAGAZINE SPRING.

PISTOL INSIDE OF STOCK, COMPLETE WITH SHOULDER STRAP CARRIER.

CARRIER FOR 100 7.63MM OR 9MM CARTRIDGES. FITS 2 BOXES OF SHELLS. FOR BELT OR PACK USE.

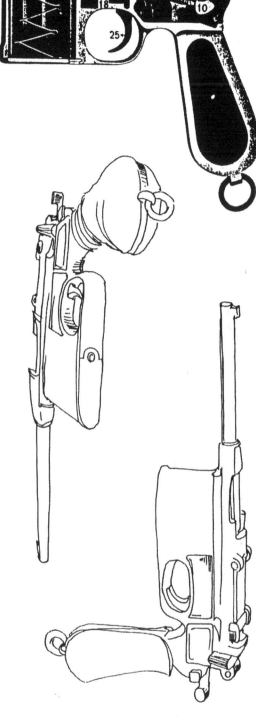

123

A COUPLE OF RANDOM FACTS REGARDING AMMO

Newspaper accounts of pistol ammunition "pulverizing" organs, ripping limbs off of grown men and blowing bowling ball-sized holes in people is all a buncha propagandistic crap. The smarmy little weasels running the major papers and networks incessantly bellyache about magic hollowpoints with the power to vaporize entire communities and the hideous effect "dum-dum" bullets are having on the very soul of civilization. Where are they getting their information? Special correspondent Steven Segal?

The neocommunist editorial staff at the L.A. Times would have us believe that if we don't outlaw Bullets That Hurt - and soon - we are all going to die. Listen, ya pukes: while you're lounging around the pools behind your fashionable Brentwood bungalows worrying about a hailstorm of hollowpoints, maybe you should read up on the subject, or better yet, get your oh-so-fabulously-tanned-and-aerobicized asses off the massage tables, get behind the phone - er, *wheel* of your precious little red Beemers and visit the pistol range ten minutes away in Beverly Hills. Learn something, you worthless larvae!

Very briefly, here are a few ammo facts to keep in mind the next time you argue with (instead of just kill) some snively little cretin who *likes* being sodomized by the mainstream media:

First we'll talk about **caliber**. Most of you already know all about caliber and how it's measured, etc., but what the hell, it's fun to read about anyway. Caliber is simply the diameter of the bullet. Americans have traditionally measured caliber in inches, while Europeans measure it in millimeters. This can be confusing. For example, the 9mm cartridge traces its lineage to Europe, even though there are hundreds of different 9mm pistols designed, manufactured, sold and fired in the United States (by the way, I've heard several otherwise well-informed gunnies state that Adolf Hitler invented the 9mm cartridge, which is bullshit. Hitler's greatest achievement was the Volkswagen, not the 9mm). We still call it a nine millimeter, even though to measure the diameter of the bullet American-style we would come up with .357" (look familiar?) This doesn't mean the .357 magnum and the 9mm are interchangeable in any way! But guess what? You *can* fire a .38 special in a .357 magnum revolver. You *can't* fire a .357 magnum cartridge in a .38 special revolver (see the paragraph on magnums for a better explanation). For some weird reason, I don't know why, a .38 is called .a 38 even though its diameter is .357". Most other calibers are a little more honest. A .45 is .45" and a fifty caliber is a half-inch in diameter.

Gauge (as in shotgun) goes like this: Look at your shotgun barrel (keeping your finger out of the trigger housing!) and imagine how many spheres of lead exactly the diameter of the inside of the barrel it would take to weigh one pound. With my shotgun it would take twelve spheres of lead - 12 gauge. That's why when you're talking shotguns, the smaller the gauge, the bigger the gun. One exception: the .410 shotgun, for reasons unknown, is measured in caliber - .41".

The all-time favorite villain of the PC set was, ironically, designed with political correctness in mind. These are the so-called **"cop-killer"** bullets which got so much hysterical media attention that they were swiftly banished from the known universe. They supposedly had the potential to penetrate police body armor. In fact they were regular old revolver cartridges, the bullets of which having a nylon coating designed to significantly reduce lead particles in the air of indoor firing ranges. Pretty scary bullets, eh?

And of course there's the **hollowpoint**. I like hollowpoints. These are efficient population-controllers for several reasons: first and most obvious is the fact that the bullet mushrooms on impact, which serves the noble duty of creating a larger wound cavity. Ow! The greater surface area resulting from the expansion also slows the bullet during its tour of the target's innards, causing loss of kinetic energy (energy loss = stopping power). Other factors contributing to the hollowpoint's efficiency are light weight (the bullet is hollow, after all) which aids the slowing process when the bullet enters the scumbag, and the lightweight bullet naturally travels faster *before* it hits. According to Evan Marshall's exhaustive study *Handgun Stopping Power*, the most effective all-around handgun round is the Federal .357 magnum 125 grain jacketed hollowpoint, which (with one shot) has proven to *kill punks dead* something like 97% of the time.

Nowadays the term **magnum** just means a powerful round. All sorts of rifle cartridges and shotgun shells (and even rifles and shotguns) are referred to as magnums in flashy ads in gun magazines, seemingly without regard to historic fact or precedent. Real magnums started with the .357, which is a .38 Special stuffed with a super-hot load of powder. They made the cartridge case a little longer so dumbfucks can't stick a .357 round into a gun designed to fire the .38 Special. The converse works just fine, however; you can fire .38 Special rounds from a .357 magnum revolver all day long, and it's a heck of a lot cheaper that way (just not as fun - if a .357 is a roll in the hay with Traci Lords, a .38 is a kiss on the forehead from your grandma). Why the numbers are different, I don't know - a .38 caliber slug is actually .357" in diameter (or exactly 9mm, to further confuse things). The .44 magnum is likewise a feisty version of the .44 Special, also with a slightly lengthened case. As stated above, ammunition manufacturers are throwing the term "magnum" around rather recklessly these days, which is having the effect of blurring the distinction and cheapening the name. I wish they'd shut up and just make ammo.

For the record, **"dum-dums"** are not some kind of mysterious, exploding astro-bullets, nor are they the commonly-thought-of bullets with crosses cut into the tips, a la Travis Bickle in *Taxi Driver*. The dum-dum bullet, in FACT, was a semi-jacketed softpoint .303 rifle bullet manufactured at the British Arsenal in Dum Dum, India, in the latter part of the 19th century. Look at almost any centerfire hunting round manufactured today, and it'll have a jacketed bullet with the soft lead tip exposed. Essentially a "dum-dum," and rarely used in a criminal fashion. Another cockamamie pile of media-poop is that dum-dum bullets were flat outlawed worldwide by the Geneva convention. Lordy, can't they get anything right? Here's the real scoop: the Hague Conferences of 1899 and 1907 declared the use of expanding bullets *in warfare* unlawful (you can kill the enemy, but don't kill 'em too dead!), but it doesn't apply to hunters shooting animals or cops shooting street scum. To this day military small-arms ammo is of the full metal jacket variety, even though it's not nearly as effective as the common hunting round. And that's the story of the mighty dum-dum. Don't let anyone tell ya different.

Velocity is another word you'll hear often among the guys hanging out in gun stores and your better barber shops. It means how fast the bullet travels, and plays an important role in the killing power of a particular round. While the .357 magnum is really fast for a handgun round (right around 1,400 feet per second [fps]), that velocity would be considered fairly mild for a rifle. A 7mm Remington Magnum (ooh, there's that *M* word again!) with a 140-grain bullet, for example, is a pretty standard, run-of-the-mill hunting round and whizzes along at around *2,830 fps*. At that kind of velocity, bodies do indeed become damaged. A lot of autopsies performed on gunshot victims (dead ones) who were hit with rifle bullets have shown cracked bones and badly damaged organs which were nowhere near the wound channel. This, the theory goes, is due to shock waves, like when you throw a pebble into a still pond. Organs (and even bones, to a certain extent) have elastic qualities which allow us to be knocked around quite a bit without being seriously injured. You can get punched in the gut and your stomach, liver, intestines, etc. will be stretched around a bit, but you'll really be none the worse for wear. Everything changes, however, when something hits you doing about two thousand miles per hour. Your insides get stretched way beyond the point of elasticity, which means they break. Which means you die.

Pollyanne briefly mentions the **Glaser "Safety"** round in her Beretta article in this issue. A lot of folks have heard the name, but don't know what the heck it is. Well, it's basically a shotshell in the form of a handgun cartridge. Little teeny balls suspended in some kind of gelatinous compound (does Rep. Charles Schumer come to mind?) which upon impact travel willy-nilly throughout your target's guts. The frequency of one-shot kills in the Strasbourg Tests surpassed even the royal .357 magnum. There is another cartridge quite similar to the Glaser in design and effectiveness, but I can't remember the name, and I'm too tired and cranky right now to look it up. If you're wondering what the **Strasbourg Tests** are, you're in for a treat.

First of all, lets get this straight: I'm no fan of France or anything French, as I think they're a bunch of snooty, arrogant motherfuckers who deserve to still be under Nazi occupation. But one thing you can say for the showerless bastards is that they don't knuckle under to the doctrine of PC. They still eat tons of meat, drink a lot on a daily basis and smoke like chimneys. And in Strasbourg, France, they held the Tests. This could never happen in ACLU-occupied America: they tested handgun ammo on live goats. They'd shoot 'em and measure how much time it took for the goats to die. All very scientific-like, and fuck Greenpeace and PETA.

There you have it, boys & girls, another worthless filler article on things loud and fast. Things which I hold dear.

This story is mostly true. I say *mostly* because it's a hunting story, and no hunting story is 100% true. This one may be more truthful than most, however, on account of its shameful nature and the fact that I didn't gloss over any of the uglier moments:

A BARBAROUS QUEST FOR
WILD BOAR
IN CENTRAL CALIFORNIA

In the strictest sense, no one needs to hunt; we have farms and ranches and supermarkets to supply us with meat. But if you look beyond the human stomach, you encounter the human spirit, and that part of us needs to hunt as much as it needs to compose music, or write novels, or record history, or worship a higher being. Hunting, as much as anything, made us what we are, and the week or two we spend with a rifle is the pivot on which the rest of our year balances.

- David E. Petzal

Hunting wild boar can be dangerous. The goddamn things can weigh upwards of 600 pounds and have been known to literally rip human beings to pieces. Big, hairy, mean, ugly motherfuckers with tusks five inches long. They kill cheetahs and mountain lions just for kicks. They eat anything and everything. They're horrible creatures, and so abundant now in central California that hunters are encouraged to kill as many of them as possible. A book of *five* boar tags only costs $7.90.

It was like a call to duty. Red, Byron, Ted, Emory and I heeded that call, and loaded Old Bloody Knuckles (my Volkswagen bus) with guns, ammo, knives, Red's dad's old police baton, two cases of Hamm's, a bottle each of tequila, scotch, ouzo, Jager Meister, some more bottles of I don't remember what, a couple of dozen four-foot long beef sticks called MaxiPeps, some firecrackers the size of road flares which Emory had picked up in Mexico, sleeping bags, coats, hats and some rope with which to drag the dead pigs out of the woods and lash them to the roof of the bus. Most of the gear fit on the shelf above the engine, behind the back seat, which seats three across without much trouble. Between the back and front seats is a large expanse of floor, on which rode the beer cooler and an impressive stack of guns and gun stuff.

We all piled in at around nine o'clock on Friday evening and headed north.

Ted, Hollister, Emory, Red, Byron. Let no boar escape our mighty wrath.

The first three hours of the trip were pretty uneventful, the bus taking the Grapevine in mostly third gear, but everywhere else a smooth 65 mph was the norm. Just like any other Friday night, we drank beer and talked about guns. And just like any other Friday night, Red had to eventually do something to piss me off. North of Bakersfield on I-5 is the San Juaquin Valley, a very boring, quiet drive through mostly flat farmland that lasts about five hours if you were to keep driving north. It kind of lulls you into a peaceful, introspective trance if you let it, and this was happening to me when rude reality came back with a **CRACK CRACK CRACK CRACK CRACK.** Goddammit, Red.

I just about crapped my pants. I inadvertently jerked the wheel and sent the bus careening into the next lane. The boys were laughing in the back seat, HAW HAW HAW HAW. My ears were whistling from the sudden burst of gunfire.

"Goddammit, Red!" I hollered over the din in my ears.

"You fuckin' fool!" Byron yelled, who was sitting up front and was as startled as myself.

"HAW HAW HAW HAW," the boys were laughing.

"Got-*damn*," Red said as they settled down a bit, "did you see that fuckin' thing shatter?" He was cradling the SKS rifle in his lap and grinning like a child.

"Jesus!" Ted was still laughing and was wiping tears from his eyes, "I can't believe you did that!"

I could believe it. Red.

Every quarter of a mile on California's freeways are call boxes mounted on poles, used for emergencies. They have little solar panels on top which serve to power them. They're pretty nifty devices, so of course Red had to stick his SKS out the wing window and blow one all to hell.

"Goddammit, Red," I said again, my hearing not having fully returned. "You know what's gonna happen if the cops pull us over? Huh? They'll confiscate our guns is what'll happen!"

"That'd suck."

"You fuckin' A right it'd suck. Jesus H! Gimme a beer." I reached my hand back behind me expecting a cold can to be slapped to me like a baton at a relay race. Instead there was clatter, a thump and another **CRACK**, this time embellished with exploding glass and a sudden burst of cold wind. Shit.

"WHATINNAFUCK!" I shrieked.

Red had stepped forward with my beer in one hand and his SKS in the other, and had stepped on his own spent shell casings, which rolled out from under him as efficiently as ball bearings. When he went down, the SKS went off and blew out the middle right side window.

"Fuuuck," he mused.

"Goddammit, Red!" That was his new name, Goddammit Red. "How many times do I have to tell the whole fuckin' world to goddamn KEEP YOUR (at this point it became a groaning, eye-rolling chorus from the back seat as everyone joined in) FINGER OUT OF THE TRIGGER HOUSING UNTIL THE WEAPON IS ON TARGET!"

Most of the glass had blown out, thank God, rather than in, but there were enough little shards for everyone to enjoy; we kept finding them in our hair, in our pockets, boots and sleeping bags for the duration of the weekend. Meanwhile the icy wind was bound to put us all in a shitty mood.

"Now somebody please gimme a beer," I said, and somebody gave me one. "A new window costs about fifty bucks and the rubber seal is about sixty or seventy. And it's kind of a bitch to put in."

Red said, "I'll pay for the goddamn window. Christ, you act like I just shot your kid."

I opened my can of beer and, predictably, it started to rain.

Our destination was Fort Hunter Liggett up in Monterey County, which is about the cheapest place to legally hunt wild boar; you just have to pay four bucks at the wildlife check station, tell 'em when you expect to come back (so they can look for your remains if you don't), sign in and go huntin.'

Just be careful to stay out of the artillery impact areas; Hunter Liggett is still an active military base. I've been there before, in an official capacity. I was a grunt in a rifle company with the 7th Infantry Division a few years ago, and we used to go out there and raise all kinds of hell. In the summer of '81 or '82 some sad-sack shitbirds in the 218th Field Artillery nearly caused a world-class disaster when they caught one of their ammo trucks on fire; there were terrible explosions, six dead and several maimed, a forest fire which eventually consumed more than thirty thousand acres, and they had to

cancel training maneuvers which involved the Marines, the Navy, the Army and the Oregon National Guard and had taken more than a year to plan. The sight of the explosion is still off limits to anyone, and nothing will grow within about a fifty-meter radius of the original blast.

By the time we made the coast highway it was raining pretty good, and the guys in the back had abandoned the seat and were sitting on the floor with their backs against the left side panel, trying to stay out of the wind and rain. Emory had covered the gear in the back with his poncho, which was keeping the stuff reasonably dry. The beer was gone. We had finished the bottle of scotch and were working on the ouzo, which I had wanted to save for the actual hunt, but didn't say anything, as the guys were looking cold, miserable and dangerous. They weren't laughing; in fact, they weren't even talking. Byron, in the passenger seat, glared straight ahead and like the others, was not talking. I offered cigars all around, and no one spoke or accepted the offer. They were Punch Maduros, my favorite. I bit the end off one, lit it and pretended that everything was just peachy. We still had time to buy some beer if we could find a store within the next twenty minutes or so. It looked as if our lives may very well depend on it.

As luck would have it, I spotted a mom 'n pop-looking gas station/convenience store about three minutes before 2:00, the cut-off time for buying beer in California. And as luck would have it, they were closed, apparently the only store for miles in either direction. Great. Only the big Texaco light was on; a nasty prank whether it was intentional or not. I pulled in under the awning next to the gas pumps and shut 'er down.

"Any of you dour sonsabitches need to take a leak?" I asked.

"Yeah," said someone, I couldn't tell who. Some *bitter* motherfuckers, boy.

"Shit," Emory spat. It was clear that he was wound up tight enough to become a liability. "How could they be closed? This is BULLSHIT! We need some fuckin' BEER, man! Some fuckin' BEER!" The last *beer* kind of echoed and died away into the

night. The feeling was disappointment and futility.

Emory doesn't kid around when he feels like being violent. He once chased his ex-wife and her boyfriend (his ex-best friend - you figure the rest) around Van Nuys at very high speeds - him in his Ford F-250 pickup and them in an Isuzu Trooper - ramming them hard now and then just to remind them of their folly, until they finally found a police station, where they thought they could find refuge. Wrong. They skidded to a stop in front of the station, whereby Emory sent the Trooper and its adulterous cargo sailing into the next block. They managed to make it around the block a time or two, hoping desperately to flag down a cop. Where are they when you need them? Emory got in a few more good blows with the big Ford, and the perfidious couple tried a last-ditch desperation attempt at getting into the station. They drove the defeated Trooper right up the front steps, scampered out of the vehicle with its engine still screaming and burst through the front doors into the welcoming lobby of the police station. Thank God! Safety! About this time Charlie (his real name) was tackled to the floor by a righteously enraged Emory and pummeled mercilessly while Kim (her real name) screamed dementedly and wet her pants. It took six cops to peel Emory away from Charlie.

We were all out of the bus and peeing in the still night air. It had almost stopped raining. There was the crash of a window breaking behind the store, and everyone was in sight but Emory.

"What the fuck is he doing?" Byron measured the words like an angry father who'd had enough. Byron is the Boilermakers' drummer, and although it takes more to get him there, like most drummers, he's no slouch in the temper department.

Red said, "He's stealing beer!" with more than a hint of glee in his voice.

I was in the driver's seat and had the engine running before I even had my pants zipped up. The boys were scrambling into the bus like we were taking mortar fire, screaming (*encouragement?*) at Emory to hurry hurry hurry c'mon c'mon c'mon let's get the fuck outta here etc. etc. He came barreling around the corner from behind the store like an all-star running back packing three cases of beer and did a head-first Pete Rose into the open side door of the bus. I stomped on the gas pedal, side-stepped the clutch and got out of there as fast as a 1600cc engine lugging five guys with hunting gear could go. Not very fast.

After about ten minutes of white-knuckle adrenaline it appeared that we were safe.

"Gimme a beer."

It was Rainier Ale, and nothing good ever comes of a night with Rainier Ale. Oh, well. We had beer, and the collective mood was now one of cheer and accomplishment. We were driving through some dense fog, but it had stopped raining, and by that time nobody really minded the cold wind whipping in from the missing window. We were excited about the hunt, and were eagerly anticipating the horrified looks we were going to induce by parading around Hollywood with big bloody dead pigs strapped to the top of the bus.

We were getting close to Hunter Liggett, and it was high time we stopped at the first cheap motel we could find and get a little shut-eye before the big hunt.

There were no motels.

"Hell," Ted said, "even if we find one, by the time we check in and get the bus unloaded it'll be time to pack up and go. I say let's just pull over somewhere and take a nap."

"I'm game," Red belched.

"It'll be crowded," I said, but didn't really care. I was feeling peaceful and harmonious with my fellow man. "Alright. Hey, someone gimme another beer."

I pulled into what looked like a fire road which dipped down for a ways, then back up, was bumpy as hell, and found a spot that felt fairly level. I shut the motor off and absorbed the stillness for a minute. Our voices had a muffled, hollow ring which I normally associate with being in a small tent. It felt like we were camping. We *were* camping, I suppose. We clambered out of the bus and breathed, walked around, pissed, opened beers and generally

appreciated life. It was still overcast, and the night was pitch black. I couldn't believe we didn't bring a flashlight.

"How much beer we got left?" Red asked, as I heard the distinctive sound of a magazine being rammed into his .45 and the slide crunching home.

"At least two cases," Byron answered. He was sitting in the passenger seat under the interior dome light, drunkenly dropping cartridges into his Ruger Blackhawk .357 mag.

It was going to be a good night. I rummaged through the heap of firearms and related accouterments and pulled out my Uncle Mike's black nylon shoulder holster, which contained my Smith & Wesson Model 586 .357 magnum. I love that gun. I was strapping in when Red chopped up the night air with the first volley. It sounded glorious. Emory let loose with six quick ones from his S&W 686. *Damn!* The .357 magnum is decidedly louder than the .45. My pulse was quickening and my ears were howling pleasantly when Byron and Ted started blasting away in unison. Dueling Rugers. God, it was beautiful. Soon we were all going at it; firing and loading, firing and loading. Ted impressed us all by pulling out his Mossberg shotgun and firing off some tracer rounds he had picked up at a gun show in Phoenix. We weren't shooting at anything - we couldn't *see* anything - but the noise and all those flames were better than a goddamn thousand bagpipes screaming *Scotland the Brave*.

The firing tapered off after fifteen minutes or so, and we were getting seriously plowed on that cursed Rainier Ale. They don't call it the Green Death for nothing. Emory lit one of his firecrackers, threw it and it went off about four feet away from him. Damn those Mexican fuses. It was so loud it made my testicles ache. Ted was passionately telling us a very sincere story about his grandma or something. No one could make out a word he was saying. Red was missing and Byron kept yelling at everyone to shut up. It was vaguely irritating. I was seeing double in the feeble dome light no matter how hard I tried to focus, and the ground would come up now and then to smack me

in the head. I lost my Smith & Wesson somewhere and was crawling around trying to find it and Byron kept screaming at everyone to shut up. Ted kept yammering on about God knows what, and Emory had crawled under the bus and was singing *Blue Moon of Kentucky*. He sounded pretty good. I found my gun in the dark and it felt all muddy, but what the hell. I holstered it *keeping my finger out of the goddamn trigger housing* and crawled to the driver's door of the bus, climbed in and slumped over the steering wheel. I had a mild case of the spins, but was too tired to get out and puke. I wanted *sleep*.

I was dreaming of Red yelling at me with his face right up next to mine as he was firing that goddamned SKS. CRACK CRACK CRACK CRACK it was going and he just wouldn't stop. He was yelling and yelling and shooting and shooting and I started drifting toward consciousness like a diver surfacing in a muddy pond. He kept yelling and shooting and soon it was Byron who was yelling. I mean *really* yelling. I was wide awake now and the CRACK CRACK CRACK CRACK was a goddamn freight train smacking the right front corner of the bus as it roared by doing about seventy. Oh, Lord God Jesus please please please start. I got the bus into reverse and *eased* it away from the railroad track which I had nearly parked right on top of the night before. The train quickly passed and in a few seconds was completely gone. The sun was high and very, very bright.

Byron was still yelling from the passenger seat beside me, "We almost died! The fuckin' train was that close to me!" He held his thumb and forefinger about an inch apart, right in my face.

"It wasn't that close to you," I said. I was trembling slightly.

"We almost died, Goddamn you!"

Someone else was yelling. It was Emory. Byron opened the door and got out and then yelled some more.

"Shit! You ran over Emory!"

I opened my door, stuck my foot out and fell to the ground. The cold mud felt refreshing somehow. I looked under the bus and, sure enough, I had run over Emory.

129

"GET THIS FUGGIN' THING OFF A ME!" he was screaming. The right front tire was on his leg.

"Alright, hold on," I said and pulled myself up to release the parking brake. Byron and I pushed the bus back about a foot and saw to Emory, who was lying pitifully in the mud, his face a grimy broadcast of hatred and pain.

"YOU FUCKIN' RAN OVER ME, YOU PRICK!"

"What the hell were you doing under there, anyway? Is your leg broken?"

"I DON'T KNOW! YOU FUCKIN' RAN OVER ME!"

"Yeah, well..." I was standing out of fist range, just in case.

A monumental hangover was creeping up on me, and I was in no condition to handle an emergency. But the bus is not all that heavy, and it looked like the tire just pushed his leg down into the mud. We helped him up and he limped around, cursing my ancestors.

The scene around the bus was revolting. There were dozens of beer cans strewn about (at least they were green), empty brass was everywhere, Ted's shotgun was lying in the mud, apparently having been stepped on several times throughout the night. Torn cardboard from ammo boxes and red plastic ammo trays were scattered around as if something had exploded. We were in a small clearing in the woods where the dirt (mud) road crossed the railroad tracks. The coast highway was about 200 yards behind us, to our west. There was a small creek to the east on the opposite side of the tracks, and beyond that were wooded hills. This was the general direction we were firing during the night, and if there was anything still alive out there, it owed its life to dumb luck. We were muddy from head to toe, and I discovered that I had peed my pants, either sometime during my sleep or, more probably, when I realized we were being slapped around by a freight train. The damage to the bus was surprisingly spare; a dent about the size of a big watermelon surrounded the area where the right headlight used to be. It was kinda grisly looking with the headlight gouged out and its wires hanging

there like the optic nerve. Red was still missing.

And then there was Ted. He was curled up on the floor of the bus, sleeping like a baby. None of the commotion had bothered him at all. There were chunks of vomit and mud in his beard and hair, which was tangled across his face like soggy dead grass. Ted hadn't stepped foot into a barber shop since he was probably twelve years old. His boots and jeans were caked with mud. He was wearing a cowboy-style gun belt, and there was mud stuck in most of the empty bullet loops, as well as on the grip of his Ruger. Surrounding him on the rubber floor mat were empty beer cans, cigarette butts, dirty rifle carrying cases, shotgun shells, shattered window glass, empty and full ammo boxes, hundreds of spent cartridges, the beer cooler tipped onto its side, a couple of half-eaten MaxiPeps and a scattering of sodden pork rinds. He was peacefully blowing little spit bubbles, oblivious to the world.

Ted is a biker to his very soul. His main transportation is a Harley Shovelhead, and his backup is a Triumph Bonneville. He is never out of uniform; engineer boots, jeans, Harley T-shirt, Langlitz leather jacket and about six pounds of chains and keys and shit hanging from his belt. And when it comes to being disgusting, none of us can hold a candle to Ted. He used to work at Nabisco, maintaining and cleaning big machines and ovens which make cookies by the zillion. He had a contest with another Nabisco employee to see who could wear the same pair of socks the longest. Every day they'd show up at work and pull these foul socks from their lockers and put 'em on. After a month or so, Ted's opponent caved in; he could take it no longer. Ted, however, being the consummate showman, opted to persevere. He wore the same pair of socks for more than a year. The management threatened to fire him, but he stood firm by his worker's rights. The employees with the surrounding lockers stopped using them altogether. Ted's achievement permeated the entire locker room with an eye-watering stench. He said that

the socks were rigid like cardboard when he put them on at the beginning of his shift, but soon would warm up and become viscous. He said it felt like he was walking in raw eggs. The company finally found a way to fire Ted the day he spotted a guy bent over underneath a dough machine sporting a good-sized plumber's crack, walked over with an air hose, rammed it down between the guy's cheeks and gave him about 150 psi. The startled employee jumped and conked his head hard on the machinery, resulting in a gash requiring several stitches to close up. Think of Ted the next time you eat an Oreo cookie.

My hangover was reaching psychedelic status. I thought about having some beer to try and kill it, but we were out, and besides, Rainier Ale is not a morning beer. I had finished off my entire canteen of water and was still parched. The creek looked dirty and smelled bad. I decided to hold off.

"I wonder where the hell Red is," Byron wondered.

"I hope we didn't shoot him," said Emory.

"Jesus, I didn't think of that," I said. "Maybe we should look around for his body."

"He's probably lost out there somewhere," Byron said, casually waving his Ruger in the direction of the woods. "Let's fire a few rounds in the air. Let him know where we are."

It sounded like a good idea. Besides, maybe some gunfire would be good for the hangover. I unholstered the Smith & Wesson for the first time since I found it in the mud the night before. It was pretty well caked. I opened the cylinder and dumped out the rounds - four of them unfired - and found a half-full can of beer. To the astonishment of Emory and Byron, I began pouring the beer all over the gun, rinsing off the mud.

"These things are tougher than people give 'em credit for," I said, pleased with the negative attention and making a mental note to get some oil on the gun *soon*.

The three of us loaded and fired. The noise was horrific and beautiful and Ted stirred a little, then went back to sleep. I reloaded and holstered the big Smith; no sense in carrying an unloaded gun. I lit a cigar, and by the time I had it drawing well it was making me dizzy.

"So we're supposed to be fuckin' BOAR hunting!" Emory exclaimed.

My sentiments exactly. None of us had a watch, but it looked to be about eleven a.m., far too late for the best hunting. Wild pigs are most active in the early morning. After that they hide in little beds which they dig in the middle of thick brush. You can crawl through brush to try and flush 'em out, but then you're on their turf, and you don't have much room to maneuver when the violence ensues.

For safety's sake, the boys and I like to carry sidearms as a backup while hunting boar. In addition to my M1 Garand I carry my Smith & Wesson. It rides comfortably in the Uncle Mike's shoulder holster beneath my army field jacket. It's of course against the rules to carry handguns *as well* as long guns while hunting, but we're talking about confronting and killing vicious man-eaters. Ted and Byron prefer shotguns loaded with three-inch slugs - Byron also packing his New Model Blackhawk and Ted carrying his Ruger Security Six (both .357 magnums) - while Emory and Red both use their SKSs equipped with 30-round magazines (we're not sure if it's legal to hunt with those things or not, but they sure are effective!). Red relies on his Colt M1991A1 .45 ACP for his backup and Emory assigns the job to his S&W model 686 .357 mag.

My choice of the M1 rifle is based mostly on sheer power. I know some guys who hunt boar in Hawaii with M1 Carbines, but I like to be *sure* the beast goes down before it gets a chance to chomp on me, and the .30-06 round is most definitely up to the task. The SKS, with its feisty .762 x 39mm round is also good, but I haven't had mine long enough to be comfortable in a chaotic moment of savagery.

Something was crashing down the hill and through the brush a couple hundred yards out in front of us; something big and unwieldy and unnatural. It had to be Red.

He emerged from the bushes across the creek to our howls of laughter. He was muddy, slightly bleeding and scratched from head to toe, carrying his police baton and wearing nothing but his Red Wing hiking boots.

"Fuck you," he said. "You guys got any fuckin' clothes?"

And so it went. After the laughter subsided (this took a while) Emory gave him his spare jeans and a T-shirt. Nature Boy couldn't very well piece together the events of the previous night, but he remembered commandeering the bottle of Jager Meister and resolving to kill a boar before sunrise. He stalked and hunted all night with that big billy club and chased after anything that moved. He thought he might have killed a possum or a raccoon, but he couldn't be sure. He had no idea where his clothes might be. Fortunately, he had left his .45 in the bus before he took off on his aboriginal quest.

Red had his moment in the limelight the night Magic Johnson announced to the world that he was HIV-positive. It was November 7, 1991 and the same characters in this story, plus one Charlie Lenz (before he ran off with Emory's wife, of course) were at the King King nightclub down on 6th and La Brea drinking beer and sake and livin' large. The Reverend Horton Heat was playing that night, and things were just about as beautiful as things can get. Red naturally got out of hand. After closing time he chased Ted and myself down the sidewalk with surprising speed, swinging maniacally at us with one of those orange road cones. This sort of activity was just not doing it for Red, however. He needed action. In the parking lot of the Ralph's Market on 3rd, which was being remodeled at the time, was a Condor Lift (commonly called a cherry picker) which has four wheels, a diesel engine and a telescoping lift, on top of which is a platform surrounded by a rail. On this platform are the controls with which to drive and steer the vehicle, as well as to lift the platform (and the driver) into the air as high as sixty feet. This was too much for Red to resist. Within a few minutes Red was sixty feet in the sky, screaming that the Lakers were a bunch of faggots and revving the diesel, the strange vehicle looking like

*something from the War of the Worlds as it lumbered across the parking lot toward La Brea. Red was going to drive the thing over the Cahuenga pass to Burbank; to hell with the power lines. He got it stuck in some kind of flower garden in the parking lot, however, and was ramming it into reverse, forward, reverse and forward, trying to get it unstuck and swaying dangerously from side to side when about eight cop cars pulled up. Red hollered at the cops for a while, telling them to get out of his way and that Magic Johnson is a **FAG**, man, but when they threatened to shoot him down he finally agreed to lower the cherry picker and surrender peacefully. At first they weren't sure what to charge him with. Grand Theft? He didn't even make it out of the parking lot. Criminal Mischief? Well, he didn't hurt anything but a few scraggly flowers. There is one thing, however...*

"Mr. Kowalski, put your feet together please, and stand straight. Now put both arms straight out to your sides, close your eyes, lean your head back and try to touch the tip of your nose..."

They slapped him with a DUI, and by the time he was cuffed and arrested there were more cop cars there than I have ever seen, and I found out later that the reason for this was that they had simply wanted to get a look at "the nut trying to steal the crane." He was a celebrity of sorts down at Wilshire Division before he was even booked. A couple of cops had their pictures taken with him in front of the stuck cherry picker, and nearly everyone at the station had a respectfully smartassed remark for him. He ended up getting his driver's license revoked for a year, and to this day he claims it was worth it.

Red put on the jeans and T-shirt, yet was still nowhere near presentable. "Jesus, dude," he said, "Your van's fucked up."

"It's a *bus*. Only rapists and contractors drive vans," I replied a little testily. "We got hit by a fuckin' train a little while ago."

"It SUCKED," added Byron.

Red didn't believe us and I didn't really care. Just standing there was taking all the strength I had. I felt

131

nauseous and cold. It was the stupidest fucking hunting trip I'd ever been on. We were a bunch of oafish, city-dwelling drunkards playing with guns and raping the environment. Los Angeles had driven us insane, I thought as I surveyed again the carnage of the night before. What the hell happened? We used to be real men! My soul has Herpes. I'm a dead piece of walking meat with no purpose or function on this planet. A mean-spirited maggot. Useless. Sick...

Emory and Byron were laughing about something, and Red was taking a dump on the railroad tracks. I dropped to my hands and knees and did a shuddering Old Faithful through my mouth and nose. I barely had time to gasp for air between the torrents of blistering sewage before the episode finally segued into a few painful dry-heaves. All of this of course was seen by the boys as spectacular entertainment.

"Yo! Yak-master Kopp!" Red shouted. He was gesticulating wildly and trying to sound like a rapper from his obscene crouch.

"MaxiPep?" asked Emory oh-so-innocently while shoving one of the ghastly things directly under my nose. It was then I realized that I must have eaten a half-dozen of them throughout the brutally drunken night.

"Fuck you," I said. I spat a little residual puke on the ground and pulled a remarkably stringy piece of saliva from my lips and wiped the stubborn thing off on my pants. My nasal passages were seared and I snorted some chunks into the back of my throat which nearly triggered again the gag reflex, but I held on.

Byron offered me some pork rinds from the bus, "a little soggy, but nutritious," he insisted.

"Fuck you," I said again, my vocabulary being a bit limited under the circumstances. I was feeling much better, though, and glad as hell to note that my Smith & Wesson hadn't fallen out of its holster and into Lake Vomit; it had been through enough abuse already. I was pulling myself together enough to feel macho again, and said, "Let's go huntin' you grubby bastards!"

"We're out of beer," said Emory, "and it's too late for huntin' anyway."

"We'll go GET some beer. And it's not too late for hunting, we'll just tromp around through the bushes 'til one of the fuckers takes a charge at us, and we'll blow the holy shit out of it."

"Might as well give it a try," Red said.

Byron said, "Sounds good to me," and it was settled. We'd get some fucking beer and go fucking hunting.

I pulled Ted's shotgun out of the mud, opened the action to have a look-see into the chamber - it wasn't loaded, to my surprise - and tossed it into the bus. We piled in and Ted stayed asleep. Incredible. I navigated the bus astern for a bit, then swung around through the awful mess we had generated, beer cans crunching beneath the tires. I headed us north on the highway in search of food, gas and beer. Red was stuffing cigarette butts into Ted's mouth to the delight of Emory & Byron. Jesus, we're never going to grow up.

After only a couple of miles (good thing we were firing *eastward* the night before!) we found a '40s or '50s-looking motel/gas station/cafe/convenience store nestled picturesquely off the road with a huge totem pole lording over its weedy gravel parking lot. A backwoods mini-mall.

I pulled up next to a gas pump to the disdainful stares of two old geezers wearing greasy baseball caps and a soulless, flabby middle-aged woman in a pink jogging suit and poofy yellow hair. They were sitting on an old wooden bench that looked like a church pew, and I figured they must be either employees or residents. Their looks of contempt changed to caution when Byron got out and opened the side door to let the boys out (except for Ted, who was still asleep). I thought with some amusement that we must be quite a sight. I walked up to geezer number one and told him I was going to fill it up on pump number three and shoved a twenty at him.

"Pump first, pay after," he grumbled. I immediately liked the grouchy old fuck.

The boys went to the cafe to order a bunch of burgers for the road, and the pink jogging suit lady said something to geezer number two,

whereas they both followed the boys into the cafe. Must be the cook and the waitress.

Filled up with gas, stocked up with beer, ice and two bottles of Wild Turkey and wolfing down surprisingly good cheeseburgers was the situation fifteen minutes later as we drove south, back to the scene of the previous night's insanity. We had decided at the gas station that if we were going to get any hunting done at all, we had better find a place soon, and the old campsite was as good a place to start as any. Besides, we could save the four bucks we would have had to pay at the wildlife check station. I guess *technically* it would be poaching, but...

Ted stirred a little, groggily propped himself up on one elbow and moved some mud-and-puke encrusted hair out of his face. "Got a burger for me?" he asked. He must have swallowed the cigarette butts Red put in his mouth! (I can't wait 'til he reads this.)

"Here ya go," Red said, stifling a twisted little smile as he handed him one.

Ted looked around and said, "Did you guys go out in public like that?"

I laughed for a second until his question suddenly made sense. We were all wearing goddamn cannons.

"Aw, Jesus!" Red said, wide-eyed. "No wonder that lady was so fucking weird to us!"

Emory was cackling at the thought.

"Wow," said Byron, "It's amazing they didn't call the cops. Or shoot us."

"Maybe they did call the cops," I speculated.

It dawned on me that they had to know about the previous night's break-in just a few miles south of them, and what better suspects could one hope for than five lewd and stinking guys driving a thrashed-out VW bus and packing guns? Damn.

I made a left onto the road from which we had emerged earlier and first-geared it through the pot-holes and ditches back to the filthy campsite, this time taking care to park a safe distance from the railroad. It was still a nice day weather-wise, and the mud had lost its soupiness, giving way to a much more tolerable dough-like consistency. We got out of the

bus and armed ourselves to the proverbial teeth.

We all agreed to hike due east for a few miles and maybe we'd get lucky and find a boar or two up in the hills, and maybe even discover Red's clothes along the way. We gulped down a couple of beers each as Ted field-stripped his Mossberg and cleaned most of the mud out of it. We played rock-paper-scissors to determine who would carry the pack first - it contained twelve cans of beer, one of the bottles of Wild Turkey, the rope and a few MaxiPeps - and struck out for the high country. We guessed it to be around 2:00 p.m. Byron got to carry the pack.

I always love being in the woods. I feel at peace there more than anywhere. Long, long ago (and far, far away from this wretched state) when I was a kid I would sometimes spend entire days by myself in the woods exploring, climbing trees, trying to catch fish with just a sharpened stick (it worked once - I speared an 8" speckled trout, bashed its little head in, cooked it over a fire and ate it, bones and all. It was the best-tasting fish I've ever had) or just sitting quietly long enough for the animals and bugs to forget my presence and resume their daily routine.

Red, who was walking point, suddenly stopped and put his hand up. It was about an hour into our trek, and I figured it would be about the time we might find something. I crept up next to him and he pointed to a patch of thick brush which had a small stream running beneath it, not 50 feet in front of us. I heard it too, and nodded with him. Something was in there. Red and I simultaneously took aim, and the boys, who were stopped in their tracks, took aim as well. They couldn't hear the hesitant rustling from where they were planted, but what the fuck, they wanted in on the action too. We waited tensely for something to SEE. I took deep, slow, silent breaths and mentally practiced reloading the M1 with the clips in the pockets of my field jacket. I had ten of them, as if I would ever need eighty rounds to kill a boar!

Red suddenly cut loose with a withering barrage from his SKS. I still couldn't see anything, but fuck it. Spray the whole thicket. Everyone else was firing. The gunfire was positively maniacal, and I still couldn't see the boar. There were limbs falling from trees. Brush, dirt and sticks were flying in all directions. There was a hailstorm of hot brass, a couple of shells finding their way down the back of my shirt. OW! The fusillade reached a terrifying crescendo that would have made

Sam Peckinpah proud. They kept firing, and so did I. I reloaded and fired until I was out of ammo for the M1, so I dropped it and fired six fast shots with the magnum. I had one speed-loader ready to go, but that was it for handgun ammo. I reloaded the Smith and kept it at the ready, not wanting to use up the last of the last unless I really had to. The gunfire eventually dwindled to a few sporadic shots, after the area was reduced to a pathetic heap of splintered twigs and mangled leaves. *Where the hell was the boar?*

"PLEASE STOP!" came the pitiful wail from the annihilated thicket. Whoopsie.

A human hand was waving tentatively from behind the shallow bank of the creek. The guy must have crawled in there when the shooting started. None of us said or did anything - what does one do in that situation? After a few moments of uncomfortable silence, first one, then two grease-painted camouflage faces appeared where the waving hand had been. Bow hunters.

Now there's a wacky subculture for you. Bow hunters live for the hunt. They spend *lots* of money on all the creepy trappings of the hardcore survivalist. They paint themselves up like Ted Nugent, dress in the latest camo fashions and sneak through the woods carrying compound bows that look like Dr. Seuss contraptions and launch arrows faster than you can see. The arrows are made of finely machined aluminum with razor-sharp tips. The smell of blood gives these guys hard-ons. They love nothing better than to kill things in a savage and primitive way. Pretty respectable if you ask me.

The bow hunters stood up, soaking wet from the creek and shivering like puppies. Incredibly, they hadn't been hit. I wasn't sure which was more embarrassing - shooting at fellow hunters or throwing hundreds of rounds at something without hitting it. The boys and I were feeling a bit sheepish at that point, and I guess it showed. One of the bow hunters - the one who first raised his hand - had stopped shivering and his terrified expression was giving way to one of explosive fury.

"YOU DUMBFUCKINSONSABITCHES!" he barked. He sounded like a drill sergeant on a 'roid rage. "WHAT THE GODDAMN SHIT! YOU STUPID MOTHERFUCKERS! COCKSUCKERS LIKE YOU COME OUT HERE AND RUIN IT FOR EVERYONE! WHY DON'T YOU GO BACK TO LOS ANGELES AND FUCKING STAY THERE!" (Jeez, was it that obvious?) "GODDAMN YOU...!"

Byron aimed his Ruger at the guy like a poker-playing cowboy, cocked it and said simply, "Shut up."

Byron displays the cool reserve of a torture expert at a prison camp. Not much gets him riled, but when he does cross that line he can be a sonofabitch. Emory was eating Cheese Nips one time and offered Byron some, whereas Byron, mistaking this gesture for a racial slur (he's half Japanese), nearly hauled off on the unsuspecting Emory.

Besides drums - he can play circles around almost any drummer in L.A. - his forte is drunk driving. He's the best. We (the usual crew, except for Emory) spent a roaring, two-fisted, fire-breathing evening in Tijuana on my birthday in (I think) 1992, with a rented Odlsmobile Delta 88 which barely survived the trip. After swaggering through town guzzling

mescal (we each had our own bottle), eating dangerous tacos from dirty little vendors, leering at the ugliest hookers on earth and barely escaping several fisticuffs with the locals - and somehow feeling that we needed more mescal, we assigned Byron with the task of driving us back to the cheap motel we had rented earlier in anticipation of getting too drunk to make it back to L.A. We could barely walk, let alone uphold a sense of direction in unfamiliar territory, but Byron got us there. I remember being slammed to the side in the back seat and pinned there by centrifugal force and Red, as Byron spun doughnuts in some parking lot, the car careening sickeningly and the tires screeching and smoking as if we were in an episode of The Dukes of Hazzard. I also remember Byron expertly smacking trash cans with the big Olds at high speed just to watch them (and their contents) fly, all the while maintaining the casual stoicism that has become his trademark.

Back at the motel we yanked the mattresses off of the beds and tossed them onto the floor, converting a two-bed room into a four-bed room, and Red learned to never, ever step on Byron's sleeping bag. Without so much as an angry word for warning, Byron deftly sent Red sailing across the room with some kind of crazy karate kick to the back. It was a side of Byron rarely seen, and awesome to behold.

After a nerve-jangling silence, Emory said at a near-whisper what was going through everyone's mind: "What are you doin,' Byron?"

"We have to kill 'em."

"Oh, Jesus..." the loudmouth bow hunter's parade had just been rained out.

Ted took a healthy swig of Wild Turkey and started mimicking *Dueling Banjos* (the theme from *Deliverance*), "Den de-de den den den den den..." It was a chilling display of Ted-humor.

"Um, Byron..." I said.

"What? We have to kill 'em, that's all. We can't let 'em walk outta here and tell the cops or the rangers about us."

"I really don't think what we did is against the law. I mean, it was an honest mistake."

Byron thought about this for a moment, all the while keeping the magnum trained on the target, who, along with his partner, had turned a sickly pale. "Okay," he said, "but at least we gotta take away their bows and arrows so they don't hunt us down on our way outta here and kill *us*."

He had a point. "Alright, we'll leave their stuff by the highway," I said, "I don't want to actually *steal* from 'em. Hell, shootin' at 'em was bad enough."

"We'll take their clothes, too," Byron said.

"What the fuck for?" asked Red, who knows a little about nudity in the woods.

"They probably have knives and shit on 'em. We can't take the chance."

"So pat 'em down!"

"You pat 'em down!"

"I'm not touchin' the fuckers! They might be fags! What do you suppose they were doin' in the bushes together?"

"This is Bullshit!" Emory yelled. "Fuckin' bullshit!"

Ted kept up his *Dueling Banjos* routine, just to create the right atmosphere, I suppose. It was clearly getting on the bow hunters' nerves.

Byron was still holding a bead on the loudmouth. "You!" he said to him, "On the ground! Face first! You too!" he said to the other guy, who quickly obeyed. "I'm not playin' fuckaround here! Where's your shit?" he demanded, and the quiet one pointed to a spot just a little down stream.

Red and Emory walked over to where the hunter had pointed, looked around a bit and started to gather up gear. I felt pretty bad doing this to obviously cool guys, but it seemed necessary. Our pack was on the ground next to Byron, and I reached in and found the last beer. *Mine!* I opened the beer and squatted down next to the quiet one.

"Look," I said. "I really hate to do it this way, but you gotta understand. I don't want you fuckers hunting us down and ambushing us, which is something I would do if I were in your position right now. I don't know where you guys parked your rig, but just over the hills that way about a mile and a half is the coast highway. Just follow the beer cans. You'll see a clearing with railroad tracks running through it. Look around there and you'll find your stuff."

He nodded slightly.

"Oh, aren't you mister fuckin' nice guy!" Byron said. "Since when have you been queer for bow hunters?"

"These guys just survived the fuckin' Tet Offensive, f'r chrissake! Show a little respect!" I responded.

Byron slugged back a little whiskey, curled his lip Elvis-like and said, "Sheeit."

"Let's go!" growled Red.

They had gathered the bow hunters' gear. It looked expensive.

"Yes, sir, commander fuckin' Red!" said Emory. "You're the one that started all this bullshit. What the fuck did you think you were shooting at, anyway?"

"You were shootin' too, numbnuts."

"We ought to tie you up and leave you with these guys."

This gave Byron an idea. "Hey, let's tie 'em up!"

Ted laughed with fairly disturbing enthusiasm.

"Aw, man, c'mon!" I said. "You're a brutal motherfucker, Byron."

He directed his gaze at the hunters, who were looking cold and

beaten lying face-down on the freshly mutilated ground.

"If you bastards move within the next fifteen minutes, I'll fuckin' pepper ya," he told them. "And you know I'm not kidding."

"Let's go!" Red hollered again, reaching into the pack. "Hey! Who took the last beer?"

I quickly drained what was left of the last beer, tossed the empty can aside and said, "Let's go!" and, slinging the M1 over my shoulder, walked off toward the campsite. There was more beer in the bus.

On rare moments I feel proud to live in Los Angeles

DECEMBER 31st 1994: AN L.A.P.D. HELICOPTER MOVES FROM SITE TO SITE TRYING TO QUELL OUT OF CONTROL CELEBRATIONS WITH ITS SPOTLIGHT.

FINALY, AT MIDNIG IRRITATED PARTY GOERS BROUGHT DOWN WITH SMALL ARMS FIRE.

THE MORAL OF THIS STORY IS . . .

(A) CHILDREN SHOULD READ THE BOOK OF VIRTUE

(B) WE NEED STRICTER GUN CONTROL LAWS.

(C) COPS SHOULD NOT FUCK WITH MEXICANS ON NEW YEARS EVE.

↑ Those were the days! (ad circa 1960)

RED'S LAST WORD

JAKE JOSEPH L.Z. KILROY KOWALSKI AKA RED

WELL FUCK IT WAS TIME TO HEAD BACK TO FUCKING BURBANK FOR THE FUCKING HOLIDAYS...LOTS OF FUCKING BEER...AMMO...FOOTBALL AND THUMPING FUCKING FAG NATIVITY SCENES WITH FUCKING EGGS AND FUCKING WATER BALOONS...I WAS GOING TO FUCKING TELL YA HOW TO KILL POLITICIANS AT THE HIGHEST LEVEL AND HOW TO MAKE FUCKING BITCHIN C-4...BUT SOME FUCKING LAWYER ADVISED AGAINST IT...I WAS ALREADY IN TROUBLE WITH THE FUCKING FAGGETY-ASS JACKBOOTED FEDS FOR TAX EVASION...GUN RUNNING...WIRE FRAUD...SELLING BOGUS HILLARY RODHAM SOILED PANTIES TO THE FUCKING JAPANESE AND FUCKING PHOTOS OF CHELSEA WEARING A FUCKING STRAP-ON TO N.A.M.B.L.A....FUCKING HOLY FUCKING FUCK...I WAS IN A WORLD OF DEEP FUCKING SHIT...SO FUCKING DEEP I MIGHT DO FUCKING TIME IN LEAVENWORTH...WHO WOULD FEED MY FUCKING DOG AND GET MY TWO SONS OFF TO

SCHOOL...PRISON IS FUCKINGBEER...NO MAGPACKS...JUST A CRAZED ASS INSANE ALL WALKS OF LOW S...SPADES...BEANE FUCKING ASIANS...A HAJIS...THEY ALL ASS SHIT...LIFT BUGGER EACH AND DRINK HOME SHIT MADE FROM TOE URINE...FUCK...KIL GET RID OF PRISONS INTO THE FUCKING FROM FUCKING PRISONS...I DID DISCO 70S AT FOLSOM FOR FOR SHOTGUNS IN MY SHOP...DID THREE YEARS...GOT OUT ON DRANK A LOT OF STAR GARDEN TITTY NO FUCKING FUN...NO GUNS...NO LOT OF FUCKING MOTHERFUCKERS FROM LIFE...SKINHEAD RS...GOOFY ASS FEW FUCKING DO THE SAME CRAZY WEIGHTS AND FUCKING OTHER...SHOOT METH BREW...SOME FUCKING JAM BUTT CHEESE AND L EM ALL AND LET'S AND PUT THE MONEY MILITARY...I KNOW EXPERIENCE ABOUT TIME IN THE LATE FUCKING CHILIHOLE SAWING OFF FUCKING HIGH SCHOOL METAL FUCKING LONGASS MY 21ST BIRTHDAY AND BEER AT THE FUCKING BAR WITH MY FATHER

AND DECIDED TO NEVER GO BACK TO THE FUCKING JOINT...FUCK...ALSO DECIDED TO GET THE FUCKING WEASEL WHO DROPPED A DIME ON ME...HIS NAME IS BILLY HUGHES...HE RATTED CAUSE I SLAMMED HIS FACE INTO THE GRINDING WHEEL ON A DARE FOR A 40 OUNCER OF MICKEY'S...I WAS TRYING TO REMOVE HIS HAIRLIP...KIDS WILL BE KIDS...I GOT MY REVENGE THE DAY BEFORE HIS WEDDING WITH AN ICE PICK TO THE SPINE...AT LEAST I LEARNED SOMETHING AT FOLSOM...HE GOT MARRIED IN A WHEELCHAIR...TODAY HE IS THE FUCKING NIGHT MANAGER AT TOMMY'S...THE ONLY FUCKING HANDICAPPED HONKY TO EVER WORK AT TOMMY'S...AFTER THAT I JOINED THE NAVY AND WENT INTO SUBS...DIDN'T LAST LONG...THE FUCKING NAVY HAS NO SENSE OF HUMOR...ONCE WE SPOTTED A RUSSKIE SUB...WHILE JUST BELOW SURFACE I RAN A CONFEDERATE FLAG UP THE FUCKING PERISCOPE...SEEMS THEY HAVE A FEW BROTHERS IN THEIR NAVY TOO...A BIG

FUCKING ARTICLE FIFTEEN CAME MY WAY FROM SECRETARY OF THE FUCKING NAVY HIMSELF JOHN LEVY...FAG...WELL HOW I GOT INTO TROUBLE WITH THE FEDS IS A STORY OF GREED...IGNORANCE...DRUNKEN DUMBASS BLIND AMBITION...ME AND FOUR

DOPE SMOKING STUDENT SO- THOUGHT WE GOVERNMENT OF FUCKING LIVING ON AND FUCKING SHITS AT A WERE BLAZING TALKING COUNTRY...I SOME TALLBOYS...D BORING...THE DEXTER FOUR COMMANDER OFF...HE THREE COMMAND WAS LANCE...THE UP HIS LUNCH AFTER YOU FLUSHING HIS OF BROWN TO ROLL HIM

IDEALISTIC QUEER COLLEGE CALLED REVOLUTIONARIES COULD ACTUALLY OVERTHROW THE OF THE ALMIGHTY FUCKING U.S. A...THEY WERE RICH KIDS THE DOLE FROM FUCKING MOMMY FAG DADDY...MET THE LITTLE DEAD SHOW IN SAN DIEGO...THEY ON WINDOWPANE AND OUZO AND ABOUT OVERTHROWING THE SAID FUCK YEAH I'LL SELL YOU GUNS...AFTER ABOUT 20 PBR EAD SHOWS ARE REALLY FUCKING LEADER OF THE GROUP WAS NAMED YOUNG...THE BRIGHTEST OF THE DUMBSHITS...I CALLED HIM PECKERHEAD...PISSED HIM DEMANDED RESPECT FROM HIS STOOGES...DEXTER'S 2ND IN A PHP STUDENT NAMED KIND OF KID WHO WOULDN'T GIVE MONEY IN JR. HIGH SCHOOL EVEN POLITELY ASKED FOR IT BY SCRAWNY HEAD IN A TOILET FULL WATER...THEN YOU WOULD HAVE DOWN A FLIGHT OF STAIRS...THE

10 COMMANDMENTS OF THE PLAYGROUND CALLED FOR IT...IT WAS THE FIFTH I BELIEVE...I SHALL GIVETH UP MY LUNCH MONEY WHEN ASKED FOR IT...HE BOUGHT THE GUNS ON HIS FAG DADDY'S A-MAX CARD...I SOLD THE FOUR WEATHERMEN...HOW FUCKING ORIGINAL...SIX RUSTED SKS'S AND FOUR STOLEN BARREL-WARPED BERETTA 9MM'S FOR EIGHT GRAND...I TOLD YOU THEY WERE FUCKING DUMBSHITS...I MADE THEM BELIEVE IT WAS STATE OF THE FUCKING ART WEAPONRY...I DIDN'T WANT THEM TO HURT ANYONE...I DIDN'T WANT FUCKING BLOOD ON MY HANDS UNLESS I DID THE FUCKING SHOOTING...UNLIKE BUTCH DYKE ATTORNEY GENERAL JACK RENO...WELL THAT'S HOW I GOT INTO TROUBLE WITH THE FUCKING FEDS...I WAS STAYING AT THE FUCKING HIPPIE COMPOUND IN THE MOJAVE DESERT FOR THREE FUCKING HOT WEEKS IN OCTOBER...THEY WANTED ME TO

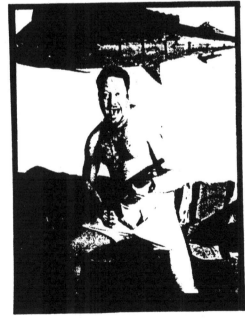

THEIR MILITARY STYLE FUCKING FUCKING HOURS A JUST WANTED TO DRINK BEER BIKES AND GAWK AT FUCKING WAS A CLASH OF FUCKING GOALS COMMITMENTS...I'M ONLY HAVING NO GOALS...LANCE'S MAX BILL CAME DUE AND HE HAD EXPLAINING TO DO...HE JUMPED HIMSELF A SLIMY LITTLE LAWYER AND WENT CRYING TO A FEDERAL GRAND JURY ON NOTHING OF HIS FUCKING FAG WAS NOW A FUCKING POSTER BOY FUCKING QUEER LIBERALS...IT WOODY...I DECIDED TO LAY LOW WHILE AND TAKE IN SOME AND COCKFIGHTS...WELL FUCKING FUCK AFTER THREE DAYS AND ONE FUCKING FUCKING HANGOVER I DECIDED

PARTICIPATE IN EXCERCISES 12 DAY...FUCK...I AND RIDE DIRT MAGPACKS...IT AND COMMITTED TO FAG DADDY'S A- A LOT OF SHIP...GOT WEASELHEAD FUCKING ME...SAID COMMIERADS...I FOR THE GAVE ME A IN T.J. FOR A DONKEY SHOWS FUCKING HOLY SHITTY FUCKING CONTINUOUS TO GO BACK TO

THE FUCKING U.S. OF FUCKING A...I WAS
TIRED OF T.J....A FUCKING CESSPOOL OF WALKING HUMAN SHIT THAT YOU COULDN'T
KILL WITH A BOTTLE OF MESCAL AND A FUCKING .45...PLUS THE FEDERALES WERE
AFTER ME AFTER I SHOT THAT MATADOR IN THE ASS WITH MY CROSSBOW...FUCKER WAS
TOO SLOW...BACK AT MY TRAILER BY THE SALTON SEA I GAVE THE FAGASS FEDS A
CALL... ``SPECIAL AGENT FRANKDICK''... ``HEY CRANKLICK IT'S JAKE KOWALSKI
HOW THE FUCK ARE YA''... ``IT'S FRANKDICK ASSHOLE''... ``ALRIGHT SPANKPRICK
ASSHOLE...DO YOU WANT MY ASS OR DO YOU WANT TO HAVE A TURKEY SHOOT AT A
BUNCH OF DOPED UP HIPPIE REVOLUTIONARY QUEERS WITH INOPERABLE WEAPONS...''
...HE THOUGHT FOR A MOMENT... ``IT COULD BE FUN...WE MAY GIVE YOU A BREAK
JUST FOR HAVING THE BIGGEST F.B.I. FILE OF ANY OF YOUR ASSOCIATES...YOU CAN
AUTOGRAPH ONE OF THE PHOTOS WE HAVE OF YOU...'' ...THIS WAS A BREAK...
``COOL FUCKING HOLY FUCKIN COOL! MEET ME ON THE ONE ELEVEN TEN MILES NORTH
OF SALTON CITY SUNDAY AT 0600...I'LL BRING THE BEER...'' ...FOR THE NEXT
TWO DAYS I DRANK HEAVILY...LOADED LOTS OF AMMO FOR THE SKS...MIXED UP SOME
FUCKING CAMO PAINT JUST FOR THE FUCK OF IT...DIDN'T REALLY NEED IT BUT IT
GAVE ME A HARD-ON...HARD TO COME BY THESE DAYS...THE FUCKING FEDS WERE

TREATING ME PRETTY WELL
FOR BEING PECKERHEADS...
THEY'VE GOT WEAPONS THAT
ARE JUST AS GOOD AS MINE...WE
COULD BE INDICTED FOR
THE SHIT WE WERE ABOUT TO
PULL...CRIMES... GONNA GO GET
THE FUCKING LITTLE
WEASELHEADS...FU CK... SPECIAL
AGENT FRANKDICK CALLED ME
SATURDAY NIGHT AND TOLD ME TO
BE READY TO BE PICKED UP IN
AN APACHE MORE LOADED THAN
ME...THE FUCKING CHOPPER LANDED
EARLY...I JUMPED INTO THE
FUCKING APACHE WEARING ONLY
MY BAGGY FUCKING SEARS BOXER
SHORTS CONVERSE HIGH-TOPS AND
JOHN DEERE CAP...I ONLY
HAD TIME TO GRAB THREE PBR'S
AND MY POTATO GUN...WE FLEW
IN SILENCE FOR ABOUT TEN
FUCKING MINUTES...WE
SPOTTED THE WEASELHEADS'
CAR AND THE FUCKING PILOT
OPENED UP...FUCKING
ALL FUCKING HELL FUCKING BROKE

LOOSE...LOOSER THAN A FUCKING WEST HOLLYWOOD CHICKEN BOY'S ASS THE MORNING
AFTER A GAY PRIDE PARADE...ROCKETS AND MISSILES AND FUCKING MACHINE GUN
FIRE...THERE WAS NOTHING LEFT OF THE CAR...FUCKING HOLY FUCKING FUCK...I
HAD THE WORLD'S MOST MAJOR WOODY...SO DID THE FUCKING FEDS BUT THEY DIDN'T
SHOW IT BEHIND THEIR FOSTER GRANTS...AFTER THAT WE HEADED NORTH TO VENTURA
COUNTY TO HUNT CALIFORNIA CONDORS WITH MY POTATO GUN...WE DRANK BEER ATE
BEEF JERKY AND TOLD SEA STORIES...LATER THAT DAY AND 300 FEET ABOVE THE
SANTA MONICA BAY THEY THREW ME OUT OF THE FUCKING CHOPPER...SONS OF FUCKING
BITCHES...I FUCKING SMACKED MY NUTS ON THE COLD HARD SALT WATER AND TOSSED
UP A STOMACH FULL OF BEEF JERKY AND YELLOWISH PBR...NEXT FUCKING ISSUE I'LL
BE REPORTING ON THE LAUGHLIN HARLEY RIVER RUN WITH BIG TED...THE FUCKING
MICHIGAN MILITIA'S FUCKING ANNUAL EASTER SUNDAY RABBIT SHOOT...THEY WANT ME
ON BOARD AS A TECHNICAL ADVISOR FOR METH AND EXPLOSIVES...FUCK...I'LL BE
HEADING OUT IN A RYDER TRUCK FULL OF ALL FUCKING SORTS OF COOL SHIT EVERY
KID SHOULD HAVE...I MIGHT STOP AT THE NEW GOVERNMENT THEME PARK CALLED
WACO-WORLD...MAYBE VISIT OKLAHOMA CITY...I'M GOING TO BUY SOME STOCK IN
DUPONT...FUCK...

BUNCHA GUN FAGS

Molly Keily, whose beautiful work graces this here issue, has just moved. As soon as she gets a P.O. box at her new locale, she'll let me know, so if you have some work for her (or just a good word) drop me a line and I'll put you in touch with her. Don't miss her genius comic *Diary of a Dominatrix*, available at your local newsstand or from Eros Comix, ████████████████, ████, ████████.. Look for **Pollyanne's** articles in *Ben is Dead* and other fine publications. She also did the silk-screen you see to your right. A note of caution here for all of us who pack heat: Pollyanne had her Beretta and her Walther snatched away by the coppers a couple of months ago, and lordy what an ordeal to get 'em back! A thousand bucks for a worthless shyster lawyer! $800 fine! Eighty hours of picking up trash along the freeways with a bunch of dirtbags wearing orange vests! All this just for a having a concealed weapon, something that should be *encouraged*, especially among women... Aside from his monthly pub *Attack Cartoons*, **John Bergstrom** is working for Warner Bros Animation these days. Pretty lofty status, eh? I hope he remembers who his friends are! Look for his work in *Slick Times* as well... In my **Francisco Martin Duran** article I mentioned that Francisco should have had a copy of *ANSWER Me!* with him at the time he shot at the White House. Well, coincidentally, it turns out that he had some pages of *AM* #2 in his truck, which prompted his attorneys to fly **Jim Goad** (the publisher) out to Washington for a deposition! Jeezus! It's only a magazine, folks!... Gun fag cartoonist **Kjartan Arnorsson** publishes *Savage Funnies*, which features a cute lil' homicidal squirrel. He's at ███████████████████████ He also supplied me with the cartoon at the bottom of this page by **William Haskell** ███████████████████████████, ████████████.. Thanks to the **Rev Smitty**, who performed Mr. & Mrs. Kopp's perfect wedding (and who wrote a perfectly angry piece for this issue) and **Rufus T. Alligator**, who provided GFM with the article by the **Company of Freemen** and the photo on the inside front cover. Maybe I doctored the photo a little. I didn't want to be left out... Thanks especially to **Mrs. Kopp** for putting up with Mr. Kopp and for being a crack shot with a Thompson submachine gun!

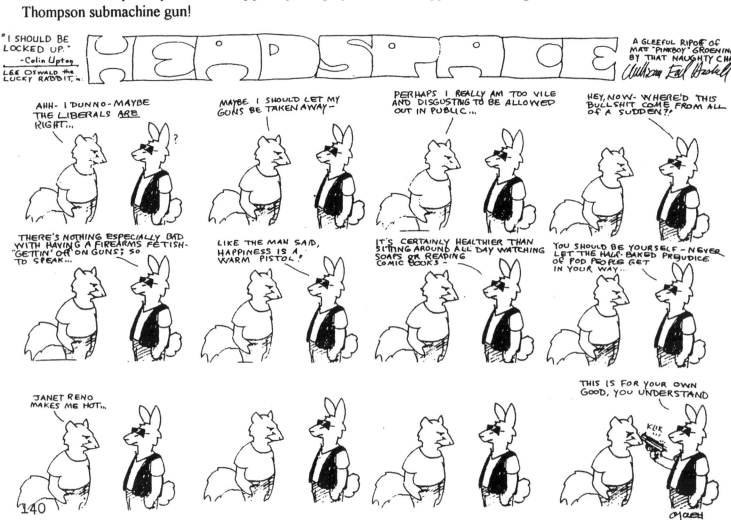

"I SHOULD BE LOCKED UP."
— Colin Upton

LEE OSWALD the LUCKY RABBIT, in:

HEADSPACE

A GLEEFUL RIPOFF OF MATT "PINKBOY" GROENING BY THAT NAUGHTY CHA...

AHH- I DUNNO- MAYBE THE LIBERALS ARE RIGHT...

MAYBE I SHOULD LET MY GUNS BE TAKEN AWAY-

PERHAPS I REALLY AM TOO VILE AND DISGUSTING TO BE ALLOWED OUT IN PUBLIC...

HEY, NOW- WHERE'D THIS BULLSHIT COME FROM ALL OF A SUDDEN?!

THERE'S NOTHING ESPECIALLY BAD WITH HAVING A FIREARMS FETISH- "GETTIN' OFF" ON GUNS; SO TO SPEAK...

LIKE THE MAN SAID, HAPPINESS IS A WARM PISTOL!

IT'S CERTAINLY HEALTHIER THAN SITTING AROUND ALL DAY WATCHING SOAPS OR READING COMIC BOOKS -

YOU SHOULD BE YOURSELF - NEVER LET THE HALF-BAKED PREJUDICE OF POD PEOPLE GET IN YOUR WAY...

JANET RENO MAKES ME HOT...

THIS IS FOR YOUR OWN GOOD, YOU UNDERSTAND

KLIK

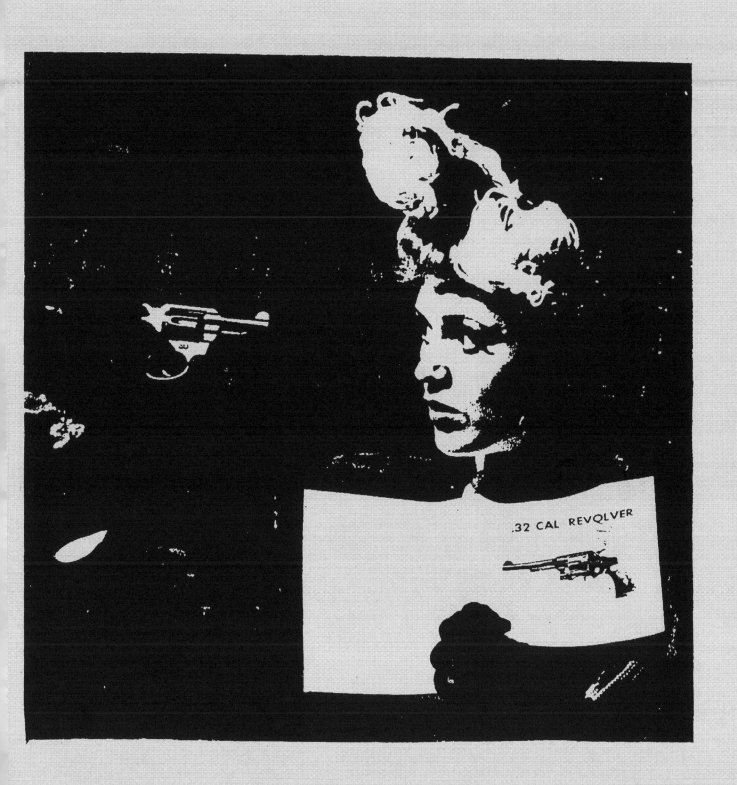

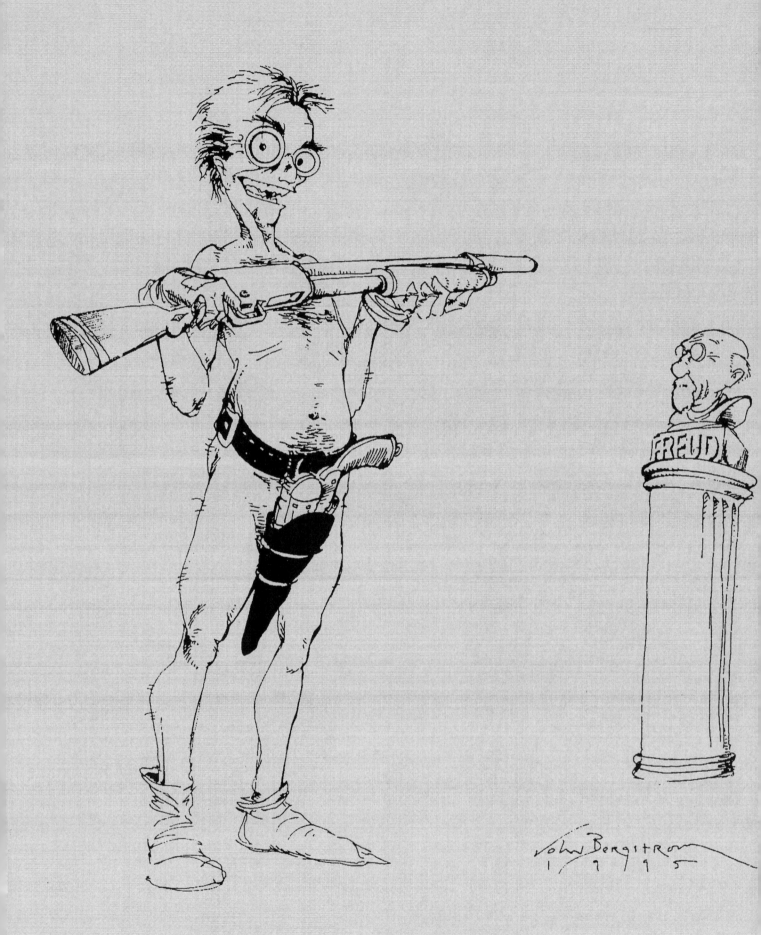

Made in the USA
Las Vegas, NV
02 November 2024

10908057R00079